Commercial Recreation & Tourism

Commercial Recreation & Tourism

$\bullet$

An Introduction to Business Oriented Recreation

Susan A. Weston
Montclair State University

Brown &Benchmark
PUBLISHERS

Madison   Dubuque, IA   Guilford, CT   Chicago   Toronto   London
Caracas   Mexico City   Buenos Aires   Madrid   Bogota   Sydney

Book Team

Publisher *Bevan O'Callaghan*
Project Editor *Scott Spoolman*
Publishing Services Coordinator *Peggy Selle*
Proofreading Coordinator *Carrie Barker*
Production Manager *Beth Kundert*
Production/Costing Manager *Sherry Padden*
Production/Imaging and Media Development Manager *Linda Meehan Avenarius*
Visuals/Design Freelance Specialist *Mary L. Christianson*
Marketing Manager *Pamela S. Cooper*
Copywriter *M. J. Kelly*

Basal Text *10/12 Palatino*
Display Type *Helvetica*
Typesetting System *Macintosh*™
  QuarkXPress™
Paper Stock *50# Mirror Matte*
Production Services *Shepherd, Inc.*

PUBLISHERS

Vice President of Production and New Media Development *Vickie Putman*
Vice President of Sales and Marketing *Bob McLaughlin*
Vice President of Business Development *Russ Domeyer*
Director of Marketing *John Finn*

A Times Mirror Company

Cover design by Kay Fulton Design

Cover image © David Falconer/Tony Stone Images

Copyedited by Shepherd, Inc.; Proofread by Barb Callahan

Library of Congress Catalog Card Number: 95–76258

ISBN 0–697–21992–5

Printed in the United States of America by Times Mirror Higher Education Group, Inc.,
2460 Kerper Boulevard, Dubuque, IA 52001

10   9   8   7   6   5   4   3   2   1

DEDICATION

This book is dedicated to the memory of my mother.

Marie R. Weston 1920–1970

I make this dedication, not so she will see it and be proud, but so that you will understand the power that this book and all books can have on your life.

My mother did not have an easy life. Yet, like every mother she wanted a better future for her children. She knew that education was the tool that allowed people to see the possibilities that existed beyond the walls of their world. She instilled in me a love of learning and of books. She made me understand that ultimately I was responsible for what I learned and that this process involved work on my part. She also taught me to reason and to question what I learned and what I read.

While you read this book remember that every book contains both truth and folly. Your job is to use your intellect to sort them out and embrace the former while questioning the latter. Above all, **read** this book and your other textbooks as well, and use them as a platform to expand the walls of your world.

CONTENTS

7   Lodging, Food, and Beverage   148

10 Looking Toward the Future   207

Appendices

Index   264

FOREWORD

Writing this book has led me to confer with practitioners and academics in many areas discussed to this text. The results of these exchanges have been revealing and are best reflected in this poem by John Godfrey Saxe.

The Blind Men and the Elephant

It was six men of Indostan
    To learning much inclined,
Who went to see the Elephant
    (Though all of them were blind),
That each by observation
    Might satisfy his mind.

The *First* approached the Elephant,
    And happening to fall
Against his broad and sturdy side,
    At once began to bawl:
"God bless me! but the Elephant
    Is very like a wall!"

The *Second,* feeling of the tusk,
    Cried, "Ho! what have we here
So very round and smooth and sharp?
    To me 'tis mighty clear
This wonder of an Elephant
    Is very like a spear!"

The *Third* approached the animal,
    And happening to take
The squirming trunk within his hands,
    Thus boldly up and spake:
"I see," quoth he, "the Elephant
    Is very like a snake!"

The *Fourth* reached out an eager hand,
    And felt about the knee.
"What most this woundrous beast is like
    Is mighty plain," quoth he;
"Tis clear enough the Elephant
    Is very like a tree!"

The *Fifth* who chanced to touch the ear,
    Said: "E'en the blindest man
Can tell what this resembles most;
    Deny the fact who can,
This marvel of an Elephant
    Is very like a fan!"

The *Sixth* no sooner had begun
    About the beast to grope,
Than, seizing on the swinging tail
    That fell within his scope,
"I see," quoth he, "the Elephant
    Is very like a rope!"

And so these men of Indostan
    Disputed loud and long,
Each in his own opinion
    Exceeding stiff and strong,
Though each was partly in the right,
    And all were in the wrong!

Moral

So oft in theologic wars,
    The disputants, I ween,
Rail on in utter ignorance
    Of what each other mean,
And prate about an Elephant
    Not one of them has seen!

The Oxford Book of Childrens Verse in America—Ed. by Donald Hall NY: Oxford University Press, 1985.

From talking to others it has become clear to me that there is an enormous profit-oriented industry at work that is based on our need for recreation and leisure. The fuel for this industry comes from our desire to experience and purchase recreation and leisure products, and services.

I have also come to believe that, like the poem, many of us see only the parts of the industry that directly relate to us and that we see neither the interrelatedness of the parts nor the whole. It is my hope that by reading and discussing the parts of the whole presented in this textbook, we will all arrive at a better understanding of our entire industry.

PREFACE

This book is different from previous texts written about profit-oriented recreation businesses (commercial recreation) and tourism. Other textbooks have emphasized this field as an entrepreneurial career choice that falls mainly outside the boundaries of traditional and corporate business. This is not the focus of this book.

Past texts, in an effort to define what professionals in commercial recreation and tourism do, have incorporated chapters exploring topics such as management, budget and finance, marketing, and other recognized business subjects. There are no chapters on these topics in this text. Instead, there are chapters exploring the different industries that comprise the total industry of commercial recreation and tourism and a look at the career options that await students who study this area. Management, marketing, program planning, budget and finance, and the other courses needed to acquire the competencies necessary to be successful in the field should be studied in separate courses that are part of the total curriculum.

When using this book, chapters 1 and 2 should be read first. Chapter 1 introduces the reader to the industry and presents a brief overview of how commercial recreation and tourism has been defined by different authors. This chapter also explores the variety of names and titles used to describe the commercial recreation and tourism industry and discusses career opportunities by function.

Chapter 2 explores the origins of commercial recreation and tourism and identifies six major factors that have helped to shape the industry over time. Although this chapter offers information that is more comprehensive than what has been included in most previous texts, it does not come close to covering the amount of historical material available in this area. Volumes have been written on such topics as the history of aviation, the carousel, and historical travel, making it impossible to cover to everyone's satisfaction these topics within the confines of a chapter.

Chapters 8, 9, and 10 should be read last and in order. Chapter 8 discusses the allied industries that support and influence commercial recreation and tourism and aspires to define the scope and importance of these often forgotten industries to the total industry. It also points out that career opportunities are available in this area for those who are drawn to this field but who do not feel fully connected to the career options and areas discussed in the first part of the book.

Chapter 9, on career management, has been added so that individuals can start to identify their interests, talents, and skills, and to think about how they might integrate these attributes with the career options discussed in the text. This chapter is also designed to alert individuals to the support services that may be offered by colleges or universities and to get them to take personal responsibility for their own careers.

Chapter 10 looks toward the future and discusses the process of prediction. While indulging in some future speculation, it also tries to identify those trends and movements that are currently in force and that will influence the future of our industry and our lives. It is meant to be a serious yet fun chapter for both student and instructor. After all, as the chapter points out, another word for prediction is guess.

The remainder of the chapters, 4 through 7, could probably stand alone and do not have to be read in order (although they would probably make more sense if they were read that way). Readers may have difficulty with chapters 5 and 7.

Chapter 5 introduces the concept of event management. Some readers will neither like nor agree with this chapter. It is hoped that they will remain open-minded and consider the possibility that besides meeting professionals, special events professionals, and other planners, there is another category of event-oriented individuals who (in this book) have been called event managers. In addition, these individuals possess their own shared, collective set of competencies, duties, and responsibilities.

The content of Chapter 7, lodging, food, and beverage, is true to the nature of the industry but has not been called hospitality. Some readers might find this upsetting. Again, it is hoped that they will remain open-minded and consider the idea that hospitality is attitude—a corporate or personal mode of conduct and behavior. It is neither an academic discipline nor is it the sole possession of one specific area of our industry or of any other industry.

Some of these issues should become a platform for discussion regarding who we are, what we do, and how we relate to one another. This is one book, an introductory book, that deals with an immense industry and it does not and cannot cover in depth the areas and issues presented. Instead it is meant to serve as the starting point for exploration of the topics introduced and to allow students, faculty, and interested readers the opportunity to bring to the book other issues, experiences, and philosophies.

To guide you in your reading of this text, chapter objectives and additional readings have been included. In addition, Appendix H contains a time line of events that have impacted on commercial recreation and tourism, and Appendix G lists professional organizations that represent different areas of the industry. Use these materials to help you sort through and understand the text.

The cooperation that I received from all of the individuals, companies, and agencies mentioned in the pages of this text was overwhelming. They promptly and cheerfully forwarded documentation, pictures, statistics, and other information. They returned my telephone calls and/or spent their valuable time meeting with me. Thank you for your generosity and help.

Two individuals deserve special thanks. The first is my friend and colleague Jerry G. Dickason, Ph.D. Jerry is the individual who is responsible for my making the decision to write this book. When I was asked to do this project, it was Jerry who sat me down and told me that I *could* and *should* go ahead with this commitment. Thank you Jerry, for believing in me.

While Jerry was the catalyst, it was my good friend Gina Balestracci who kept fanning the flames. Gina is my best critic. She read every line of this book as it was being written and not only told me what was good, but more importantly, she told me what was atrocious. When I would falter or get tangled in the complexities of this project, it was always the calm reasoning words of Gina that started me moving again. Thank you Gina for being my best critic and for telling me "gently" both the good and the bad. . . .

I would like to thank all who were instrumental in the development of this book. I am grateful to my reviewers, Sandra Little, Ronald H. Simpson, and S. Harold Smith, for their comments. Your suggestions were much appreciated, and I have tried to incorporate them into this text whenever possible. Your constructive criticism helped me work through issues, and to rethink my justification for making choices concerning content and presentation. Thank you.

Finally, I am indebted to Scott Spoolman, my editor, and his assistants, Jean Thompson and Kim Olsen, and to Heidi DiDonna. Thank you for your patience and for answering all of my questions. A special thank you goes to Rick Hecker. Thank you Rick for your expert editing skills and for correcting and improving my errors without changing my ideas. I appreciate the help, guidance, and support that all of you provided and consider myself fortunate to have worked with all of you.

Introducing the Industry

LEARNING OBJECTIVES

1. *To introduce the variety of names and titles used to describe commercial recreation and tourism enterprises.*
2. *To describe the mission of commercial recreation and tourism services.*
3. *To explain and discuss the differences between goods and services.*
4. *To introduce sites where commercial recreation and tourism activities may take place.*
5. *To present career opportunities by function for commercial recreation and tourism graduates.*

Introduction

Have you taken a vacation recently or gone to a concert? Have you bought a new tennis racket or gone out to dinner with friends? If you have done any of these things, then you already know something about the commercial recreation and tourism industry.

Commercial recreation and tourism is a relatively new name for a rapidly growing industry. Not everyone refers to this new field as "commercial recreation and tourism"; other names include: commercial and leisure services (Bullaro and Edginton 1986); recreation business (Kelly 1895); commercial recreation (Ellis and Norton 1988); and commercial and entrepreneurial recreation (Crossley and Jamieson 1993). In colleges and universities, curricula with names such as travel and tourism, culinary arts, sport and event management, commercial recreation, and hospitality, may indicate that a recreation-oriented business program exists.

Why can't everyone seem to agree on a name for the industry? One reason is that the number and diversity of the disciplines involved in this area is very large. In addition, the rapid expansion of the field means that the defining and sorting process is still going on. Old titles and concepts are difficult to shed, and while the terms "leisure" and "recreation" are not new, they do carry with them the vestiges of systems that have undergone rapid change in the last fifteen to twenty years. New names and titles incorporating the traditionally understood concepts and philosophy of leisure and recreation are undergoing transformation in an effort to accurately describe the current state of the industry.

Public Recreation Roots

Most people are familiar with public recreation services. Perhaps you took swimming or tennis lessons from your town recreation department or attended a summer band concert that was arranged for you by your county recreation agency. If you have visited a national park, recreation area, or historic site, then you have participated in a recreational experience provided by the federal government.

Historically these agencies have provided many of the recreational opportunities that citizens experience. Traditionally supported by taxes, public recreation occurs on the national, state, county, and local levels. What these services have in common are their funding base (taxes) and their availability to all members of the community.

Originally public agencies submitted budgets and were given tax monies to support their parks, programs, and facilities—but times changed. Funding became difficult and many of the government agencies that were supported by taxes faced severe budget cuts. Fiscal realities forced governments and citizens to make difficult choices. The mandate to the public recreation sector regarding the spending of funds quickly changed from counting

Established in 1872 for "the benefit and enjoyment of the people," Yellowstone National Park became the world's first national park. With borders in three states, Wyoming, Montana, and Idaho, Yellowstone contains Old Faithful and some 10,000 other geysers and hot springs. Photo courtesy of the National Park Service.

Introducing the Industry

Early visitors wading in hot pool at Great Fountain Geyser, Yellowstone National Park.

Photo courtesy of the National Park Service.

Jupiter Terrace of the Mammoth Hot Springs serves as backdrop for this bus and tourist car as they take off on the Grand Loop Tour Road which still follows essentially the same route today as it did when Yellowstone Park was opened to motoring.

Photo courtesy of the National Park Service.

Visitors on footbridge at Black Sand Basin, Yellowstone National Park.

Photo courtesy of the National Park Service.

on expendable monies to self-reliance. Departments were restructured to ensure the continuance of programs, and user fees and charges became common. While profit was not the principal motivator for public recreation, those who provided services looked more and more to the business sector, and to those commercial recreation enterprises that were already in existence, to learn how to survive.

> Public recreation is any department of government—local, federal, or state—with primary responsibility for the provision of recreation facilities and programs to meet public needs. Many such programs are open to all members of the community regardless of ability to pay.
> However, the trend in public recreation is to charge fees for services. This does not mean that public agencies have gone commercial. It merely reflects the need of public agencies to draw on additional sources of revenue. Because of this trend it is no longer possible to make a distinction between public and commercial recreation agencies based solely on management techniques, cost of service, or source of payment for services (Ellis and Norton 1988: 2).

Breaking even, or at least recuperating the majority of expenses, became one of the primary goals of public recreation. Without this change in orientation regarding monies, public recreation would, at the least, have had to severely decrease its program offerings and ability to maintain its facilities and grounds. At the very worst, some public recreation departments would have been cut.

Public recreation did not disappear: it learned, adapted, and endured. Meanwhile, the world's appetite for leisure and recreation experiences continued to grow and made the recreation market an economic force. In 1970, Americans spent 6.3 percent of their personal consumption dollars for commercial participant amusements. By 1980 that figure had jumped to 12.5 percent, and by 1990 it had reached 19.2 percent. (Statistical Abstract of the United States 1992: 383) Having fun, relaxing, and enjoying themselves in a variety of forms had definitely become very popular with John and Jane Q. Public. In addition, the idea that they would spend their money to participate in commercial amusements had increased 12.9 percent.

An Old Industry Enters a New Era

There is no doubt that an old industry has entered a new era of importance and growth. While there does not seem to be agreement about what it should be called, there does seem to be agreement regarding its mission.

> For our purposes *commercial recreation* is any for-profit or non-profit enterprise whose business is providing recreation or leisure services not funded by tax monies or charitable contributions (Ellis and Norton 1988: 2).
> Therefore, *a recreation business provides goods and/or services for organized leisure through the market sector of the economy.* A recreation business is organized to obtain a price for goods and services adequate to pay the costs of materials, labor, and capital plus an incentive to engage in the business, a profit (Kelly 1985: 6).
> (Commercial recreation is) . . . the provision of recreation-related products or services by private enterprise for a fee, with the long-term intent of being profitable (Crossley and Jamieson 1993: 6).

All three of these definitions recognize that making a profit is the essential component of the industry. In addition, it is private enterprise, not tax-supported agencies, that will be providing the goods and services for consumption.

We all know what it is to consume something. We live in a society where as consumers we are barraged daily by all forms of media enticing us to buy and use goods (products) and services. The recent popularity of shop-at-home television shows and infomercials attest to our insatiable appetite to see and to own whatever is new and popular (whether or not we really need a diamond-studded fishing rod is another issue). Our definitions have stated that the provision of goods and services for a profit are the essence of the industry. What are goods and services, and what kinds of goods and services do commercial recreation and tourism professionals provide?

The United States has been changing from a manufacturing-based economy to a service economy comprised of service industries. In 1985, 20,879,000 people were employed in manufacturing in the United States. This number dropped to 20,434,000 by 1991. Meanwhile, for the same years, the figure for those employed in the service industries went from 33,322,000 to 39,705,000, an increase in excess of 6 million jobs (Statistical Abstract of the United States 1992: 632). The shift to a service-based economy in the United States and in other nations of the world that historically have had manufacturing-based economies, has occurred for a variety of reasons. The

The Broadmoor—
Colorado Springs,
Colorado.
The Broadmoor has a
colorful and interesting
past. Established in 1891
as a gambling casino
when James Pourtales, a
Prussian count, formed
the Broadmoor Land and
Investment Company, the
Broadmoor has become
one of the world's
premier Mobil Five-Star
resorts. Located at the
foot of the Colorado
Rockies, it has 550 guest
rooms, nine distinctive
restaurants, 100,000
square feet of meeting
and exhibition space, and
numerous on-site and off-
site sports and recreation
activities, including three
indoor heated swimming
pools. The Broadmoor is
truly the grand dame of
the Rockies.
Photo by Bob McIntyre.

emergence of the European Union, energy control, supply, price, and competition by emerging nations with more favorable economies of scale are just a few of the reasons.

Service industries have been described as "organizations primarily involved in the provision of personal services" (Morrison 1989: 26). A few examples of service-based businesses in our field include travel agencies, special event companies, destination resorts, and theme parks.

These businesses share a common goal; to provide us with an intangible commodity—service. The goal of a travel agency is not to sell us a plane or a hotel, but an exciting experience that we will remember long after our trip is completed. Could we plan our own travel arrangements? Absolutely—but by using the services of a competent travel agent we are tapping into their expertise and experience and trusting that the information we receive will ensure us a pleasurable and hassle-free trip.

How is a product (or good) different from a service? Unlike a service, which cannot be held in the palm of our hand, a product has form and substance.

> Products such as automobiles and personal computers can be tested
> before you buy them. You can do so much evaluation because products are
> tangible. On the other hand, services cannot be tested and evaluated in the
> same way. They are **Intangible** and you have to experience them to 'know
> how they work' (Morrison 1989: 27).

The provision of a service is often more difficult than the provision of a product. Most of us like to "kick the tires" a few times and take a couple of spins around the block to "see how it handles" before we buy. We cannot do this when we purchase a service. Service industries rely on their good name to tempt consumers to buy, and the success of their business rises and falls based upon their reputation for delivering what they promise. Most people know that a product has a reasonable life expectancy and that eventually it will need to be replaced, but a service that has been provided and does not meet the buyer's expectations is often mourned and talked about for years. Experience with a disagreeable or disappointing service becomes a story recounted at a party or told to friends around the dinner table. The story often contains creative embellishments, and usually is told at the expense of the agency or company who provided "the worst experience of my life." Service definitely belongs in the definition of the new industry; it is the underlying tenet of what we are about.

What about products? How do they fit into the industry and are they really important? Products are very important. Without product development and sales, we would not have the numerous activity choices available to us today. New fabrics have made it possible for us to camp, hunt, ski, and snowmobile in comfort. Lightweight materials for both clothing and equipment make it easier for us to move about and to transport the tents, bicycles, stoves, boats, and other recreational equipment and supplies that we have come to depend on for our enjoyment. In addition, companies like American Tourister promise to provide the "gorilla-proof" luggage for our trip. Other companies make and sell the cameras and film that we use to record our experiences. Language and currency converters help us find the way to the hotel in multiple languages, while we try to figure out how much it will cost in our currency. The range and availability of products for recreation and travel have exploded, and the companies that develop, manufacture, and supply them have taken full advantage of the interest in these areas.

The athletic footwear (formerly referred to as "sneaker") industry is a good example of a business that has rapidly expanded and exploited the interest in recreation to the fullest. These companies have taken product differentiation to its zenith. At one time, sneakers came in two models—high tops or low tops. There was also a wide range of color choice—black, white, blue, and (in the more daring stores) red. Have you purchased athletic footwear lately? Today's sneakers not only expand to fit the unique features of your foot, but they light up as well. There are special models for basketball, tennis, jogging, aerobics, weight-lifting, cross-training, walking, and almost every other conceivable activity. How did we ever manage to participate effectively in different activities before the age of specialty footwear?

The athletic footwear industry is not alone. The producers of other recreation and leisure products have shown the same zeal and enthusiasm as their counterparts when it comes to manufacturing and marketing their products.

Defining Commercial Recreation and Tourism

Where does this leave us in trying to understand the scope of the industry? For several years now academics and practitioners have been busy trying to define, categorize, label, and diagram the commercial recreation and tourism industry. All this activity has not resulted simply because of ego, but more out of a need to find commonalities between and among the different providers of goods and services. Understanding the relationships and interrelationships of industry components could lead to the identification of common strengths, weaknesses, and difficulties. This in turn could lead to shared power and influence, along with the resolution of mutual problems. John Kelly in *Recreation Business*, states:

> Recreation business is not a simple phenomenon.
> Nevertheless, some framework of classification can help sort out the variety and complexity: In general there are two types of recreation business. The first type is the *direct* supplier of goods and services related to recreation. The second is the *indirect* type (Kelly 1985: 3).

Kelly calls these two entities Retail Recreation Suppliers I and Retail Recreation Suppliers II. Type I, the direct suppliers of goods and services, make the recreational experience possible by providing the equipment and environment necessary for the activity. Type II, the indirect suppliers:

> are a step removed from our experience with the recreation occasion. For example, they advertise the products, edit trade periodicals for the business managers, and provide capital for new and expanding businesses. They develop the locales in which the direct providers operate, the shopping malls and centers or the residential locations for the community pool or golf course. . . . They are the business services along the highway leading to a national park, including those where cars are repaired, equipment fixed, and sundries purchased. They are the infrastructure of the market economy that makes available the many articles required to take the leisure trip, visit the leisure locale, or engage in the recreation activity (Kelly 1985: 3).

Kelly's explanation of the industry deals with recreation-related businesses, and his definitions recognize that there are two types of forces at work in the industry and that the difference between them is a matter of distance from the consumer.

Bullaro and Edginton have taken a more expansive view of the industry. While acknowledging that it is possible to generically classify the industry in terms of producer, retailer, or wholesaler, their system recognizes five different business areas:

1. Travel and tourism
2. Entertainment services
3. Leisure services in the natural environment
4. Hospitality/food services
5. Retail outlets

(Bullaro and Edginton 1986: 19)

This definition is more comprehensive than the classification offered by Kelly. In addition it has an interesting category: leisure services in the natural environment. Bullaro and Edginton recognize that some services offered are dependent on natural attractions, not manufactured environments. While it may be fun and exciting to go on a log flume ride, the outcome of the experience is just not the same as traveling down a real river. Both activities have their positives and negatives, and both have a place in the industry. We have the technology and the creativity to manufacture and manipulate environments in a variety of settings (artificial ski slopes and wave pools, for example), but when nature is polluted, overused, and mistreated, it is very likely to be lost. A loss of nature results in a loss of tourists and customers, which (for those among us who are not altruistic) means a loss of revenue.

Taylor Ellis and Richard Norton (1988: 18) have elected to use a four-category system of classification: tourism, local commercial recreation, retail sales, and manufacturing. Tourism is defined as services for nonresidents and includes not only the destination but the mode of traveling to the site and the activities that are either made available or are naturally present. Local recreation is divided into outdoor recreation, indoor recreation, and clubs. Local residents are the primary users of the service or experience, although it is unlikely that a provider would turn away a tourist.

Retail sales include the selling of recreational equipment and supplies to consumers. There are a variety of different distribution options for the selling of recreational merchandise. There are specialty stores (tennis or ski

Warner Bros. Studio Stores have been opening in major tourist areas across the United States. While other retail operations like the Studio Stores have been in existence for years, most of them have targeted children as their primary market. The Warner Bros. Studio Stores have departed from this orientation and offer merchandise that appeals not only to children but also to adults.
Photo Courtesy of Warner Bros. Studio Store.

shops), general merchandise stores (sporting goods chains or clothing stores), discount stores, and catalogue sales.

Finally, there is the manufacturing of the products needed to support our recreation habits. If you think that this is a small-time proposition, ponder this: In 1990 1.3 million people owned sailboats that were used for recreational boating (Statistical Abstract of the United States 1992: 240). Someone had to design, manufacture, and sell (to a retailer) the thousands of flotation devices, flares, rain gear, sails, lines, navigational instruments, maps, and other chandlery used by these individuals. Also in 1990, the total number of motorized homes, travel trailers, folding camping trailers, and truck campers manufactured and shipped was 380,300. The retail value of these shipments was $8,223,000 (Statistical Abstract of the United States 1992: 1006).

Like Kelly, Ellis and Norton realize that the categorization of the industry is complex.

> There is a tremendous amount of overlap in the commercial recreation field. A person traveling to see a theme park such as Disneyland is an example of the tourism (sic). However, to nearby residents Disneyland is a local attraction. This illustrates some of the problems involved in trying to sort commercial recreation into mutually exclusive categories (Ellis and Norton 1988: 18).

By now you should realize that the formulation of a classification system for the industry is difficult to construct. As the preceding example illustrates, nothing can be categorized as black and white when at the same time a "gray" area of overlap exists.

John Crossley and Lynn Jamieson have proposed a classification system that recognizes the overlap that exists in the industry. Their model has three components: the travel/transportation industry, the hospitality industry, and the local commercial recreation industry. Each of these areas has a "purist" aspect as well as subindustries that cut into the primary components of the industry as a whole. Consider, for example, the travel and transportation industry. Crossley and Jamieson identify airlines, rental cars, bus lines, and railroads as "purist"; most of us would agree that these industries are involved in travel and transportation, but what about boat dealers, travel campgrounds, and expedition companies? Would you consider them to be in the travel and transportation business? Crossley and Jamieson (1993: 9) see them as subindustries that overlap with other component industries.

Finding Common Ground

Regardless of which term personally appeals to you to describe the new industry, and regardless of which definition you like, there are commonalities that everyone seems to agree on. Commercial recreation is:

1. A service-based industry
2. Business oriented
3. Profit motivated
4. A market for the manufacturing and delivery of recreational services and products

At each and every opportunity, ardent recreational sailors travel to marinas located on lakes, rivers, and coastal shores to rig their sailboats and take to the water. They represent only a portion of the total population of recreational boaters, all of whom support the industry through their purchase of boats, trailers, and related supplies and equipment. In addition, they rent boat slips, purchase insurance, and support local industries by spending their dollars in the surrounding community.
Photos courtesy of Nancy Giardina.

There is a fifth dimension to understanding the industry that has not been stated, but basically implies that people who have studied commercial recreation and tourism are most qualified to deliver the products and services for the industry. Consider this: You are studying commercial recreation and tourism, a system that specializes in the delivery of recreation and leisure-oriented goods and services for a fee. Why are you enrolled in this type of curriculum?

There are many ways of arriving at the same destination, and a comprehensive curriculum in commercial recreation and tourism is designed to help you gain entry into the industry. You should acquire business skills in the areas of management, marketing, and finance. At the same time, you will study the history and philosophy of leisure, recreation, and travel. Courses in these areas will help you understand the derivation of our attitudes towards work and play. What makes our attitudes different from those of the Japanese or the Dutch? How do today's commercial recreation and tourism enterprises fit into the evolutionary framework of recreation and leisure? What roots, if any, do we still share with other forms of recreation? Exploring these issues will give you a unique perspective and understanding of an intertwined and multidimensional industry. The emphasis on understanding how leisure and recreation relates to the lives of individuals and nations gives you an advantage not shared by those who study concentrated areas of information.

Career Possibilities

Commercial recreation and tourism graduates can be found in a variety of industries and businesses in which they function under assorted job descriptions and titles. Here is a list of some of the sites where you will find them and of some of the career opportunities available to them.

Places Where Commercial Recreation and Tourism Occur

Theme parks	Convention and visitor bureaus
Hotels and motels	Transportation companies
Tour operators	Catering companies
Travel companies	Special event companies
Sporting goods stores	Destination resorts
Corporate meeting centers	Campgrounds and hostels
Clubs	Concessions and vending companies
Sports arenas and facilities	Bed and breakfast establishments

Career Opportunities in Commercial Recreation and Tourism

Management	Advertising
Sales	Program/event delivery
Marketing	Facility maintenance and safety
Promotions	Market research
Customer relations	Manufacturing and distribution
Human resources	

The types of business configurations in which the transactions of the industry occur range from sole-proprietor (single owner) companies to large corporations. Some individuals elect to become entrepreneurs, others choose to work for established companies and corporations. The decision is a personal one, usually based on individual strengths, weaknesses, and needs. There is no correct choice, only one that best suits the individual.

Entrepreneurial or corporate, owner or employee, management or sales, the choice is yours. There are endless opportunities waiting for those whose vision and understanding of the industry are not limited, and who commit themselves to studying and mastering the knowledge and skills necessary to compete.

Summary

The leisure service delivery system is large and comprised of many different distribution channels. Public, military, and church recreation are some of the means of delivering recreation programs and experiences to individuals and groups. Commercial recreation and tourism is another segment of the total recreation delivery system that is recognized as an expanding and economically powerful component.

Although it has existed for centuries, only recently has commercial recreation and tourism been recognized as an organized area of study. In an attempt to identify the parameters of the industry, individuals have proposed definitions and drawn models of the various parts of the whole. While these definitions and models differ, they do have certain commonalities. Everyone seems to agree that commercial recreation and tourism is:

1. A service-based industry
2. Business oriented
3. Profit motivated
4. A market for the manufacturing and delivery of recreation services and products

The fact that commercial recreation and tourism is still being defined and delineated means that we may find programs that are housed in various departments in colleges and universities. These programs are listed under a variety of names and include, but are not limited to, the following titles: travel and tourism, culinary arts, sport and event management, commercial recreation, and hospitality. Regardless of what these programs and the industry are called, there is no doubt that many career opportunities are available in commercial recreation and tourism. These opportunities occur in areas such as management, sales, customer relations, promotions, and program and event delivery. The venues where these opportunities occur range from corporate settings to theme parks and entrepreneurial enterprises.

Commercial recreation and tourism professionals need to be service oriented, knowledgeable about the role and function of leisure in our lives, and have the necessary business skills to integrate the components of the leisure industry into a total delivery package that provides for profit-oriented recreational experiences and programs.

Discussion Questions

1. What forms of recreation, other than public recreation and commercial recreation and tourism, are included in the leisure service delivery system?
2. What is the relationship of the different forms of recreation contained in the leisure service delivery system and commercial recreation and tourism?
3. Besides the classification systems for commercial recreation and tourism discussed in this chapter, what other systems might be possible?

Chapter Exercises

1. Interview employees of a public recreation agency on the local, state, or national level to determine how the mission and funding of the organization have changed during the last ten to twenty years.
2. Visit two different sites where commercial recreation and tourism activities take place and discuss the similarities and differences between these sites.
3. Interview two industry professionals to determine their duties as described by their job descriptions.
4. Identify examples of goods that are necessary for the carrying out of ten different services that may be supplied by the commercial recreation and tourism industry.

References

Bullaro, John J., and Christopher R. Edginton. 1986. *Commercial leisure services managing for profit, service and personal satisfaction.* New York: Macmillan Publishing Company.

Crossley, John C., and Lynn M. Jamieson. 1993. *Introduction to commercial and entrepreneurial recreation.* 2nd ed. Champaign, IL: Sagamore Publishing.

Ellis, Taylor, and Richard L. Norton. 1988. *Commercial recreation.* St. Louis: Times Mirror/Mosby College Publishing.

Kelly, John R. 1985. *Recreation business.* New York: John Wiley and Sons.

Morrison, Alastair M. 1989. *Hospitality and travel marketing.* Albany, NY: Delmar Publishers, Inc.

U.S. Department of Commerce, Economics and Statistics Administration, Bureau of the Census. 1992. *Statistical Abstract of the United States: 1992.* Washington D.C.: Government Printing Office.

Additional Resources

de Grazia, Sebastian. 1964. *Of time, work, and leisure.* Garden City, NY: Anchor Books.

Dickason, Jerry G. 1983. The origin of the playground: The role of the Boston women's clubs, 1885–1890. *Leisure Sciences* 6:83–98.

Doell, Chas. E., and Gerald B. Fitzgerald. 1954. *A brief history of parks and recreation in the United States.* Chicago: The Athletic Institute.

Dulles, Foster Rhea. 1965. *A history of recreation: America learns to play.* New York: Meredith Publishing Company.

Ellis, M. J. 1973. *Why people play.* Englewood Cliffs, NJ: Prentice Hall, Inc.

Goodale, Thomas, and Geoffrey Godbey. 1988. *The evolution of leisure.* State College, PA: Venture Publishing, Inc.

Huizinga, Johan. 1955. *Homo ludens: A study of the play-element in culture.* Boston: Beacon Press.

Knapp, Richard F., and Charles E. Hartsoe. 1979. *Play for America: The National Recreation Association, 1906–1965.* Arlington, VA: National Recreation and Park Association.

Kraus, Richard. 1994. *Leisure in a changing America: Multicultural perspectives.* New York: Macmillan College Publishing Company.

Leisure Sciences: An Interdisciplinary Journal. New York: Taylor and Francis.

National Recreation and Park Association. *Journal of Leisure Research.* National Recreation and Park Association.

Van Doren, Carlton S., and Louis Hodges. *America's park and recreation heritage: A chronology.* 1975. U.S. Department of the Interior. Department of Recreation and Parks. Washington, D.C.: Government Printing Office.

Origins of Commercial Recreation and Tourism

LEARNING OBJECTIVES

1. *To identify and discuss six major factors that have shaped the commercial recreation and tourism industry over time.*
2. *To describe the historical origins of the major areas of today's commercial recreation and tourism enterprises.*
3. *To demonstrate through retrospection the conditions that existed in the early development of the industry so that they may be compared to the industry as it exists today.*

Introduction

Attitudes toward work and leisure have changed throughout the ages as societies have examined and redefined the concepts of work and leisure. As these changes occurred, a new philosophy often arose to replace the earlier views of expected conduct and behavior. Recreational activities and pursuits evolved into an accepted part of daily living, and society began to realize the enormous economic potential of leisure activities and industries. A new industry was constructed to service the new philosophy.

Examining the Threads

There are many forces that cause change in our world. Six major factors have deeply influenced the evolution of the industry. These factors are: the changing concept of the relationship of work and leisure; the redefinition of the roles of men, women, and children; the sophistication of marketing and consumers; the mobility of populations; the existence of a global village; and the impact of technology. Each of these factors has pushed and shaped the industry into its present form. Each is important and all are intertwined. We could try to follow the threads independently, but that would distort the true picture. The evolution of the industry did not happen in that manner. While one factor might dominate for a while, all factors are influential and all factors are influenced.

The Changing Concept of Work and Leisure

Primitive humans were hunters and gatherers; they followed the available game and went where the wild plants grew. For these people, there was no distinction between work and leisure. They did not go to an employment office to apply for work, and they did not inquire about paid holidays and fringe benefits. There was no office Christmas party and no company picnic. Their days consisted of those activities that were essential for survival. Without those markers that divide our days into segments specified as work or leisure, they had no clear-cut division of time. Without a market or a mall to go to, primitive humans were generalists who had to provide for their own basic needs of shelter, food, and clothing.

This scenario changed as people settled down and towns and villages formed. Generalists gave way to specialists. Basket makers, carpenters, blacksmiths, and other tradesmen appeared. Just as the land was divided into parcels for individuals and for communities, the day and the week also started to be divided into work and nonwork times, giving people an opportunity to attend fairs and theaters and to travel and play.

Colonists with varied motives came to America from England and other countries. Some came to establish trading companies, while others were lured by the vision of vast riches. Some sought adventure and discovery and some sought new beginnings and a chance to escape religious persecution. It was this last group that brought with them an ethic that prevailed in parts of America for many years. The ethic is called the Protestant or Puritan Work Ethic. In its simplest form, this belief system stressed the virtue of hard work, thrift, and self-denial. Paradise and your reward for adhering to the ethic would be received in the next world, not on earth. In order to reach Paradise it was imperative to follow the moral good—hard work, thrift, and self-denial.

Today vestiges of the Puritan Work Ethic live on in some places in the United States, but most Americans no longer feel the pressure to conform to such a rigid doctrine. Americans of today love their fun, and the leisure and recreation industries are booming. The decline of the Puritan Work Ethic is one of the factors that made it possible for people to enjoy themselves in new and free ways and for a new industry to arise.

Throughout time the concepts of work and leisure have changed. Tied to many social, political, religious, and economic variables, they will continue to change shape as peoples and societies define and redefine their philosophies. The shape that evolves and the meaning and importance assigned to it will determine to a large extent the way that people spend their leisure time.

The Redefinition of the Roles of Men, Women, and Children

Bob Dylan, the folk singer, once sang a song in which he stated that "the times they are a-changing." Times have changed, and society is sometimes out of breath trying to keep up with all of these changes. Men and women of the 1960s, '70s, '80s, and '90s have been struggling to redefine themselves and to establish new ways of relating to one another. Women have been entering the workforce in increasing numbers, and many men have been assuming more responsibility for household chores and for childcare. The definition of what constitutes a nuclear family has been altered to include stepparents, half brothers and sisters, single-parent households, households with no children, and households with no blood-related relatives at all.

The scenes depicted in the television shows of the '50s and '60s, such as "Leave it to Beaver" and "Father Knows Best," no longer describe what constitutes a typical American home. Perhaps they never did: father no longer knows what is best, and "the Beaver" probably will be spending this weekend with his father, who has weekend visitation rights, and his "new" family.

These are not the only times that men and women have found their roles changing. The Industrial Revolution and the flight of many families to the city drastically changed America and other parts of the world. The rise of machines and of cities demanded workers. For the first time, some of these workers were women. The rest were men who gave up their agricultural lifestyle to punch time clocks and to work in factories. Recreation now happened in cities, not on farms, and women and men looked to the city to provide opportunities to escape the boredom of the factories.

The role of children has also changed over the years. Children were once viewed as miniature adults, and portraits of them painted throughout the sixteenth, seventeenth, and eighteenth centuries show them dressed in clothing that mimicked that of adults. Males wore tiny breeches and vests complete with child-sized ruffled shirts and hats. Little girls were dressed in tiny gowns and dresses that, once again, mirrored the dress of their mothers. Boys and girls were not only seen as being miniature adults but were treated accordingly. Their activities mirrored those of their elders, and the toys that they had were child-sized replicas of everyday objects; dolls, guns, carved farm animals, and other items representative of the time were their toys.

Eventually society began to realize that children were not miniature adults. We began to see that children were different; their needs were not the same as those of their parents. Their dress no longer reflected the dress of adults, and many people came to view play as the "work" of the child. Older children, particularly teenagers, were also recognized as a distinctive group with unique problems and needs of their own.

As a result of increasing life expectancy, society as a whole began to segment the population, by age groups, into categories that reflected the different phases of life. Over the course of three to four generations a forty-year-old person was no longer thought of as being old.

Origins of Commercial Recreation and Tourism

The Sophistication of Marketing and Consumers

For many years a product labeled "Made in America" symbolized the finest in technology, safety, and reliability. American goods carried warranties and guarantees that assured consumers that the product they were purchasing was a quality item. Products from developing nations such as Japan and Taiwan were viewed as inferior and poorly made. They were low cost but also low quality.

Ralph Nader, the consumer advocate, is largely credited with alerting the American public to the problems that existed in the American automobile industry. The inquiry and the close examination of this most powerful American business brought about sweeping changes not only in the manufacturing of automobiles but in other industries as well. Americans became acutely aware for the first time that perhaps the label, the guarantee, or the sales pitch, was not to be trusted. Perhaps, just perhaps, the consumer would have to become more discriminating and ask more questions. It was time to learn to read "the fine print."

The result of this experience was that a generation of consumers learned to question and to ask why. New consumer laws were passed and a magazine was created solely to report on the reliability, safety, and effectiveness of products. To remain uncompromised, the magazine refused to carry advertising or to endorse products.

Labels began appearing on items. Food products in particular listed ingredients as well as calories, fat content, additives, etc. Cigarettes and eventually alcoholic beverages also came with warnings regarding their use. Individual and class action lawsuits became common as consumers sought restitution from those companies that they felt had failed to warn them and/or to protect them from products that were harmful. The former innocence of the consumer gave way to a new breed of informed and demanding buyer.

In order to keep up with this change, American companies had to rethink their marketing strategies. Brand-name recognition and loyalty was no longer enough to keep market share. The developing nations in the world were knocking hard on the walls of the American marketplace, and the new consumers were willing to listen to and evaluate what they had to say.

American companies responded by reevaluating their product lines and by stepping up their marketing efforts. Companies established Marketing Information Systems, which helped them identify target markets and allowed them to broadcast their messages to the appropriate audience. Consumer buying behavior was analyzed, and advertising and promotion of products became fiercely competitive. Products could no longer rest on their laurels but had to keep pace with the times and the needs of the consumers. Both marketing and consumers reached a new level of sophistication.

The Mobility of Populations

Americans, and other peoples of the world, have become more mobile during the last couple of generations. The concept of the "family homestead" has disappeared for many individuals; instead we find that people move frequently. No longer do they live and die in the same town.

The tendency to move within the United States is tied many times to the movement of companies and corporations from one region to another. Looking for better tax laws, transportation options, wage requirements, or just better living conditions in general, these companies and corporations are willing and very often eager to relocate. Employees who wish to retain their jobs must move with them.

Companies also expand outside of their national borders. American companies are expanding into foreign markets in an effort to go international, and middle- and upper-level employees may have to relocate to foreign countries to help establish the company. Very often they take their families with them. Europeans have also extended their boundaries by establishing an Economic Union (EU) that has redefined the national boundaries of the member nations. Citizens of the community move freely from country to country, extending their understanding of the world and taking new customs and beliefs with them to their host nations.

Individuals also choose, for personal reasons, to move from one area to another. Retirees in major metropolitan areas often find it difficult to keep pace with prices on their fixed incomes, and high school students contemplating college often look to other areas of the country for adventure and freedom.

The result of all of this moving is that individuals are exposed to different patterns of living within their own country or in other countries. They also take with them their personal or regional customs and mannerisms. The mobility of populations allows for the easy transportation of ideas and culture from one area to another.

The Existence of a Global Village

The arrival of television allowed individuals to see how other people on the planet lived. Before television, we were restricted to gaining such information from newspapers, magazines, and movies. Television made it possible for us to see other cultures and countries almost immediately. Here were living, moving people in far away places that did not resemble "Kansas" at all. Not only were Dorothy and Toto surprised, but the rest of us had our horizons vastly expanded as well!

The heralding of the age of communication satellites increased the potency of television and caused a further shrinkage of the world. Satellite transmission of television pictures made it possible to see the actual wedding of a prince and a princess as it occurred. We could be at the sites of disasters and demonstrations, speeches and spacewalks, events and invasions. We had become global voyeurs.

The world also decreased in size with the arrival of airplanes that were capable of taking us to faraway places in record time. Now it was possible to see and to talk to those individuals and groups that we had been watching. We could smell the smells, taste the tastes, and experience firsthand what we had been watching on our television sets. Not only could we see them, but now they could see us as well.

The world became a much smaller place. World consciousness and the realization that we were becoming a global village were confirmed by the fact that gas prices here could be deeply affected by actions taken "over there"; that acid rain and nuclear accidents had no respect for boundaries; and that a terrorist could alter, with a pull on a trigger or the placing of a bomb, the lives of citizens throughout the world.

Earth, the center of our universe, became a planet in a solar system that was filled with other planets and spheres. Somehow Earth had become a lot smaller. . . .

The Impact of Technology

If there is a single thread that runs throughout all of what we have been examining, it is the role of technology in our lives. Technology has been the "driver" for much of what has happened in the other five factors. It is technology that not only influenced the concept of work and play in early America during the Industrial Revolution, but it is also technology that is redefining our current workplace. Robotics, computer chips, new communication venues, and the potential for the peaceful industrialization of space are some of the areas that are vastly changing the workplace and the way that we live.

Technology is also responsible for helping us to rethink the roles of men, women, and children. As the workplace changes, so have the expectations of individuals and the jobs that are required. Brute force is no longer a factor in many of today's occupations. Women are capable of competing on an equal level with men in most areas, while men are finding that washing machines, dishwashers, synthetic fabrics, microwave ovens, prepackaged foods, disposable diapers, and other housekeeping miracles are allowing the chores formerly thought of as "women's work" to be done by everyone—children included.

Technology has also had a large impact on consumer demands and marketing strategies. Consumers demand the newest in technology. Amusement rides must be more realistic, more exciting, and more creative in order to attract customers, and travel offerings to unique and potentially hostile environments (under the sea or to Antarctica) are now accessible to the general public because of technological advances. Indeed, technology (the automobile, airplane, ship, and railroad) makes it possible for us to get to these places, often faster and more economically than ever before.

The sophistication of marketing has been enhanced by the creation of lasers, computers, and other technological devices that have allowed us to create special effects of extraordinary quality. Max Headroom, the California Raisins, dancing gasoline pumps, and red dots that jump off 7-UP cans and dance in the kitchen are the invention of clever individuals who rush to keep pace with the insatiable appetite of the American people for innovative and entertaining advertisements.

Finally, the mobility of populations and the rise of the global village could not have happened without technological advances. Wagon trains and stagecoaches are not an efficient way to travel. Wireless machines and smoke signals do not foster effective and extensive communication. The technological advances in the areas of transportation and communication are what have helped shrink our world, and further advances in these areas will shrink it even more.

The forces that have impact on our profession have brought us where we are today and will determine to a large extent what our tomorrow will be like.

Amusements and the Amusement Industry

The carousel, Ferris wheel, roller coaster, and other rides that we know today, have a long and interesting history. In fact, the amusement industry itself is not a recent phenomenon but has roots that reach back to the establishment of towns and villages both here and in other parts of the world.

The Pleasure Garden

During the seventeenth century, large parks known as pleasure gardens began appearing in France and soon spread throughout most of Europe. The pleasure gardens were beautifully landscaped and offered an opportunity for patrons to participate in a wide variety of sports and activities. The gardens were places where people could meet one another, and many of them contained fountains, walking paths, and stands that sold food and drinks. In the evenings torches were lit, and the pleasure gardens were transformed into a dazzling display of various colored lights. Most people during this period spent their evenings at home in a dimly lit house, and this novel activity alone was an enticement for them to come to the pleasure garden. The pleasure garden was a place to go to socialize, to be entertained, and to be surrounded by an interesting and stimulating environment.

By the early 1700s the pleasure gardens began to offer a larger variety of entertainment. Balloon ascensions and parachute jumping were two of the more exciting additions. There were also more traditional activities such as dancing, concerts, and acrobatic exhibitions. Gambling began to appear in the pleasure gardens, as well as prostitution and increasing alcoholic beverage consumption. These activities began to give the parks a disreputable image.

French pleasure gardens were designed mainly as gardens, but English pleasure gardens were established around an inn or a tavern. Vauxhall Gardens in London was opened in 1661 (Mangels 1952: 6) and became the first internationally known pleasure garden. There was no admission charge, and patrons paid only for those amusements that they enjoyed. Vauxhall Gardens closed on July 25, 1850, after almost two hundred years of success, a victim of the same problems that haunted the gardens in France.

Just about the same time that Vauxhall Gardens was closing, the Prater in Vienna, Austria, became the most popular pleasure garden in Europe (Mangels 1952: 13). In 1873, it became the site of the Vienna World's Fair. The Fair introduced a new concept of outdoor entertainment to the world. Visitors who attended found new and exciting attractions and amusement rides. The quiet, relaxing atmosphere of the typical pleasure garden was broken by the introduction of primitive forms of the Ferris wheel, carousel, and roller coaster. These attractions appealed to the international visitors, who wanted the excitement offered by this new form of park. When these visitors left, they took back this new concept of entertainment to their own countries, and amusement parks began appearing in other parts of the world. One of the countries most enthusiastic about the new form of park was the United States.

The Amusement Park in the United States

In America during the late 1800s a brand new industry, public transportation, was emerging, and electric traction companies (trolley or streetcar companies) were appearing. The streetcar lines run by these companies were directly responsible for the development of amusement parks. In most cases, the electric light and power companies were charged a flat fee for the electricity used to run the trolley cars. Regardless of how much or how little electricity was used, the trolley company paid the same price. Most customers patronized the trolley cars from Monday through Friday, and the owners of the companies realized that they could increase their profits if they could find a way to convince passengers to ride on the weekend (Griffin 1974: 1). The solution was the placement of an attraction at the end of the line. The attraction could be anything that would get the people to ride the trolleys. Usually it was a merry-go-round. This idea started in New England and spread so rapidly that merry-go-round builders had difficulty keeping up with the demands. The Sunday trolley excursion was an inexpensive way for families and individuals to spend a day. They rode the trolley to the end of the line, where they picnicked, listened to music, and rode the rides.

Early Amusement Rides and Attractions

By the late 1800s the first comprehensive parks were being built on the fringes of major cities. These parks included roller coasters, Ferris wheels, spin and twist rides, shows, exhibits, games, and a variety of choices for eating and drinking. Many of the original parks—like Coney Island—were designed for adults, and initially the patrons paid an individual price for each ride. In 1903, George Tilyou of Steeplechase Park streamlined the system by inaugurating the concept of "pay one price" (P.O.P.).

The Carousel.   The carousel is one of the oldest and most popular rides of all time. The earliest visual record of the carousel is from Byzantine times, and the word can be traced to the twelfth century Arabian games of horsemanship called *carosellos* or "little wars" (Dinger 1986: 9). The carosello was a series of tests of dexterity and equestrian skill that involved the tossing of perfumed clay balls between two men. The object of this test of skill was to catch the fragile clay ball without breaking it. Losers were easily identified. The concept of the *carosello* spread to France, where it became a lavish pageant called a *caroussel*. The most celebrated of all caroussels was Le Grand Caroussel planned by Louis XIV to impress his teenage mistress, and thousands of people attended to view this spectacle of horsemen and other entertainments.

Eventually the carousel became a training device for young French noblemen. The noblemen rode legless horses attached to rods that rotated in a circle. The object of this activity was to provide practice for spearing contests by having the young men lance rings as they rode (Dinger 1986: 9). A servant supplied the necessary power to move the carousel by walking in a circle either above ground or in a pit dug below it. Later carousels were powered by systems of gears turned by men, and eventually (much to the relief of the men) by horses, mules, wooden-powered steam engines, and finally electricity.

Although the carousel was used by noblemen to practice for their contests, the general population took to it as a form of amusement. Carousels were built in many forms. While the traditional horse was still popular, exotic animals, boats, airplanes, and even replicas of blimps appeared. As technology advanced, some carousels were built on two levels instead of one, they became larger, music was added, and elaborately decorated

At far right, Henry Auchy, the founder of the Philadelphia Toboggan Company (PTC), stands on a fancy PTC carousel. Note the ornate chariot on the left of the picture and the facade carvings on the top of the carousel.
Photo courtesy of Charlotte Dinger, author of *Art of the Carousel*, Carousel Art, Inc., Green Village, NJ.

panels depicting popular themes replaced the canvas roof that covered early rides. Patrons looked for new and novel carousels, and those parks that had the most modern and elaborate rides were sure to draw crowds.

The Ferris Wheel. Like the carousel, the Ferris wheel has a long historical background. The primitive pleasure wheels enjoyed in European and Asian countries were the forerunners of the Ferris wheel. Unfortunately (at least for some individuals), early pleasure wheels were also powered by men who stood on the ground and operated the wheel by hand.

Originally called swings, pleasure wheels, and perpendicular roundabouts, the name Ferris wheel was coined when George Washington Gales Ferris built a 264-foot wheel for the 1893 Chicago World's Fair. The wheel came about as part of a nationwide contest to determine if Yankee ingenuity could beat the star of the 1889 Paris Exposition, the Eiffel Tower.

> The thirty-six carriages of the great wheel are hung on its periphery at equal intervals. Each car is twenty-seven feet long, thirteen feet wide, and nine feet high. It has a heavy frame of iron, but is covered externally with wood. It has a door and five broad plate glass windows on each side. It contains forty revolving chairs, made of wire and screwed to the floor. It weighs thirteen tons, and with its forty passengers will weigh three tons more. It is suspended from the periphery of the wheel by an iron axle six and one-half inches in diameter, which runs through the roof. It is provided with a conductor to open the doors, preserve order, and give information. To avoid accidents from panics and to prevent insane people from jumping out, the windows will be covered with an iron grating (*Scientific American* 1893: 8+).

Each car on the Ferris wheel also contained a new and novel communication device called a telephone, which enabled the conductor to contact the ground if a problem arose.

It took twenty minutes for the Ferris wheel to make one revolution, and rides consisted of two complete nonstop revolutions. Patrons stood in lines that stretched a city block and paid the exorbitant price of fifty cents (the equivalent of the exposition admission price) to ride the wheel. Without a doubt, Ferris's wheel was the darling of the exposition, dazzling all who rode or gazed on this engineering marvel.

The Roller Coaster. The roller coaster was born in Europe. Its ancestors were the Russian ice slides, which were used for public amusement (Griffin 1974: 42). The Russian ice slides were elaborately built of sculptured hard-packed snow and were made even harder by the application of water, which froze to create an extremely slippery surface. The slides could reach heights of seventy feet and were supported by timber frames. A guide selected from a group at the top escorted riders up the slide. The guide would lead passengers up a staircase to the top of the hill; there he would seat himself on a wooden sled approximately two feet long and seat the passenger in his lap. When everything was just right, the guide and his passenger would launch themselves off the slide. The ride carried them down the slope to the bottom of the hill, and then up another slope to the top of another slide. There the

Chicago World's Fair Ferris Wheel.

Courtesy of *Scientific American.*

[Entered at the Post Office of New York, N. Y., as Second Class matter. Copyrighted, 1893, by Munn & Co.

A WEEKLY JOURNAL OF PRACTICAL INFORMATION, ART, SCIENCE, MECHANICS, CHEMISTRY, AND MANUFACTURES.

Vol. LXIX.—No. 1.
Established 1845.

NEW YORK, JULY 1, 1893.

$3.00 A YEAR.
WEEKLY.

THE WORLD'S COLUMBIAN EXPOSITION—THE GREAT FERRIS WHEEL, 250 FEET IN DIAMETER, 36 CARS, 40 SEATS PER CAR.—[See p. 8.]

riders would disembark, carry their sled to a parallel track, and ride back to the top of the original slope.

At the end of the eighteenth century, a Frenchman returning from Russia wanted to introduce the idea of the Russian ice slide to the citizens of Paris, but the warmer climate made this impossible. The Frenchman adapted the ride to the area by constructing a hill made of wood and using small carriages that rode on a track. This was the beginning of the roller coaster as we know it today.

The first roller coaster, built in 1804 in a public garden in Paris, was called the Russian Mountains. This coaster was so high that many were frightened as the car started down the incline, and there were many serious accidents. Passengers also found the climb up to the top of the slope tiring and boring. Needless to say, safety features were virtually nonexistent.

Eventually technology overcame these problems, and the roller coaster took on new and interesting variations. In 1879 the first coaster using an oval design was developed (Griffin 1974: 43). In another unusual configuration, passengers sat in cars that accomodated six people and looked like park benches. During the ride, which returned to its original starting point, the passengers sat sideways so that they could see the scenery. In 1885, Phillip Hinkel built the Coney Island Coaster. This coaster had a powerful chain elevator that took loaded cars up the initial incline.

The Flip-Flap at Coney Island.
United States History, Local History and Genealogy Division. The New York Public Library. Astor, Lenox and Tilden Foundations.

In 1888, the flip-flap or the loop-the-loop coaster appeared (Griffin 1974: 46). The loop-the-loop was a gravity ride that had a complete loop at the bottom of the slope. Centrifugal force kept people in the coaster as they went through the top of the loop upside down. Gravitational forces were very uncomfortable, and riders complained of aching necks, hurting backs, and various displacements of their insides. The coaster was dismantled after its second year due to the lack of repeat riders.

Unusual Rides and Attractions.   Human imagination has been pushed to its outer limit in the quest for new and unusual rides and attractions. Some of these ideas have been unique and relatively benign; others are out and out bizarre.

Water attractions have been popular throughout the ages. Two of these inventions were the forerunners of the log-flume ride and the water slide. The first was patented in 1890 by James Inglis of Montreal, Canada (*Scientific American* 1890: 162). It was called "Inglis Artificial Water Slide for Pleasure Resorts." Inglis' idea consisted of a tank filled with water, one-half of which had a ramp that emptied into the artificial lake created at the bottom of the tank. Riders walked up a staircase on the outside of the tank, entered a boat that was stationed at the top of the ramp, and then were pushed off the ramp into the water below. A hoist system that was suspended over the entire structure returned the empty boats to the top of the ramp. Pumping machinery circulated water from the lake up to the ramp. The ride was cumbersome to operate and difficult to move from site to site.

An even more creative device was the "New Toboggan Slide for Bathers," which allowed bathers to slide into the ocean.

> This new toboggan slide for bathers is 23 ft. in height from the bottom to top of platform and 12 ft. 6 in. in width at the bottom, tapering up to the top of the platform to 6 ft. The framework is made of hemlock timber. On one side are steps built for bathers to ascend to the platform. They are 32 in number. On the other side is the shute [sic]. The shute [sic] is connected to the platform at the top, and runs down and out into the water for about 10 ft (*Scientific American* 1891: 169).

Bathers carried their toboggans, each weighing 18 to 20 pounds, to the top of the slide. The slide itself consisted of a series of rollers that provided the sliding surface for the toboggans.

> The greatest angle in the shute [sic], which is about 45 deg., is about 25 ft. from the starting point. When the slide strikes this point it goes down like a shot and out into the water, if it is not too rough, to a distance of about 200 ft. (*Ibid.*).

The entire ride from the top to the bottom of the slide took approximately 1.5 seconds. The entire apparatus rested on 16-inch wooden wheels, which were used to move the slide back and forth as the tide rose and fell. You could purchase this device for 600 dollars.

The popularity of horses led to several "horselike" rides. In 1891, the Paris Garden offered an adult version of the rocking horse. These rides

New Toboggan Slide for Bathers.
Courtesy of Scientific American.

called Hygienic Horses (presumably because you did not have to clean up after them) were very popular (*Scientific American* 1891: 214). As participants rocked their horse, it moved along a rail. A ratchet system kept the horse from sliding backwards as patrons raced to the finish line.

Besides Hygienic Horses, there were electric horses that ran around circular tracks (*Scientific American* 1890: 151+) and horses that were arranged in a circular manner and pedaled by the riders.

Illusion was also used to make interesting rides. The Haunted Swing was a popular ride in Atlantic City, New Jersey and at the Midwinter Fair near San Francisco, California (*Scientific American* 1894: 379). Patrons entered a completely furnished room. Suspended from a bar near the ceiling was a giant swing that looked much like a swinging platform. People sat in the swing while an attendant gave it a push to start it moving back and forth. The attendant then left the room, and the swing appeared to pick up speed and eventually even seemed to rotate completely around the bar. Actually it was the room that rotated, while the passengers were in a swing that was basically stationary. Furniture, including an apparently lit kerosene lamp, moved over their heads. Pictures hanging on the walls, tables, chairs, and a cupboard full of china all helped to disorient the riders, who gripped the sides of the swing to keep from falling out.

Equally as baffling as the Haunted Swing, was the illusion created by "The Cabaret du Neant" (Tavern of the Dead), a dinner show that was imported from Paris (*Scientific American* 1896: 152+). Spectators entered a long hall hung with black and entered a special restaurant. Coffins lined the walls of the restaurant, each with a burning candle placed on its lid. The center of the room was dominated by a chandelier made from what appeared

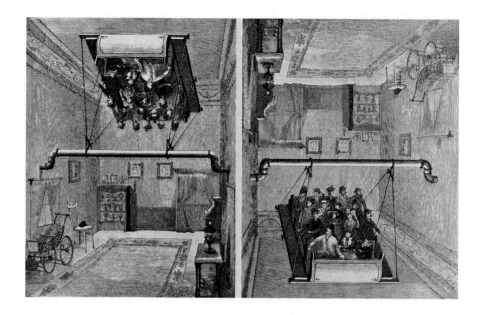

to be bones and skulls, and dinner was served by a gloomy man who appeared to be a mute. The room was full of pictures, which were pointed out to the diners by a lecturer. When the light of the room was ordinary, the pictures looked normal. As the light changed, and the pictures were illuminated from behind, they changed into skeletons.

After dinner, participants entered a second chamber. There, one of them was placed in a standing coffin and his body wrapped in a sheet. As the audience watched, he was transformed into a skeleton. These illusions continued in a third room, where a variety of specters appeared before the crowd. This performance was, in some ways, reminiscent of the Haunted Mansion found today at Disneyland and Walt Disney World.

Two of the oddest attractions were the exhibiting of premature babies by a man named Martin Couney, and a proposed device to drop people from a height of 1,000 feet into a well full of water. Martin Couney was a doctor who specialized in the treatment of premature babies. His stint as a showman started in 1896 at the Berlin World's Fair, when Dr. Pierre Budin asked him to supervise a display of incubators. Couney persuaded the staff of the Berlin Charity Hospital to let him take six babies and display them in his "child hatchery." He had hoped to be able to clear expenses but found instead that this was not a money-generating idea. To his credit, he never took money from the parents of the children and managed to save 6,500 of the 8,000 babies placed in his care.

The proposal to drop passengers from a height of 1,000 feet into a well filled with water is one of the more bizarre rides created. The idea was to place fifteen people into a capsule that looked like a bullet and suspend them from a tower that was located over a well dug into the earth.

A tower several meters in height and a closed cage constitute the plant. The maneuver is simple: The passengers enter the cage, which is afterward allowed to drop freely from the top of the tower. At the end of 100 meters fall the velocity acquired is 45 meters per second, at the end of 200 meters it is 77 meters. Now the fastest trains make scarcely 30 meters per second and descents into mine shafts never exceed 15 meters per second (*Scientific American* 1891: 114).

Whether or not this ride was ever manufactured or tried is unknown; at least no one "alive" claimed to have attempted such a feat.

Tourism and the Travel Industry

There have always been travelers, but the reasons for traveling have changed throughout the centuries. During medieval times the main reason for travel was war, and the great crusading waves of the late eleventh and twelfth centuries gave people a vast amount of geographical information about the Middle East and Europe. During this time both men and women traveled on land and across the seas.

Early Travelers

Pilgrims were early travelers. They journeyed to many places, but the three great pilgrimages of the Middle Ages were to Jerusalem, Rome, and Compostela. Other reasons for early travel included social occurrences, such as tournaments and feasts, which might be held following a special occasion like a knighting ceremony. Sometimes ambassadors were sent to represent rulers who did not, or could not, travel to witness marriages, coronations, and the formal ratifications of treaties. People also traveled to attend funerals and to return the body of the deceased to the land of his or her origin.

The early travelers and pilgrims had some of the same problems that bother travelers of today. Passports are not a modern-day invention. Passports (literally a pass that lets you travel through a port) originated in 1388 when King Richard II required English citizens to acquire and carry a permit before they could travel to France (Howell 1989: 22). (An earlier version of a passport was also issued in ancient Rome.) In the United States, the first issuing of passports occurred in 1796. The original passport announced the bearer as a U.S. citizen. In 1827, the passport format was changed to include a description of the person whose name was on the document. Passports were free until July 1, 1862, when the government decided that it needed additional revenue. The original fee was three dollars (Sutton 1980: 46).

Additional concerns involved the changing of money into local currencies, booking the best passage, and deciding what to pack. Early travelers did not have the advantages of drip-dry fabrics, disposable products, or modern-day grocery stores. Collecting the necessary items for traveling was probably an exasperating experience. Often the traveler needed to pack his own bedding, towels, and food. Needless to say, the early traveler did not throw a few things in a suitcase, but carefully packed his or her trunks for the often long and difficult journey. In addition to clothes and bedding, an early packing list might have included the following items: confections, cordials, laxatives, restoratives, spices, and dried fruit.

Like modern-day travelers, early travelers also had guidelines and guidebooks. In medieval times, the Venetian government licensed special guides who were stationed in the Piazza or on the Rialto. These guides were expected to serve as interpreters and "honest middlemen."

During the seventeenth and eighteenth centuries wealthy gentlemen and some ladies took the Grand Tour (McIntosh and Goeldner 1990: 25). The Grand Tour started during the Renaissance when young men began to travel in search of culture and learning. It was also taken by scholars, businessmen, and diplomats who traveled to Europe (the Continent) as an educational experience. By the eighteenth century it had become an extended trip, sometimes lasting several years. Eventually the Grand Tour evolved into the packaged tour.

The packaged tour consists of combined arrangements for transportation, lodgings, sightseeing, and other features. Thomas Cook was the first person to organize packaged tours on a large scale (Howell 1989: 209). Cook was born in England in 1808, and when he was twenty years old became a Baptist missionary and a strong supporter of the temperance movement. During the summer of 1841, Cook was working for a Baptist publisher in Loughborough. He was on his way to a temperance meeting in Leicester when it occurred to him that a special train running from Loughborough to Leicester would allow more people to attend the temperance meetings held there. Cook negotiated for a train, and on July 5, 1841, the first "Cook's Tour" took place. This was the first publicly advertised excursion train run in England. Five hundred and seventy people crammed into nine seatless third-class cars that were open to the elements. Cook negotiated a special fare of one shilling per person, arranged for a picnic lunch to be served, and set out tea for a thousand people.

Cook went on to run his first international tour in 1855, when he marketed tours to the Paris exhibition (van Harssel 1985: 17). He eventually had offices and contacts in other European countries that could help him overcome the obstacles of language, money, exchange rates, cultural differences, and border-crossing formalities. By 1864, Cook had offices from New York to Rome, and over 1 million people had used his services.

Early Forms of Transportation

The modes of transportation used by travelers have been varied. Early travelers journeyed by foot, by animal, or by boat. The Egyptians are credited with inventing the sail around 3200 B.C. (Howell 1989: 114). Before sails, boats were poled or rowed. The invention of the sail permitted boats to travel faster with less effort (at least on the part of the men) and therefore allowed for further exploration. With the arrival of the sail, the first cruises were organized approximately 5,000 years ago in Egypt. The first journey was made for peace and tourism by Queen Hatshepsut. She visited the lands of Punt (now believed to be Somalia) in 1490 B.C., and descriptions of this tour are recorded on the walls of the Temple of Deit El Bahari at Luxor. Later tourists also left their mark when they traveled, and the Colossi of Menon at Thebes have on their pedestals the names of Greek tourists of the fifth century B.C. (McIntosh and Goeldner 1990: 23).

In the United States, the first regularly scheduled transatlantic passenger service was established in 1818 by the Black Ball Line, and in 1819 the first steamship, the *Savannah,* crossed the Atlantic (Howell 1989: 115). Iron hulls replaced wooden hulls, propellers replaced paddle wheels, and steam turbines and later diesel engines made ships a faster, more comfortable mode of transatlantic transportation. By 1840 100,000 people were crossing the English Channel each year, and the Cunard Line had become the first line to offer scheduled steamship service across the Atlantic.

The cruise lines steadily improved their service and the level of comfort found aboard the ships. Ships now had private baths, hot and cold running water, wonderful food, and spacious, elegant common rooms. Liners, ocean-going ships that ran over a fixed route on a regular schedule, had become large luxury ships with names like the *City of Paris,* the *Lusitania,* and, of course, the *Titanic.*

The death knell for the large ocean liners occurred in the early and middle 1950s. High labor costs had helped to push the United States out of the passenger market. This, along with the introduction of jet aircraft, marked the end of an era. The new planes had increased passenger capacity, which

The Cunard Ship—The Mauretania—1939 to 1965.
The Mauretania and its sistership, the Lusitania, were known as the pretty sisters. Both of these ships were turbine propelled and were the first British liners to be fitted with a new apparatus that allowed all watertight compartment doors to be closed from the bridge. Note the two towering masts on the bow and the stern of the ship. They are a reminder of the sailing history of ocean crossing vessels.
Courtesy of Cunard Line, Ltd.

meant that ticket prices could be reduced. Also, air travel to Europe took eight hours as opposed to four or five days by ship. By the late 1950s, the number of passengers crossing the Atlantic by air equaled the number traveling by sea. With the introduction of the new airplanes, the reign of the modern ocean liners ceased.

Americans and Europeans also traveled by railroad and stagecoach. During the sixteenth century a primitive railroad, powered by horses on wooden tracks, was used to haul coal and iron ore. In the early 1800s, this early form of the railroad yielded to the invention of the steam engine, the real ancestor of the modern railroad. In England in 1804, the world's first successful steam engine ran on a nine-mile track at five miles per hour, and by the late 1820s and early 1830s, America had established a primitive railroad system (Howell 1989: 91). The South Carolina Canal and Railroad was started in 1829 and was the first scheduled passenger line in the United States. It ran from Charleston, South Carolina, to Hamburg, Georgia, a distance of 136 miles. By the 1830s, most early American railroads, the majority of which were under fifty miles long, served most major cities on the East Coast.

The first real railroad boom happened in the late 1840s and early 1850s (Wickre 1988: 15). Lines extended from the eastern seaboard and went west and south. By 1860, the railroad served all of the states east of the Mississippi; Chicago had become the nation's rail center; the Mississippi River had been crossed with the building of a railroad bridge; and the railroads had become absolutely luxurious—George Pullman had invented the sleeping car (Sutton 1980: 57). The car was cool, clean, comfortable, and had couches for sixty-four passengers. The interiors were paneled in carved black walnut, and the seats were covered with velvet. Corridors were carpeted, damask hung at the windows, and fragrant bouquets hung from the ceiling. This was a great departure from the earlier trains, which had hard bench seats, no windows to protect you from the elements, and belching clouds of smoke and soot.

The railroad went ocean to ocean on May 10, 1869, when the Union Pacific coming from the east and the Central Pacific coming from the west met at Promontory Point, Utah. This event allowed products and people to travel everywhere, and the railroads became a fast, comfortable form of transportation. Meanwhile, other forms of wheeled transportation that did not travel on rails were evolving.

In 1670, a European stage line offered coach service between Edinburgh and London. In America, people traveled by stagecoach in the early 1800s. (The term *stagecoach* was derived from the fact that the coaches traveled in stages.) In 1802, through coach service ran from Boston to Savannah, a distance of 1,200 miles (Sutton 1980: 25). The coaches covered fifty miles a day; the entire trip took approximately three weeks and cost around a hundred dollars, including board and lodging. Boston to New York took four days and cost ten dollars, while New York to Philadelphia took a day and a half and cost five dollars. The earliest stagecoaches carried

Origins of Commercial Recreation and Tourism

twenty passengers who sat on hard seats and discovered that the ride was dusty, hot, cold, and generally miserable. Ultimately, the stagecoach yielded to the bus, which first appeared in the 1890s. The buses were more comfortable than the stagecoaches, but they ran on solid tires and did not have springs.

Along with the arrival of the bus, came the automobile. The first commercially produced automobile was the Model A built by Henry Ford. The Model A was mass produced and came in one color, black. The floorboards of the car were assembled from the box that contained the battery (Sutton 1980: 147). By 1908, Ford was producing the Model T, also called the Tin Lizzie. This car was inexpensive and the price was affordable for the average person. As more cars were sold, people began to demand better roads.

By 1912, there were dozens of makes of cars. They were powered by steam, electricity, or internal combustion and accessories became popular. One of these accessories was Bosco's Collapsible Driver. The collapsible driver sat behind the wheel of your car while you were gone and discouraged thieves. "No thief ever attempted to steal a car with a man at the wheel. . . . It's so lifelike and terrifying that nobody a foot away can tell it isn't a real live man" (Sutton 1980: 116).

Americans loved their cars. The car became an indispensable item to many people. It was this need to have a car that led the Saunders brothers of Omaha, Nebraska, to start an automobile rental business. In 1916, the brothers borrowed a car. They thought that others might also need use of a car, so they bought one and went into the rental business. They charged ten cents a mile with a three-mile limit. The business grew until, eventually, they had offices in twenty-one states (Howell 1989: 101).

While the automobile dramatically changed the way that people traveled on land, the arrival of the airplane marked the beginning of a new era of transportation and travel. Man had tinkered with the idea of flight for centuries, and in the sixteenth century Leonardo da Vinci had designed a nearly practical flying machine. In June of 1783, Joseph and Etienne Montgolfier made the first ascent into the sky in a balloon; from 1891 to 1896, Otto Lilenthal of Germany made flights in a series of hang gliders of his own design (Yenne 1988: 10); and on October 10, 1902, Wilbur and Orville Wright made their famous 57-second flight at Kitty Hawk, North Carolina. Up until World War I many people saw the airplane as a novel amusement for the adventurous few. The war led to the first push for the serious development of the airplane. It became a new weapon in the arsenal of war, and countries raced to perfect the new flying machines.

World War I left many young men interested in flying, and it was immediately after WWI that the first commercial airlines were established both here and abroad. In Europe, the Germans started commercial flights less than a hundred days after the Armistice was signed. The Deutsche Luft-Reederei offered passenger service between Berlin, Leipzig, and Weimar (Sutton 1980: 145). In 1919, scheduled passenger service was started in Europe on the London to Paris route, and passengers wrapped in helmets and flying coats flew in a converted bomber. This service stopped after nineteen months. Fear and the absence of restrooms were major reasons for discontinuation (van Harssel 1985: 19).

In the United States, the first scheduled airline was the Petersburg-Tampa Airboat (1914). Tony Jannus, the owner of a seaplane, flew passengers one at a time from St. Petersburg to Tampa. The cost was five dollars for the 22-mile trip (Howell 1989: 64). Later, in 1919 a second Florida company, Aeromarine Sightseeing and Navigation, joined Jannus' company as a tourist carrier (Yenne 1988: 24).

The passage of the Kelly Air Mail Act of February 1925, helped to increase the number of commercial aviation operators. The Kelly Act allowed for commercial rather than government air-mail carriers. Many individuals formed companies to bid on the Contract Air Mail routes (Yenne 1988: 24). This helped to bring business into the air industry and to set the stage for the commercialization of the new industry. Air routes, first for the carrying of mail and then for the carrying of passengers, were established.

In 1925, scheduled passenger service was introduced in the United States when a Los Angeles-San Diego route was formed (van Harssel 1985: 19). In 1927, Charles Lindbergh stunned the world and won the hearts of millions both here and abroad when he soloed to Paris, an unheard-of feat.

Lindbergh joined the then fledgling Transcontinental Air Transport (TAT) and helped to map, route, and set airport standards. TAT became Transworld Airlines (TWA). In July of 1929, TWA sent its first trimotor airplanes across the United States. The trimotors each carried a total of ten passengers and went 110 miles per hour (Sutton 1980: 159). Travel was primitive, and passengers sat in wicker baskets without the benefit of pressurized cabins. They flew at low altitudes, often in rough and turbulent air. Airports (if there were any) were minimal, and paved runways and lights were scarce luxuries. The plane often landed for refueling, and the passengers assisted in this procedure by debarking from the plane and helping the pilot carry gas from the pump to the plane. The trimotors flew until dark or until conditions made it unwise to fly, then the plane landed and the passengers boarded trains. Now you could cross the country in forty-eight hours using air and rail. The cost was $351.94 (Sutton 1980: 159).

On May 15, 1930, Ellen Church joined United Airlines. Church was a young nurse who had been selected for a new job: stewardess. She joined the California-Chicago route. She was such a success that she was asked to select and train seven other young women to serve with her (Sutton 1980: 181). The young women served coffee, tea, and milk. They also took passenger's tickets, carried bags, made sure the seats were bolted down, nursed sick passengers, and watched for gasoline leaks in the cabin. An early stewardess manual listed the following instructions:

- Keep the clock and altimeter wound up.
- Carry a railroad timetable in case the plane is grounded.

TWA Lockheed Constellation 049. TWA owned and operated more Constellations than any other airline. Although the Constellation made its first flight for TWA in January of 1943, the airline did not start its scheduled international passenger service using the Constellation until February 6, 1946. An 049 "Connie" made the almost 20 hour trip from New York to Paris with stops for refueling at Gander, New Foundland, and Shannon Ireland.

- Warn the passengers against throwing their cigars and cigarettes out the windows.
- Keep an eye on passengers when they go to the lavatory to be sure they don't mistakenly go out the emergency exit.

In 1933, the DC-1 was introduced by Douglas Aircraft. The DC-1 was a metal plane with a crew of two and space for twelve passengers. It could travel at 150 miles per hour and go a distance of 1,000 miles before needing to refuel. The DC-1 had two engines and flaps so that it could make low-speed approaches and landings. TWA bought twenty-five of them at 65,000 dollars a piece. Douglas lost money at this price but sold them anyway (Sutton 1980: 1890).

The DC-1 was followed in 1934 by the DC-2. The improved model carried fourteen passengers, had a speed of 213 miles per hour, and could reach an altitude of 12,000 feet. One of the interesting features of the DC-2 was its windshield. It leaked so badly that pilots often wore raincoats when flying through a storm (Howell 1989: 72).

The DC-3 arrived in 1936 and became the most adaptable and successful plane of all time. The DC-3 was not only a passenger plane but served as a workhorse during World War II. During the war, 11,000 of them were built and by the end of the war, the DC-3 had emerged as a quick, reliable means of transportation. Returning soldiers came back eager to know more about flying, and some of them pursued aviation as a profession. The soldiers had also been exposed to different people in foreign lands, and many of them vowed that they would return during peace time; thousands did return, as tourists. The advancement of the aviation industry continued after World War II. In the late 1950s the first transatlantic jet passenger plane crossed the Atlantic, and travel was never the same again.

Lodging, Food, and Beverage

No one knows when the very first inn was established, but we do know that any time people traveled they required a place to stay. We also know from stories written by authors who lived many thousands of years ago that early accommodations were very primitive and not at all like what we are accustomed to today.

The earliest places for people to stay were probably along trade routes. These routes were unpaved paths through difficult, unpopulated terrain. Often these routes were dangerous not only because they were primitive, but also because robbers waited to prey upon the traders and the merchants who used them. The robbers knew that the traders would be carrying valuables and that they were vulnerable. The inns provided a place where the travelers and merchants could rest and find safety for the night. Later, as people traveled for reasons other than trading, and highway systems improved, the demand for inns and shelters increased.

In ancient Rome, individuals needed to obtain a permit from the government that allowed them to travel. This letter was called a "letter of eviction." The Roman government had a magnificent system of roads, and citizens could travel about quite easily (Howell 1989: 21). The single system of currency found throughout the empire facilitated the payments made for food and lodging, and the Pax Romana (Roman Peace), instituted during the reign of the emperor Augustus, ensured travelers of a reasonable degree of safety. Ultimately, the decline of the empire resulted in the disappearance of the wealthy class, the deterioration of the roads, and the rise of unsafe travel.

In America, the public stagecoach arrived around 1650, and inns were placed where the teams of horses were changed along the route, usually at a tavern. These inns were very crude, and the downstairs room consisted of the tavern. There one could have a drink, purchase some food, and if not too tired, spend the evening smoking tobacco and telling stories. Upstairs were either one or two sleeping rooms, each with several beds. Guests had to share the beds often with three or more people by having everyone sleep crosswise. There was no need to supply drawers for clothes because the guests slept in them. Wooden pegs were provided for coats and cloaks. Those who needed to use the "facilities" found them located right outside the tavern door.

In 1710, the U.S. Post Office established routes between major towns called post roads, and some farmers who lived along the routes converted their houses into inns. By the early 1800s there were a variety of coach lines with names like the June Bug Line, Pioneer Line, Good Intent Line, and the Shake Gut Line (Sutton 1980: 24). Needless to say, some of the names of

Origins of Commercial Recreation and Tourism

these lines reflected the quality of the ride. Although it became easier to travel, lodgings had not improved.

Around the same time, railroads and depot hotels were being established to serve travelers. Usually the hotel was connected directly to the station. As the American economy changed from an agrarian, home-based economy to an industrial economy, the need for inns and for places to purchase food increased, and the railroad and the depot hotels handled the early traders and merchants.

Guidebooks began to appear, and in 1732 one of the first guidebooks, *Vade Mecum for America* (A companion for Traders and Travelers), listed the roads and taverns from Maine to Virginia. It also had a directory of Boston streets for those who did not know their way around the city (Sutton 1980: 21). Information and directions for travelers going abroad were also available, and in 1824 a guidebook was published in London to give directions and advice to travelers going to the continent.

> Ten drops of essential oil of lavender, distributed about a bed will drive away either bugs or fleas; and five drops of sulphuric (sic) acid, put into a large decanter of bad water, will make the noxious particles deposit themselves at the bottom, and render the water wholesome . . . (Sutton 1980: 51+).

The first hotel built in America was the City Hotel, built in 1794 in New York City (Howell 1989: 141). It had 73 rooms and was designed specifically to be a hotel, a term and a concept imported from France. The City Hotel was followed some thirty-five years later by Tremont House. Tremont House, built in 1829 in Boston, was the first luxury hotel. It had 170 rooms and was the first hotel to have indoor toilets and private bedrooms with locks on the doors. Tremont House had single and double rooms, free soap, French cuisine, room service, bellboys, and a staff trained to provide polite service. For the traveler, this was paradise.

The early 1830s saw the importation of an idea from Europe. Up until this point lodgings usually included meals, but now hotels gave guests the option of paying only for their rooms and having the freedom to eat wherever they pleased. A week's lodgings ranged from $2.50 to $3.50, and a one-plate meal cost from 12.5 cents to 31.5 cents (Sutton 1980: 40).

With the invention of the elevator in 1853, hotels were built upward (Howell 1989: 141). Ellsworth Statler made a study of the hotel industry, and in 1908 opened his first hotel in Buffalo, New York. Known as the Buffalo Statler, it had new features that included fire doors, door locks with keyholes above the door knobs for easy access, light switches just inside the door, private baths, full-length mirrors, circulating ice water to every room, and a free morning paper for each guest. Statler also kept room rates within the reach of the average traveler, $1.50 per night.

The industry continued to change. There were tourist cabins, tourist courts, motels (a term derived from the phrase motor hotel), and motor inns. Today we have progressed to resort hotels, convention hotels, boatels, undersea floatels, etc. There is even an African hotel called Treetops, which features rooms in a huge tree where, from the safety of their rooms, guests can watch wild animals feed at night. Time-sharing has become a way for strangers to share accommodations, and there is a revival of the concept of the inn. We are calling it the Bed and Breakfast.

Putting It All Together

We have examined the forces that have influenced the development of commercial recreation and tourism, and we have looked at the evolution of specific aspects of these industries. Today's events become tomorrow's history. The amusements, modern hotels, and shiny planes of today will be the antiquated museum pieces of tomorrow. The driver of technology will work in concert with the other five factors that we have identified to keep the industry moving forward into the future. If we are to move into the future with it, then we need to keep our finger on the pulse of what is happening in our world.

Summary

The roots of commercial recreation and tourism go back to ancient times. The evolution of the industry has occurred throughout the ages and has brought us to where we are today largely due to the influence of six major factors:

1. Changing concept of work and leisure
2. Redefinition of the roles of men, women, and children
3. Sophistication of marketing and consumers
4. Mobility of populations
5. Existence of the global village
6. Impact of technology

Of the six factors, technology has been the most important driver for the development of the industry. Technology has allowed the realization of new, more realistic, and safer amusement rides. The early carousel, roller coaster, and Ferris wheel were dangerous. They lacked safety features and resulted in numerous accidents.

Technology has also changed customs and cultures by giving the peoples of the world instant access to events through the creation of television, satellites, fax machines, and personal computers. Technology has allowed us to see how other countries and cultures live and has created a desire for travel. We want to meet and experience first-hand the peoples and cultures of other countries, and they are interested in us as well. The rise of the large ships and their ultimate demise, first by prop and then by jet aircraft, only served to speed up the process of our meeting one another and the satisfying of our collective curiosity.

While technology has been and will be an important catalyst, the other five factors have also allowed change to occur. New legislation protecting workers, the entry of women into the workforce, and the realization that children are not miniature adults are only a few of the events that have allowed the industry to evolve into its present form.

The history of the industry is important, because it shows us where we have been. The factors that shaped this journey will continue to shape our future. Industry professionals need to understand and monitor these factors, and to identify other important influences, in order to comprehend the direction and the next level of evolution that commercial reaction and tourism will take.

Discussion Questions

1. Other than the six factors discussed in this chapter, what factors have shaped the industry? What impact have they had on commercial recreation and tourism?
2. Is the Puritan Work Ethic still alive today?
3. While the establishment of the global village has had many positive effects, there have also been negative ones. What are the negative effects of the global village?
4. What form do you think gender roles and family composition will take in the future? How might this change affect the industry?

Chapter Exercises

1. Research the Puritan Work Ethic. Cite examples of how this ethic came about and determine how widespread the sphere of influence of this philosophy really was.
2. List and discuss at least two early forms of industry-related amusements and games that are not mentioned in this chapter.
3. Determine the origins of, and philosophy for, the creation of the National Park System in your country.
4. Find old newspapers and magazines from the '40s, '50s, and '60s. What advertisements, articles, and news in these publications are industry related? What movies, television programs, products, and travel opportunities are listed?

References

A proposed apparatus for a fall of 1,000 feet. 1891. *Scientific American* (21 February): 114.
A novel amusement apparatus. 1903. *Scientific American* (15 August): 123.
An artificial lake and water slide. 1890. *Illustrated Scientific American* (13 September): 16.
An automatic centrifugal amusement way. 1903. *Scientific American* (9 May): 356–57.
An amusement park chronology. 1986. *National Amusement Park Historical News* 8: 4–5.
The aqua aerial trolley. 1895. *Scientific American* (10 August): 89.

Barrett, Wayne. 1982. A heritage preserved. *American Heritage* 33(4): 65–69.

Bicknell, Percy F. A review of *History of travel in America,* by Seymour Dunbar. *The Dial* 58(691): 254–56.

Braden, Donna R. 1988. *Leisure and entertainment in America.* Detroit, MI: Wayne State University Press.

Bullaro, John J., and Christopher R. Edginton. 1986. *Commercial leisure services managing for profit, service and personal satisfaction.* New York: Macmillan Publishing Company.

The Cabaret du Neant. 1896. *Scientific American* (7 March): 152–53.

The California Midwinter Exhibition. 1894. *Scientific American* (23 June).

Cartmell, Robert. 1986. Chemin du centrifuge. *Roller Coaster Magazine* 7(2): 18–23.

Dinger, Charlotte. 1986. *The art of the carousel.* Green Village, NJ: Carousel Art, Inc.

The electric race course. 1890. *Scientific American* (6 September): 151–52.

Fredriksson, Kristine. 1985. *American rodeo from Buffalo Bill to big business.* College Station: Texas A & M University Press.

Fried, Frederick. 1964. *A pictorial history of the carousel.* New York: Bonanza Books.

The great wheel at Chicago. 1893. *Scientific American* (1 July): 8–9.

Greenwood, Isaac J. 1898. *The circus—Its origins and growth prior to 1835.* New York: The Dunlap Society.

Griffin, Al. 1974. *Step right up folks!* Chicago: Henry Regnery Company.

The haunted swing—A curious illusion. 1894. *Scientific American* (16 June): 379.

Howell, David W. 1989. *Passport—An introduction to the travel and tourism industry.* Elmsford, NY: National Publishers of the Black Hills, Inc.

Hygenic horses. 1891. *Scientific American* (3 October): 214.

Kasson, John F. 1978. *Amusing the millions—Coney Island at the turn of the century.* New York: Hill and Wang.

LaBarge, Margaret Wade. 1982. *Medieval travellers.* New York: W. W. Norton and Company.

Lancaster, Paul. The great American motel. *American Heritage* 33(4): 100–8.

Lehmann, Armin D. 1982. *Travel and tourism—An introduction to travel agency operation.* Indianapolis, IN: Bobbs-Merrill Educational Publishing.

Looping the double loop. 1904. *Scientific American* (24 June): 293.

Looping the loop in 1846. 1903. *Scientific American* (9 May): 352–53.

Mangels, William F. 1952. *The outdoor amusement industry from earliest times to the present.* New York: Vantage Press, Inc.

The mareorama. 1899. *Scientific American* (11 March): 150.

McIntosh, Robert W., and Charles R. Goeldner. 1990. *Tourism principles, practices, philosophies.* 6th ed. New York: John Wiley and Sons, Inc.

McKechnie, Samuel. n.d. *Popular entertainment through the ages.* London: Sampson Low, Marston and Co., Ltd.

McKennan, J. 1972. *A pictorial history of the American carnival.* Bowling Green, OH: Popular Press.

McLean, Albert F., Jr. 1965. *American vaudeville as ritual.* n.p.: University of Kentucky Press.

New toboggan slide for bathers. 1891. *Scientific American* (12 September): 169.

Notes from the World's Columbian Exposition—Chicago, 1893. *Scientific American* (15 July).

O'Connell, Renee. Roller coaster: Part II. 1984. *Roller Coaster Magazine* (Fall): 32–37.

The pyramidical pleasure railway. 1895. *Scientific American* (14 September): 171.

Randel, W. P. 1969. *Centennial American life in 1876 Philadelphia.* Philadelphia: Chilton Book Company.

Sutton, Horace. 1980. *Travellers.* New York: William Morrow and Company, Inc.

van Harssel, Jan. 1985. *Tourism—An exploration.* Elmsford, NY: National Publishers of the Black Hills, Inc.

Wickre, John M. 1988. *American steam.* New York: Gallery Books.

Yenne, Bill. 1988. *The pictorial history of American aircraft.* New York: Exeter Books.

Additional Resources

Allen, Leslie. 1985. *Liberty: The Statue and the American dream.* New York: The Statue of Liberty-Ellis Island Foundation, Inc.

Allward, Maurice. 1981. *An illustrated history of seaplanes and flying boats.* New York: Barnes and Noble Books.

Appelbaum, Stanley, ed. 1977. *The New York World's Fair 1939/1940 in 155 photographs by Richard Wurts and others.* New York: Dover Publications.

Braynard, Frank O., and William H. Miller. 1987. *Fifty famous liners 3.* New York: W. W. Norton and Company.

Bryan, C. D. B. 1988. *The National Air and Space Museum.* 2nd ed. New York: Harry N. Abrams, Inc.

Burnham, Louise C., and George W. W. Packard. 1993. *Central Park: A visit to one of the world's most treasured landscapes.* New York: Crescent Books.

Crouch, Tom D. 1989. *A dream of wings: Americans and the airplane, 1875–1905.* Washington, D.C.: Smithsonian Institution Press.

Davies, Nancy Millichap. 1992. *Gateway to America: Liberty Island and Ellis Island.* American Traveler Series. New York: Smithmark Publishers, Inc.

Fussell, Paul, ed. 1987. *The Norton book of travel.* New York: W. W. Norton and Company.

Gibbs-Smith, C. H. 1981. *The Great Exhibition of 1851.* 2nd ed. Victoria and Albert Museum. London: Her Majesty's Stationery Office.

Gilbert, James. 1970. *The great planes.* New York: Ridge Press.

Greenfield, Jeff. 1981. *Television: The first fifty years.* New York: Crescent Books.

Gregory, Alexis. 1991. *The golden age of travel: 1880–1939.* New York: Rizzoli International Publications, Inc.

Hawkes, Nigel. 1991. *Vehicles: The most extraordinary achievements since the invention of the wheel.* New York: Macmillan Publishing Company.

Humble, Richard, and Mark Bergin. 1991. *A World War Two submarine.* The Inside Story Series. New York: Peter Bedrick Books.

Kinkead, Eugene. 1990. *Central Park 1857–1955: The birth, decline, and renewal of a national treasure.* New York: W. W. Norton and Company.

Levi, Vicki Gold, and Lee Eisenberg. 1979. *Atlantic City: 125 years of ocean madness.* 2nd ed. Berkeley, CA: Ten Speed Press.

Mackworth-Praed, Ben, ed. 1990. *Aviation: The pioneer years.* Secaucus, NJ: Chartwell Books, Inc.

Myer, Valerie Grosvenor. 1989. *A Victorian lady in Africa: The story of Mary Kingsley.* Southampton, UK: Ashford Press Publishing.

Oakes, Claudia M., and Kathleen L. Brooks-Pazmany, comp. 1985. *Aircraft of the National Air and Space Museum.* 3rd ed. Washington, D.C.: Smithsonian Institution Press.

O'Leary, Michael. 1992. *DC-3 and C-47: Gooney birds.* Osceola, WI: Motorbooks Publishers and Wholesalers.

Reeves, Pamela. 1991. *Ellis Island: Gateway to the American dream.* New York: Crescent Books.

Smith, Henry Ladd. 1942. *Airways: The history of commercial aviation in the United States.* New York: Alfred P. Knopf. Reprint. Smithsonian History of Aviation Series. Washington, D.C.: Smithsonian Institution Press, 1991.

Taylor, John W. R., ed. 1990. *The lore of flight.* Rev. ed. New York: Mallard Press.

Taylor, Michael J. H., ed. 1989. *Jane's encyclopedia of aviation.* New York: Portland House.

Villard, Henry Serrano. 1987. *Contact! The story of the early birds.* Rev. ed. Washington, D.C.: Smithsonian Institution Press.

Wescott, Lynanne, and Paula Degen. 1983. *Wind and sand: The story of the Wright brothers at Kitty Hawk, told through their own words and photographs.* New York: Harry N. Abrams, Inc.

Willensky, Elliot. 1986. *When Brooklyn was the world: 1920–1957.* New York: Harmony Books.

Wise, David Burgess. 1992. *The new illustrated encyclopedia of automobiles.* Secaucus, NJ: Wellfleet Press.

Yenne, Bill. 1988. *All aboard! The golden age of American rail travel.* New York: Barnes and Noble Books.

3

The Amusement Industry Today

LEARNING OBJECTIVES

1. *To depict the diversity of the amusement industry today.*
2. *To trace the evolution of post-World War II amusement and theme parks to current industry models and alternatives.*
3. *To demonstrate the importance of technology by illustrating how it has shaped and changed the industry.*

Introduction

Coney Island was the undisputed capital of fun in the late 1800s. Coney Island was significant because it gave North America a glimpse of amusement parks to come. Actually a combination of three parks (Steeplechase, Luna Park, and Dreamland), Coney Island was the harbinger of cultural change.

> Boston's Paragon Park and Revere Beach, Philadelphia's Willow Grove and nearby Atlantic City, Atlanta's Ponce de Leon Park, Cleveland's Euclid Beach, Chicago's Cheltenham Beach, Riverview, and White City, St. Louis's Forest Park Highlands, Denver's Manhattan Beach, San Francisco's The Chutes—these and others large and small became meccas for a public eagerly seeking recreation. Dominating them all in size, scope, and fame was New York's Coney Island (Kasson 1978: 7).

Coney Island, and other parks like it, challenged and defied Victorian attitudes and rules. The Coney Island experience was unique. You had the sense that you had entered another world where everyday rules and laws were suspended, daily routines and inhibitions were forgotten and restrictive Victorian ways were left behind.

Ultimately the demise of Coney Island arrived. The catalysts for this event were the phonograph, radio, and movies. These startling new

Dreamland, Coney Island Park at the turn of the 19th century— Dreamland was built across the street from Luna Park. Its 375 foot Beacon Tower contained 100,000 of the one million electric lights that illuminated Dreamland and transformed it into a spectacular sight.

inventions helped to blur the distinction between the real world and Coney Island. No longer unique, the park began to lose its effectiveness as a means of escape and as a source of adventure. By the 1920s customers were getting bored. World War I, the Great Depression, and World War II were the final nails in the coffin as the mystique of Coney Island died, not with a bang, but with a whimper.

Post-World War II Parks

It was not until the end of World War II that serious interest in amusements and the amusement business returned. After all, in the last thirty years the world had witnessed the Great Depression and two world wars. Things had been grim during this time period, but as the men and women who had fought during World War II returned home, the nation was ready to enter a new era of peace and prosperity. It was time to leave the harshness of the depression and the two great world wars behind.

Many of today's amusement parks had modest beginnings as one-ride operations. An entrepreneur with a passion for fun would purchase an attraction, find a location, and sell tickets for rides. Most likely the attraction was a small carousel or Ferris wheel, and the target market was children. While owning one attraction was good, owning two attractions was better. Two attractions ultimately became three attractions, and so on. Growth progressed naturally with the addition of restrooms, souvenir stands, more attractions, and food and picnic areas. Before long an amusement park was born.

These early parks, established in the 1950s, catered to the children who were born after World War II, the baby boomers. Many of the parks were themed and became Storybook Villages and Fantasyland Parks. They were designed to entice parents into taking their small children to the parks to enjoy the attractions and the other amusements. Pumpkin houses and shoe-shaped buildings, where the old woman who lived in a shoe resided, sprung up next to kiddy rides and costumed Mother Goose characters. Here you could see Humpty Dumpty, Little Jack Horner, Miss Muffet, and the popular children's characters of the day. Although most of these parks are gone, some still exist. Although the themes have changed, the concept of a children's section lives on in designated areas of many of today's parks.

Nothing stays the same. As the World War II baby boomers grew up so did their taste in rides. Some parks either would not or could not change to keep up with the times and subsequently died; others adapted and evolved in form. The arrival of Disneyland in Anaheim, California, on July 17, 1955, was the opening salvo in the race to catch up with the new leader of the pack: Walter Elias Disney. Airfares and discretionary income put Disneyland out of reach for many people, but the opening of Walt Disney World in Orlando, Florida, in 1971, brought the Disney experience within a one- to two-day drive of the major population centers in the East Coast corridor. During the 1970s in an effort to take up the chase, huge heavily financed parks were built, and existing parks pushed to expand. The chase, however, was costly.

The Disney Influence

Disneyland

Disney was a man of extreme talent, perseverance, vision, and drive. He also happened to be a family man with two young daughters. Walt would take his daughters to the parks, which had been designed for children.

> The idea [for Disneyland] came along, Walt said, when I was taking my daughters around to those kiddy parks. While they were on the merry-go-round, riding 40 times or something, I'd be sitting there trying to figure out what I could do (*Walt Disney World 20 Magical Years:* 7).

What Walt wanted was a park for the entire family. This was not to be a typical amusement park and not a park only for children, but a place unlike any other ever built. What emerged was a huge success called Disneyland.

There were many reasons for the success of Disneyland. First and foremost was the unique quality of the experience. Like Coney Island, Disneyland became a place where reality and the presence of the everyday world were suspended, if only for a while. Unlike Coney Island, this place was clean, the employees were courteous, the atmosphere was wholesome, and the quality of the experience was exceptional. Here you could see the familiar faces of Mickey, Minnie, Snow White, and all the other popular characters that had been visible on film or television.

Van Arsdale France, a long-time Disney pioneer and founder of the Disney Universities, lists some other reasons why he feels that Disneyland is a "rare and unusual occurrence" (France 1991: 6–7). First was timing and the willingness of society to eagerly accept the concept of the family park. The opening of Disneyland capitalized upon the ending of World War II and captured the attention of the children who were born after the war—the baby boomers. Here was the perfect population for Disneyland. Born between 1946 and 1964, years that saw more American babies born than any other period of time, these new families were ripe for the Disneyland experience.

Television, a new commercial technology that emerged in the early 1950s, became the vehicle by which the Disneyland experience invaded the homes of the baby boomers. Thousands sat riveted in front of the magical screen that brought the "Wonderful World of Disney" and the "Mickey Mouse Club" into their lives. While some adults saw these shows as huge commercials for Disney (perhaps the original infomercials), the kids sat mesmerized in front of their television sets. Who didn't want to own a coon skin cap and a set of mouse ears? Who didn't want to be a Mouseketeer? Who didn't want to go and meet Mickey in person?

France also points out that the interstate highway system was created in 1956, and commercial aviation was expanding. Air travel was still expensive and highways were not nearly as accessible as they are today, but at least it was now possible to draw larger numbers of guests to the Disneyland experience.

Finally, it was Walt and his brother Roy whose vision and combined skills of creativity and business made Disneyland possible. Disneyland was the first uniquely themed park and the flagship of other Disney parks and ventures to come.

> *There are thousands of mountains in the world, there is only one Fujiyama.*
> *There are innumerable architectural gems, there is only one Taj Mahal.*
> *There are thousands of athletic events, there is only one Olympics.*
> *There are countless parks and entertainment sites throughout the world, **there is only one Disneyland** (France 1991: 6).*

France is right. Disneyland, the smallest of the Disney parks, will always be special because it was *first*.

Walt Disney World

Disney died five years before the opening of Walt Disney World. With acreage totaling one hundred and fifty times the size of Disneyland, Walt Disney World was to be a destination resort. Besides a Magic Kingdom, modeled after Disneyland, there would be hotels, recreational facilities, and an Experimental Prototype Community of Tomorrow known simply as EPCOT. More than 8 million cubic yards of earth were moved during the first phase of construction (*Walt Disney World 20 Magical Years:* 11).

Unlike Disneyland, which had become landlocked, Walt Disney World was situated on a 28,000-plus-acre site. Walt had realized that he had not purchased enough land in Anaheim for Disneyland. Surrounding properties were quickly purchased to make way for hotels, restaurants, and other

The EPCOT Center geosphere rises 18 stories above EPCOT. Inside guests can enjoy the story of the history of communication from the beginning of time to the future.
Photo: Susan Weston.

tourist attractions. As a result, businesses formed a ring around Disneyland. This would not happen with Walt Disney World. His purchase of approximately 43 square miles would ensure that guests would be able to approach the Magic Kingdom without having to sort through signs and buildings. Instead of being tucked in among commercial ventures, the Magic Kingdom would appear and stand alone amid palm trees and meticulously manicured lawns.

The total investment for the 1971 opening of Walt Disney World was 400 million dollars. Like Disneyland, Walt Disney World was a success. The

The Land in EPCOT celebrates the earth and our relationship to nature. A revolving restaurant, the Land Grill, rotates while you eat and looks down upon the attraction "Listen to the Land"—a boat trip through a South American rain forest, an African desert, and the American plains.
Photo: Susan Weston.

Florida climate and accessibility to the major cities in the East Coast corridor by car, bus, rail, and airplane, made this the perfect spot for a destination resort. Tourism grew at a tremendous rate with 500,000 tourists arriving by air in Orlando in 1970, more than 3 million in 1980, and nearly 9 million in 1989 (Braun 1991: 102). The sleepy little town of Orlando became the center of an attractions-driven tourist economy. Life in Orlando would never be the same again.

With the addition of EPCOT Center in 1982 and the Disney-MGM Studios Theme Park in 1989, Walt Disney World became three parks on one site. The twelve major Disney resorts on location offered 10,668 rooms / units for guests who could enjoy not only the three parks but the other attractions of the "Vacation Kingdom" as well. (Walt Disney World Facts and Figures Sheet—EPCOT Center, 1992) With Disney properties on both the West Coast and the East Coast of the United States, the Disney Company was ready to go international.

Tokyo Disneyland

Approximately thirty years ago the Oriental Land Company (OLC) purchased the tract of land that now contains Tokyo Disneyland (TDL). Unable to find a Japanese company capable of developing a major theme park, the OLC approached the Walt Disney Company. One thing that the president of the OLC had requested was that Tokyo Disneyland be pure Disneyland and uniquely American. Van Arsdale France describes the scene at the presentation of TDL to the Japanese executives involved in the Tokyo project.

The room was set up in rather sterile-looking quarters in a Mitsui office building. The Japanese executives were seated according to status, with the most senior men in the center front seats. Fortunately, we had been warned that they might be stone faced but they would listen. I was glad to receive the warning (France 1991: 101).

Ultimately OLC and the Walt Disney Company combined forces, and the TDL project was undertaken. While all TDL-related affairs are decided on by both companies, other responsibilities were divided. Disney oversaw the creative aspects of the park, while OLC was in charge of park operations with advice from Disney. OLC was in charge of financing, and both parties were responsible for quality control (Makanae 1993: 15).

Snow White's Castle—
Tokyo Disneyland.
Photo: Paola Zanzo.

Tokyo Disneyland opened in 1983 with an attendance exceeding 10 million. Attendance continued to rise each year with 11,975,000 guests in 1987, 13,382,000 in 1988, and 14,752,000 in 1989 (*Park World* 1991: 12). Cumulative attendance exceeded 100 million in 1992, and the park expects to accommodate more than 16 million guests in 1993 (Makanae 1993: 13). Like its sister parks in America, TDL has done well. Its impact has transcended the boundaries of the park and touched on other aspects of Japanese culture. TDL's success has spurred the development of other theme parks in Japan and has also raised Japanese consciousness concerning the place of leisure in one's life and the value of family entertainment. With parks on both coasts of the United States and one in Japan, Mickey went to Europe.

Euro Disneyland

Euro Disneyland is located in Marne-la-Vallée, a farming region approximately twenty miles east of Paris. A 400-page document detailing the agreement for Euro Disney gave Disney tax breaks and loans totaling approximately 40 percent of the cost of the project. The French received 50 percent European ownership of the park, attractions showing French and European civilizations, and an opening date of 1992. In an effort to gain acceptance for Euro Disney, the mayors and public officials of the towns surrounding the site of the park were taken to either Disneyland or Disney World. It was hoped that a visit to an existing site would serve as an educational experience concerning the potential for Euro Disney. Euro Disney management also flew approximately 200 potential investors and bankers to Disney World to help them understand the possibilities of establishing a Euro Disney and to help with the process of issuing stock to finance the park (Reeves 1991: 83).

Opened on April 12, 1992, Euro Disney is approximately the size of Walt Disney World in Orlando. Five languages are spoken in the park, which has been modeled after Disneyland with modifications made for climatic and cultural reasons. Michael Eisner, the Chief Executive Officer (CEO) of the Walt Disney Company, described the park as a "European version of the American Classic, not just a French one" (Reeves 1991: 82).

Euro Disney has not been without its controversies and problems. The French intellectual community has called it "Euro Disgrace," "Euro Dismal," and a "cultural Chernobyl." Meanwhile, critics have raised questions concerning the cost of the land, the building of a train station for the sole use of the park, and the sale of company housing at below-market rate. The hiring and training of cast members also ran into cultural differences. French unions operate differently from American ones, the Disney dress code has been received with a less than enthusiastic response, and the park was plagued with "technical difficulties" when it first opened.

Finally, the park had financial set backs. Plans to build a second site were delayed (*Park World* 1993: 12) and in October of 1993, prices were adjusted to try to recoup some of the more than 300 million dollars lost. At the same time 950 of the 11,100 jobs at Euro Disney were eliminated as part of a cost-cutting move (*The New York Times* 1993: D30). Even with these adjustments Euro Disney still did not show a profit. In Spring of 1994 Saudi Arabia's Prince al-Waleed bin Talal bin Abdulaziz al-Saud, rescued the park by agreeing to invest up to $439 million in Euro Disney. A few months later Euro Disney quietly and unofficially changed its name to Disneyland Paris in an effort to change its image and align itself with the Disneyland mystique.

Response to the Disney presence by the management of many of Europe's biggest and oldest parks has, for the most part, been positive. Park owners and managers recognized the positive aspects of the presence of Euro Disney on European parks. Olivier de Bosredon of Parc Asterix, a major park less than thirty minutes from Euro Disney, pointed out that "existing parks in Europe must continue to develop their own identities if they are to continue to operate successfully" (*Park World* 1992: 38). Paul Beck of De Efteling in the Netherlands stated that the Disney presence and higher admission rates might give other parks the opportunity to adjust their fees accordingly, and that "there are four identical Disneys, but there is only one Efteling" (*Park World* 1992: 39). Almost everyone agreed that the Disney presence would lead to higher customer expectations. European parks began to compare their facilities to Disney standards and strove to reach or to exceed them. Meanwhile, Euro Disney is still young and the Walt Disney Company remains an adaptable and extremely capable organization. Their initial entry into the European market has not been as smooth as they might have wished, but they are by no means out of the running.

World Parks

North America does not have a monopoly on the amusement industry. There are major parks, primarily in Europe, whose histories reach back long before there were parks in North America and there are countries, mainly in Asia and the Middle East, that are just starting to organize their own leisure industries.

Blackpool Pleasure Beach is the king of all European parks and ranks among the top tourist attractions in Britain. Sitting on a 42-acre site in Blackpool, England, it has its own railroad station. Admission is free and you pay-as-you-go. Founded in 1906 Blackpool has the world's only operating Steeplechase ride.

From Argentina to Saudi Arabia to Nigeria, people are enjoying and building amusement parks. They are discovering that the amusement industry is not only profitable, but fun.

Ocean Park—Hong Kong

Ocean Park is the largest theme park in Southeast Asia and is just one example of the many major parks all over the world. Ocean Park sits on a steep

The Steeplechase, a unique rollercoaster at Britain's most popular amusement park, Blackpool Pleasure Beach.
Courtesy of Blackpool Pleasure Beach.

promontory between Aberdeen and Deepwater harbors in Hong Kong. It covers 192.66 acres and is a "tiered" park with thrill rides at the top, a water-park at the bottom, and the Middle Kingdom in between. The Middle Kingdom celebrates the cultural side of China and consists of walkways, gardens, pagodas, and entertainment.

Originally visitors entered the park by riding up the side of the hill in a chairlift. The chairlift sits six people in a podlike capsule and provides spectacular views of the China Sea, surrounding islands, and the two harbors. Eventually a series of giant escalators were installed as a means of transporting those who were afraid of heights and disliked the white-knuckle ride of the lift. The escalators comprise the longest moving staircase in the world.

Because Ocean Park is a nonprofit organization, it uses its surplus revenue for development. In 1992, ten million dollars were pumped back into the park (*Park World* 1993: 6). In 1993, a 3.5-acre site was opened for kids. Known as Kids' World, the new area includes four family rides, two trains, and cost over six million dollars. Ocean Park maintains a comprehensive master plan for expansion. In 1994, a 30-meter Ferris wheel, wet-dry slide, and atoll reef with a breeding program for killer whales was added. A winter village exhibit (which should be a novelty for the occupants of Hong Kong, who do not receive snow), is scheduled to be showcased in 1996 (*Park World* 1993: 6).

Attendance at Ocean Park for 1991 was 2.7 million visitors. In 1997, when Hong Kong reverts to mainland China, Ocean Park will be accessible to large segments of the surrounding population that have never seen anything like the park. The impact of the reunification of Hong Kong with China could push attendance up dramatically.

Ocean Park in Hong Kong overlooks the Aberdeen and Deepwater Harbors. It is a tiered park that can be reached by riding a series of escalators that comprise the world's longest moving staircase.
Courtesy of Ocean Park.

Waterparks

During the 1980s, the waterpark became the vehicle for individuals, small groups, and businesses to either keep the attention of their current customers, attract new ones, or enter (on a more economical scale) the amusement industry.

The change from small parks to larger ones had been due to a combination of factors. Prime space along coasts, waterways, and around popular vacation spots was at a premium, and increased land prices and availability made the entry into the industry expensive. Unlike the years following World War II, it was difficult for individuals who wanted to enter the industry to do so. They just could not afford the cost of the land.

As amusement-park ride sophistication increased (along with price) marketers convinced many people that bigger was better, higher was required, and faster was the only way to go. Everyone was looking for a thrill and something different. It was expensive to keep up with the industry. Even if you had the land, the price of construction and of acquiring the attractions was high. Return on investment (ROI) was the bottom line in many decisions regarding land usage, and often a shopping center, condominium complex, or office building had a better ROI than a new park. Corporate interests replaced many of the mom and pop operations that did not want to be bigger, higher, or faster. The value of their business became the value of their land.

North American Parks

People have always recognized the therapeutic value, both physical and psychological, of being in the water. The fitness revolution brought with it thousands of lap swimmers whose quest was to swim to stay flexible, increase strength, and improve fitness. But, except for the diehards in the crowd, the monotonous routine in a traditional rectangular pool soon separated the truly committed from the incredibly bored.

On August 8, 1970, the first wave pool opened in North America. This was not a commercial facility but an enterprise undertaken by a municipal government. There was a surfing pool in Arizona, but Point Mallard in Decatur, Alabama, was the first pool with oceanlike waves. Europe had been building wave pools since the 1960s, and former Decatur mayor, J. Gilmer Blackburn, traveled to Germany to see a wave pool before installing one in his town. For seven years, Point Mallard was the only wave pool in North America (Bell 1990: 11). Since its inception, Point Mallard has capitalized on its original goal of becoming a unique regional facility by expanding its attractions and offerings. Some of the additions include an aquatic center, open-air skating rink, 18-hole golf course, and campground.

The United States ultimately chose to follow two paths in the development of its waterparks and facilities. The first path has been the commercial development of waterparks by profit-oriented companies. The second path is the change in programming and facility design by community park and recreation departments. The development of the commercial sites has been more rapid than that of the community agencies. Although some communities such as the Mallard Point facility in Decatur have followed a progressive path, space, money, and a historically traditional approach has made the community sector slow to respond.

In the United States, private corporations built parks as stand-alone attractions or as new attractions in already established parks. Wet 'N Wild, Raging Waters, Water Mania—the names alone reflected the intent of the experience. This was not a leisure center; this was where the action was.

Older parks with water areas tried to stay competitive by retrofitting their pools with slides, hot tubs, and appropriate "tropical" decor. The day of the barren pool environment had died. New construction included interactive water activities, spraypools, themed water areas, bigger and better slides, and any other innovative device or idea that seemed to be at least semireasonable and profitable. A study of park investments for 1993, done by the International Association of Amusement Parks and Attractions (IAAPA), saw as a conservative estimate the investment of almost 206 million dollars in new attractions worldwide (*Funworld* 1993: 32).

Hotels were not to be outdone by the parks. It was not enough to provide a room, a restaurant, and maybe some entertainment any more. Even Walt Disney World, which had its two original waterparks, River Country and Typhoon Lagoon, added Stormalong Bay; a three-acre water playground shared by two hotels.

In Canada, development of waterparks and facilities was influenced by the desirability of capturing all segments of the community. Many of the Canadian projects were built by municipalities.

Community centers that combine aquatic facilities, libraries, day care centers and many other amenities under one roof are becoming the modern equivalent of the old town square in many Canadian cities (Goldman 1992: 10).

These multiuse facilities serve as focal points for all members of the community. Cole Harbour Place in Cole Harbour, Nova Scotia, supplies a family changing room as well as separate changing areas for men, boys, women, and girls. In the family changing room young children and handicapped individuals can be helped to dress. Children can then attend swimming or dance class while their parents either work out or take fitness classes. Afterwards, everyone can go to the library or attend the theater.

World Waterparks

Parks outside of North America tend to be smaller and not as flamboyant as parks built in North America, but they have been experiencing massive construction and expansion.

'There seems to be an explosion in international park development right now,' said Al Turner, executive director, World Waterpark Association (WWA), Lenexa, Kan. 'One reason for growth in some regions is the changing political world. The culture and geography of the region also may strongly affect what can be built' (Steinberg 1993: 30).

Europe with its centuries-old tradition of "baths" was building indoor aquatic leisure centers with waterfalls, lamp areas, and other unique features.

In Europe, aquatic leisure centers are a three-dimensional environment including spas, waterslides, zero-depth entries, swim-throughs, lounging areas as well as the lap and diving pools common to most natatoria (Goldman 1992: 10).

European leisure centers usually include a swim-through feature and a hydrotube. The swim-through allows patrons to swim from one area to another, usually from an indoor pool to a small heated outdoor pool. This feature can sometimes be found in the more progressive hotels in the United States. The hydrotube is an enclosed waterslide which starts and ends in the leisure center and may extend outside the facility. Having the slide outside helps to control construction costs by limiting building size.

European parks tend to be indoors and are health, fitness, and family oriented. Many of these facilities are built and operated by local government. Because mass transit is more likely to be used by Europeans to get to the park, parking facilities do not have to be as extensive as they are in North America. Also, there is much less emphasis on fast-food facilities; Europeans tend to "dine" or to bring their own food to the park.

In Asia land is expensive, and there is less space for slides and other attractions. Some parks may be built vertically and combined with nonwater amusements. Andrew Wray of WhiteWater West Industries in Vancouver, British Columbia, sees the Asian market as two separate markets: Japan and the rest of Asia.

Rokko Island in Kobe, Japan is the world's largest waterpark installation. One tower provides the base for fifty slides that can be reached from two levels. Slides go from the tower to several small splash pools which circle the 100-square-meter area.

Courtesy of WhiteWater West Industries, Ltd.

Even in Taiwan, China, Hong Kong, the Philippines, Malaysia, Singapore, the businesspeople tend to be Chinese. The Japanese have the highest quality standards of any market. There, price is not so much an issue; whereas in the Chinese sphere, it is the major issue (Steinberg 1993: 36).

Waterpark development is influenced by weather (European parks), land price (Japanese parks), and religious and cultural laws. Religious and cultural laws are certainly a consideration in the Middle East where modesty is required; building a waterpark can be a cultural challenge. In the United Arab Emirates a project was proposed for the building of a waterpark that would really be two facilities. The women's park would be indoors, and the park for the men would be outdoors. A Libyan park built by WhiteWater West is one facility that has been split by a dividing fence. The men are on one side and the women are on the other. Another solution is to build one park and alternate days; women visit one day, men the next. Modesty laws also extend outside of Asia. Where there is a Moslem population, many people will not wear swimsuits but enter the water in more modest attire in observance of their religious beliefs.

Sunway Lagoon Waterpark—Kuala Lumpur, Malaysia.

Sunway Lagoon Waterpark is part of a larger development called Bandar Sunway. Bandar Sunway is broken up into eight activity zones with the waterpark in the leisure and entertainment sector. The park was designed to be self-reliant, while at the same time being a catalyst for the development of the resort.

Sunway Lagoon Water is the first successful international theme park in Malaysia: (top) under construction, (bottom) open to the public.
Courtesy of Australian Leisure Industries.

The waterpark occupies approximately five out of seventeen acres set aside for its development. Sunway Lagoon itself is an old quarry pit that has been transformed into a five-hectare freshwater lake.

Because no one in Malaysia had operated a theme park before, Australian Leisure Industries (ALI) not only designed and constructed the park, it also signed a management contract with the owners. The park intensively trained its staff in waterpark operations and safety. Sunway Lagoon Waterpark became Malaysia's first successful international theme park.

Pay-for-Play

The concept of paying to play was a new idea that was totally alien to many people. Why would anyone pay to play when there were playgrounds, not only at public schools but in public parks? Children could play there.

There has been a long tradition of public playgrounds in North America, but, during the 1970s traditional playgrounds were hard hit by rising insurance costs and huge settlements resulting from lawsuits. Unsafe equipment and practices coupled with an increase in litigation in general, led many communities to the conclusion that the only way to protect themselves was to dismantle their playgrounds. Those who could afford to pay the insurance premiums did so. Others became self-insured either by themselves or in conjunction with other communities. Some just removed the equipment. Why take a chance? Awards for injuries were high, industry standards were virtually nonexistent, risk management was a new concept to many, and money for maintenance and repair was scarce. It was the perfect combination for trouble.

The opening of Sesame Place in Langhorne, Pennsylvania, signaled the start of the soft play movement. Soft play minimized the hazards *and* the insurance risk. Soft, protected play elements replaced traditional playground pieces. There was no hard equipment on which to hit yourself and no hard surfaces underneath on which to fall. Opened in the early 1980s, Sesame Place was a joint venture between the Children's Television Network and Busch Entertainment. The Children's Television Network needed revenue, Busch Entertainment had the capital, and Sesame Place was the result. Sesame Place featured the familiar characters of the popular children's television show, Sesame Street. Jim Henson's Kermit, Bert and Ernie, the Count, and the rest of the Sesame Street troupe were brought to life at Sesame Place. These characters were well known to thousands of children who were barely able to stand in front of the television set. Sesame Place became their Disneyland.

Initial soft play equipment consisted of custom-made units that stood alone. Although they were expensive, they were not nearly as costly as a major amusement attraction. Eventually soft play units became modular. Modules were not only cheaper than stand-alone units, they were also safer. By confining children to a specific space through the arrangement of the modules and the use of nets, the kids could be channeled in specified directions. Dangerous situations were eliminated or minimized and unlike passive rides, soft play was challenging both physically and intellectually. This arrangement was perfect, and the children loved it.

Mass-manufactured units called "Space Stations" were the first pay-for-play soft modulars. Installed in over 200 ShowBiz Pizza establishments, they were extremely popular. Other installations of modular units for fast-food establishments followed.

> The first soft, modular units for fast-food restaurants began with the introduction of a two-level unit in a new Burger King in Charlotte, NC. The effect was electric. The play unit capacity of 70 was filled from 10:00 A.M. to 10:00 P.M., and the store's sales shot up 25 percent over projections. While the McDonald's across the street was left with an all-adult clientele, the Burger King was bursting with family business. Birthday party bookings soared. Thus was born the fast-food playground wars (Pentes 1992: 33).

The soft play wars have not subsided but have spread to other areas. Ball crawls, a form of soft play equipment, have sprung up in retail stores as a way of entertaining the kids while mom and dad shop. IKEA, a Swedish-based company selling home furnishings first in Europe and now in North America, has instituted a variety of child-friendly conveniences to help families shop. One of these features is a ball crawl. Parents can drop the kids off at the ball crawl when they arrive, shop unimpeded, and retrieve them when they are done. Retailers know that parents will spend more when not distracted by children who are bored and want to go home. As for the kids, they no longer have to stand and listen to a discussion concerning what shade of mauve will go with the lamp that Aunt Nancy sent. Ball crawls have also been a popular and cost-effective form of fun for family entertainment centers.

Family Entertainment Centers

Family Entertainment Centers (FECs) are the emerging form of family entertainment for the 90s. Part old-time arcade, part high-tech, and containing both rides and live entertainment, the FEC is both innovative and interactive.

An FEC may be built as an indoor facility, an outdoor facility, or as a combination of both. They may stand alone or be integrated with other types of business. Some of the kinds of activity found at an FEC include soft play pieces, miniature golf, simulators, pinball machines, virtual reality, and video games. There may also be roving characters and live shows. Much of what is contained in the FEC depends upon the size of the facility and the available budget. Some FECs have put in small skating rinks or laser tag games. The obvious target market for an FEC is families, but the question that operators need to answer is: What are these families like? What goes into the facility depends on the creativity of management and an understanding of the demographics for the area it serves.

Integrated Facilities

Although FECs allow smaller organizations and individual owners to enter the amusement industry, larger corporations and already established businesses have looked to increase their revenue by attracting a broader market: families. They have done this by providing integrated facilities. There have always been facilities that offer diverse services and products, but the magnitude of these new enterprises sets them apart from previous ventures.

Where are these integrated facilities appearing? At the moment there are two prime areas: shopping centers and casinos.

> One of the major changes within the theme parks industry over the last decade can be discerned in the spread of amusement industry attractions into areas more traditionally confined to retail activities (*Park World,* Sept. 1993: 70).

In 1988 the Tropicana in Atlantic City, New Jersey, became TropWorld Casino and Entertainment Resort. An 80,000-square-foot indoor amusement park called Trivoli Pier was added to the existing 1,041-room hotel and 90,000-square-foot casino. Also on site was a 1,200-seat auditorium, 80,000 square feet of meeting space, a comedy club, and retail shops. When the idea was proposed to put an amusement park in with a casino, there was snickering up and down the boardwalk (Pina 1991: 15). The snickering has since stopped, and Atlantic City's big brother, Las Vegas, embarked on its own building campaign. On May 1, 1992, The Forum Shops at Caesar's Palace opened. This new shopping center cost approximately 100 million dollars and was not only a mall but a Las Vegas happening. A vaulted ceiling covers the enclosed mall and displays a laser-driven image of the sky, which every few hours changes from sunrise to sunset. There are talking statues of ancient gods, dancing lasers, underground valet parking, and special events. Moving sidewalks carry customers in from the street, and unless you know where you are going, the only way out seems to be through the casino.

Others followed suit, and in July of 1993 Circus Circus opened "Grand Slam Canyon," a five-acre amusement complex based on the Grand Canyon. Grand Slam Canyon is covered by a vented space-frame dome that provides year-round climate control. The attractions are thrill rides and include a double-looping corkscrew coaster, 140-foot peaks, and a 50- and 90-foot waterfall. Fall of 1993 saw the opening of two additional major attractions, the 400-million-dollar Luxor Hotel and the 430-million-dollar resort, Treasure Island. The Luxor Hotel is a thirty-story hotel that is shaped like a pyramid and has an Egyptian focus while Treasure Island has a pirate theme.

Meanwhile, the MGM Grand Hotel and Theme Park opened in 1994. The MGM Grand is a 112-acre resort hotel, casino, and theme park that is based around MGM's Hollywood image.

> Designed by the Duell Corporation to resemble the back lot of a Hollywood movie studio, the park will be a one-of-a-kind Las Vegas extravaganza featuring a dozen rides, shows and attractions. There will also be 12 food and beverage outlets including the Cotton Blossom River Boat Restaurant, reminiscent of a New Orleans paddle boat, while 11 retail shops and a large crafts area where guests can see handicrafts being made will round out the variety of activities (*Park World* 1992: 4).

The park was located on the 33-acre site that was formerly the Tropicana Golf Course and has parking for approximately 8,700 cars. With the completion of MGM, the total investment in integrated facilities in Las Vegas reached over two billion dollars. All this activity has caused some to liken Las Vegas to an Orlando with gambling.

Why have the casinos changed from a gambling-only orientation to become integrated facilities? First of all, gambling is no longer the sole property of Las Vegas. The success of Trivoli in Atlantic City (despite the snickering) and the opening of casinos in other states and on Native North American Indian reservations created competition. Second, the success of destination resorts demonstrated that a family oriented market was a lucrative market to attract. Finally, the experience of integrating facilities at shopping malls had proven that while it might not be possible to be all things to all people, it was possible to be most things to most people.

In 1981, the four Ghermezian brothers opened the West Edmonton Mall in Alberta, Canada. This is no ordinary mall but a unique shopping and recreational experience that is the size of 115 football fields. Some of the indoor attractions it contains, besides 800 shops, are a zoo, a National Hockey League rink, an indoor waterpark, a lake with a submarine adventure ride, and one of Canada's largest saltwater aquariums. The mall is also home to the Fantasyland Hotel. True to its name, the Fantasyland Hotel contains rooms themed around three choices: Roman, South Pacific, and Hollywood. A themed "truck stop" room contains gas pumps, flashing traffic lights, and a truck body for a bed. Waterfalls, spas, lights, ornate plaster ceilings, and unique beds promise to make a visit to this hotel an unforgettable experience. For the less adventurous, traditional rooms are available.

Other integrated facilities opened, including Mall of America in Bloomington, Minnesota, and Woodbine Centre in Ontario, Canada. Woodbine Centre is an 875,000-square-foot mall with a Victorian theme and 50,000 square feet of rides and attractions. The building of these types of facilities continues; other projects are on the drawing board, including a proposal to build an eight-story shopping center with the top two floors dedicated to entertainment. This facility is scheduled to be built in Hong Kong (*Park World*, Sept. 1993: 71).

These are examples of new construction of large facilities. On a smaller scale, established malls are rethinking their use of space. "Mall walkers," individuals who walk in malls for fitness and to avoid the cold of winter and the heat of summer, were the first to suggest that the mall might serve a purpose other than shopping. Small malls put in FECs as a way to attract families and to provide something for everyone to do. If there was no room for an FEC, special events were scheduled to bring in the customers. The mall became a gathering place for all ages.

Technology and the Parks

Almost everyone likes to keep up with what is new and modern. Most of us would neither permanently turn in our calculator for an abacus nor our

Mall of America covers 78 acres and has 2.5 million square feet of space for retailers. Besides stores, it contains movie theaters, restaurants, nightclubs, and an indoor amusement park called Knott's Camp Snoopy. The amusement park covers 7 acres and has 23 rides and attractions, including the Pepsi Ripsaw Roller Coaster and the Screaming Yellow Eagle—a large platform that rotates 360 degrees while patrons sit theater-style on the platform. What attraction does this remind you of that was mentioned in chapter 2?

Courtesy of Mall of America. Photo: Donna Baumgaertner.

stereo system for a crystal radio set. The same principle holds true for our fun. Riding an early mule-driven carousel or the loop-the-loop coaster of 1888 might be thrilling once, but *only* once.

Most of us want to try what is new. The amusement industry knows this and is sensitive to market demands. The industry also knows that those who do not keep up, very often get left behind. It is this race to keep up that

The LEGO Imagination Center rises 90 feet to the top of the ceiling at the Mall of America and contains just under 7,000 square feet. While LEGO astronauts and a LEGO space shuttle hang from the ceiling, a little LEGO dinosaur sits among tired shoppers. In the background children play with LEGO Bricks, happily constructing their own creations.
Courtesy of LEGO Systems, Inc.

Photo: Gina Balestracci.

makes the amusement industry a natural for devising and using new and innovative technology. One of the biggest factors in this quest has been the rapid and continued development of the computer.

Computer-generated ticketing is becoming a popular method of issuing tickets at theme parks and can speed up the ticketing process.

Electric cash drawers can add at least three extra seconds to every transaction; manually imprinted credit cards another 45 seconds, difficulty in hearing through badly designed glass bandit screens eight seconds and slow ticket printing four or five seconds on every ticket. This all adds up to a delay of between 8 to 12 seconds on a typical transaction (*Park World* 1992: 26).

Besides cutting waiting time, computer ticketing makes fraud easier to spot and control. Tickets have value only when they are printed at point of sale, and daily sales can be reconciled more easily. Tickets can be printed with serial numbers and bar coded to allow park entry for only certain days and dates. Bar coding also speeds up the checking of tickets by allowing them to be scanned.

Attractive and/or personalized tickets are less likely to be thrown away and are more likely to be kept as souvenirs. Groups who buy tickets can be identified by having the same number printed on their tickets, and names and addresses of group leaders can be collected for future marketing efforts. Tickets can be personalized, welcoming groups to the park and may contain messages regarding discounts, special offers, and other inducements.

Finally, the computerized system can tell you when tickets were sold and identify peak time periods for attendance. It can collect zip codes for demographic information and record weather conditions, daily special events, or any other information that you would care to input.

Computers have also allowed parks to increase their revenues through digital imaging. Digital imaging systems allow for the instant capture and production of high-quality photographs. Taken while customers are riding an attraction, they are stored in a systems memory and sent to banks of monitors where they can be previewed by patrons as they exit. Approximately five to six percent of riders will purchase a picture. The secret to the clarity of the photograph is the digitalizing of the image. Digitalizing means that the photograph is the result of electronic signals, not of movement.

Tired of working out to get in shape? Digital imaging can give you the physique of your dreams without you even getting off of the couch. The good news is that you get to keep the body, the bad news is that it is only on film. Customers who wish to purchase customized magazine cover pictures of themselves in costume, or with another body, or any other number of additional choices can have that picture produced by a digital imaging system.

The customer selects the body he or she desires. Body/background combinations reside on hard disk in permanent memory. The facial areas of these digitized overlays are programmed to allow the output of the camera (which is focused on the customer's face) to show through. By adjusting the camera and the color, the operator fine tunes the composite image, freezes it, and fuses the overlay with the image of the customer's face (*Funworld* 1992: 27).

Digital imaging systems are also being used to promote safety. On one of the attractions in a well-known theme park, part of the attraction must be free of guests before it can continue. The solution to making sure that the area was clear was to take a series of five monochrome images when the area was known to be safe, average them, and come up with a picture of what a safe condition should look like. This ideal condition was then stored in the memory of the unit. While the attraction is operating, another five images are taken when it reaches this critical point and compared with the known photo stored in memory. If the photos agree, the attraction continues. If they disagree, the ride stops and someone is sent to make sure that the area is clear.

While digital imaging is still new, its cousin, virtual reality, is better known. Many people understood the concept of virtual reality before they knew what it was called. Star Trek fans knew it by another name. They called it the "holodeck," a feature found on the starship *Enterprise.* Every "Trekker" knew that the holodeck was the place to go to find computer-generated worlds and situations. Here you could enter a room where reality was not *really* real but *virtually* real. It was a great fantasy where you could fight an alien life-form without shedding a drop of green blood. Did you run out of power in your phaser gun? Just "freeze program" and reload.

While the diaper and toddler crowd was watching Sesame Street, the older members of the family were exploring new worlds with their own set of fantasy characters, Captain Jean-Luc Picard, Comdr. Will Riker, Geordi, and the rest of the crew were their Kermit, Count, and Bert and Ernie. Imagine everyone's surprise when the first virtual reality system came on the market. True, it was no holodeck (it wasn't even close); yet it was a beginning, and thousands stood in line asking to be beamed aboard.

Like digital imaging systems, virtual reality (VR) also relies on a computer. The computer generates an interactive story, which players enter by looking into a visor that they wear on their head. It is the interactive feature of VR that makes it so popular. Players have choices and their actions have consequences. Most of the early VR experiences were hunt-and-shoot games. Skill in mastering the handheld controls and in orientating yourself in the crude computer-generated landscape determined how well you performed in the game.

In the short time that it has been around, VR has made significant improvements in both the technology and the sophistication of the computer-generated "worlds." Sega Enterprises of Japan was so confident of the popularity and profitability of VR that it established an amusement theme park division. The charge to this new branch was to establish a network of venues. These sites will become VR arcades. Not only will there be individual VR games, but there will be mini-theaters that will link players to one another via computer. This interaction will make the experience more intense, not only between players and computer but among players *and* the computer. There is no holodeck yet, but perhaps there will be one someday.

Even garbage has gone high-tech thanks to computers. New cans for trash collection are now being designed to look like attractions. Shaped to look like animals, themed characters, or anything imaginable, people put litter into the disposal unit and a computer-generated tape requests more. Patrons delight in feeding trash to the can and may even use this event as a photo opportunity. Suction removes the garbage and places it in a wire container in the body of the waste bin. Unlike standard cans, which need to be emptied frequently, the new bins are emptied only once or twice a day. Smoke detectors and sprinkler systems are built into the unit to ensure safety, and the taped messages can be changed so that cans send patrons to other parts of the facility.

Computers have also allowed us to engage in the great "coaster wars" (Lanza 1992: 54). The roller coaster has been a staple in almost every action park built. Even Disney has added coaster attractions to its parks to enhance their image and to keep the attention of those who cannot bear one more trip through "It's a Small World." Coaster enthusiasts take the coaster wars very seriously. Who has the fastest coaster, the tallest coaster, the longest coaster, or the coaster with the steepest drop? The industry can barely keep up with the changes, and the paint is hardly dry on the newest entrant before a new contender enters the market. Computers control the new coasters and are used to draw and test them for feasibility and proper adherence to engineering principles.

Without doubt, the undisputed king of thrill rides is Six Flags Theme Parks. Founded by Angus G. Wynne, Jr., the first of the now seven parks was opened in 1961 near Dallas/Fort Worth and called Six Flags over Texas. Today there is a Six Flags park within a day's drive of 85 percent of Americans. Six of the seven parks are bigger than Disneyland, but unlike Disneyland, thrill rides including all forms of coasters are the signature of the parks.

The coaster wars were not confined to North America. Across the Atlantic in England, Blackpool Pleasure Beach had Project '94. Project '94 was the name for a 235-foot steel roller coaster that could be height-adjusted upwards. If a taller coaster was built by another park, Blackpool Pleasure Beach would simply raise their coaster. So that all competitive possibilities were accounted for, the new coaster would travel near 85 mph, and have the longest drop on the planet. Unfortunately, while Project '94 was being built other parks were in the process of executing their own plans for equally enticing coasters (*Park World*, 1993: 20).

Special effects is another area where technology and creativity have merged to produce more realistic and exciting experiences.

> Seeing a scary creature does little to chill the bone, but smelling his hot breath, hearing his grunts and roars, and shaking from the vibration of his heavy footsteps could incite your visitors to return again and again (Doggett and King 1991: 139).

Gore, blood, drool, and hot, seething monster breath are now required to complete the experience for park goers. Without the lasers, lights, giant video screens, and robots we sit and are bored. Fiber optics, holography, and High Definition Sound (HDS), coupled with VR and computer capabilities are moving us toward startling realistic experiences. Entertainment related industries have always been eager to embrace the newest and most outrageous technological advances. When we look at them, we should see more than just amusement; we should see an image of our future.

Summary

The amusement industry today is eclectic in nature. In North America, traditional amusement parks have been joined by theme parks, waterparks, family entertainment centers, and integrated facilities. The independent parks that rose after the end of World War II and that catered to the children born after the war, known as the baby boomers, have been usurped by large parks that are owned by corporations.

The Disney Company was instrumental in bringing about these changes. The opening of Disneyland in California was timed perfectly to capture the attention of the baby boomers. A generation of children grew up with Mickey, Minnie, Goofy, and the rest of the characters associated with the Disney legacy. The fame and reputation of Disney did not stop at the borders of North America but traveled abroad to introduce the children and adults of other countries to the wholesomeness of the Disney image and ventures.

As the demand for more parks began decreasing in North America, Asia and the Middle East became the fastest growing markets for this aspect of the amusement industry. Parks rose in Saudi Arabia, Malaysia, Hong Kong, and other Asian and Middle Eastern cities and countries. These parks adopted the best of the North American parks and adapted these concepts to fit their culture and their religious beliefs.

Meanwhile in North America, newly integrated facilities that intertwined multiple purposes sought to attract customers. This was done by combining gambling with amusements (Las Vegas), shopping with recreational activities (malls), or by any other combination of choices that would attract customers. New kinds of attractions included virtual reality and technologically sophisticated audio and video displays, which provided new and interesting choices to a customer base that was constantly looking for a new and different experience.

Discussion Questions

1. What effect, if any, will the emphasis on technology and engineered environments have on recreational experiences that occur in the natural environment?
2. Is it possible that the two orientations (engineered environments and traditional recreational experiences) can complement one another?
3. What might the next level of evolution be for the industries discussed in this chapter?

4. What steps concerning religious and cultural differences might park designers, planners, and managers take into effect when building and designing amusement areas and programs?
5. What might happen to areas like Las Vegas with the spread of legalized gaming and gambling to local facilities?

Chapter Exercises

1. Identify the major theme and amusement parks in Europe, Asia, and the Middle East.
2. Research the Victorian era. Are vestiges of Victorian philosophy still present in our society—other societies?
3. Visit two of the following: an FEC, waterpark, soft play facility, or a theme or amusement park. What population was present at each of these places? Was there a main attraction that drew customers to this facility? How were they similar? Different?
4. Compare the amusements discussed in chapter 2 with the amusements of today. Do you think that "everything old is new again?"

References

A goofy kind of year. 1993. *Newsweek* (18 October): 57.
Abandon all hope ye who enter here. 1991. *Games Industry* (November): 97.
The bins that talk back. 1993. *Park World* (May): 22.
Disneyland visitors up. 1991. *Park World* (July): 12.
The dreammakers. 1993. *Park World* (July): 38.
Euro Disney in sell-off fury. 1993. *Park World* (September): 12.
Europe's second D-Day. 1992. *Park World* (May): 37.
First for Las Vegas. 1992. *Park World* (October): 4.
Forrec to the fore of retail leisure. 1993. *Park World* (September): 70–71.
Get the picture! 1993. *Park World* (New Year): 27.
Grand designs. 1993. *Park World* (May): 44–45.
Grand Slam Canyon to open in 1993. 1992. *Park World* (October): 5.
Great new association. 1993. *Park World* (July): 20.
Grona Lund—Entertaining the people of Stockholm since 1883. 1991. *Park World* (July): 20–21.
Hi-tech robotics. 1991. *Games Industry* (November): 81.
High-tech ticketing. 1992. *Park World* (October): 26–27.
Hyper entertainment. 1991. *Games Industry* (November): 51.
In at the deep end! 1992. *Park World* (March): 49.
Lighting the future. 1991. *Games Industry* (November): 74.
Looking for a way out. 1993. *Park World* (May): 26–27.
Mickey and Co. come to Europe. 1992. *Park World* (April): 26.
Ocean Park expansion. 1993. *Park World* (May): 6.
Omni moves into malls. 1993. *Park World* (New Year): 8.
Park World survey—A look at the most popular attractions at parks around the world. 1992. *Park World* (March): 33.
Philips: Giant screen video pioneer. 1992. *Park World* (October): 45.

Russia—Land of opportunities. 1993. *Park World* (New Year): 6.

Saudi amusement centers company. 1993. *Family Entertainment Center* 1st Quarter: 16–17.

Snapshot by surprise. 1991. *Games Industry* (November): 85.

The sound of reality. 1993. *Park World* (May): 32–33.

Theme parks and the cultural climate. 1991. *Park World* (July): 40.

UK coaster wars loom. 1993. *Park World* (July): 6.

Waterparks invest more than $200 million in 1993. 1993. *Funworld* (April): 32–37.

What will the visitor to Euro Disneyland encounter? 1992. *Park World* (May): 42.

Wrapped up in images. 1991. *Games Industry* (November): 48.

Anderson, John. 1991. Ray Williams and the great turnaround. *Funworld* (November): 117–18.

Bell, Christopher. 1990. First U.S. wave pool turns 20. *Aquatics* (March/April): 11–17.

Braun, Raymond E. 1991. The Disney effect. *Games Industry* (November): 102–7.

Brener, Joshua L. 1993. Thrill seekers-innovative water rides command attention. *Aquatics International* (May/June): 37.

Capturing the moment with digital electronics. 1992. *Funworld* (March): 24.

Chow, Jackie M. 1993. Make a splash: Children's pools attract all ages. *Aquatics International* (July/August): 27.

Collins, Terry. 1991. Special effects, animation, lighting—A look at the latest technology. *Park World* (July): 24.

Dillard, Elizabeth. 1993. Designed for the desert—Guest comfort requires special attention in hot, arid climates. *Aquatics International* (May/June): 24.

Doggett, Tim, and Doug King. 1991. What's so special about special effects? *Funworld* (November): 139.

Doornick, Robert. 1991. Techno-marketing: A new business science for the 90s. *Funworld* (November): 149.

Ellis, Kenneth L. 1993. Community aquatics planning: The family recreation center. *Parks and Recreation* (November): 44–49.

Flower, Joe. 1991. *Prince of the magic kingdom.* New York: J. Wiley and Sons, Inc.

Fortner, Brian. 1993. Roller rinks to FEC riches. *Family Entertainment Center* 1: 28–30.

France, Van Arsdale. 1991. *Window on Main Street.* Nashua, NH: Laughter Publications, Inc.

Fuller, Rick. 1993. 15 years on the edge: Hyland Hills water world. *Parks and Recreation* (November): 34–39.

Goldman, J. David. 1990. A desert oasis—Southwestern resort creates the ultimate water playground. *Aquatics* (January/February): 10.

———. 1992. Added meaning—Canadian facilities redefine 'multi-use.' *Aquatics International* (March/April): 10–15.

———. 1991. Putting on a show—Aquatic amenities create fantasy at Orlando resort. *Aquatics International* (July/August): 8.

Hackett, V. 1992. Family center firms looking to expand: Survey. *Amusement Business* (May 11–17): 23.

Hartman, Margaret. 1993. Convivial pursuit: Part 2. *Funworld* (April): 56.

Hovey, Pauline O. 1993. Market hot for cool rides. *Funworld* (April): 6.

Hunsaker, D. J. 1991. European approach: Aquatic leisure centers can be all things to all people. *Aquatics* (March/April): 10.

Kasson, John F. 1978. *Amusing the million—Coney Island at the turn of the century.* New York: Hill and Wang.

King, Doug. 1992. Special effects. *Park World* (May): 50.

King, D. 1993. The future of FECs? *Family Entertainment Center* 1: 32–36.

Lanza, Joseph. 1992. Coaster wars—The glory and the hype. *Park World* (April): 54.

Makanae, Masa. 1993. Tokyo Disneyland—The Godzilla of Japan's amusement parks. *Funworld* (April): 12.

Pentes, Jack. 1993. Children at play. *Family Entertainment Center* 1: 10–14.

———. 1992. The evolution and elements of pay-for-play. *Funworld* (March): 32–33.

Pina, Michael L. 1991. Taking a gamble on Trivoli Pier. *Funworld* (November): 15.

Reeves, Melissa. 1991. Mickey moves to Europe. *Funworld* (November): 82–87.

Reicher, Scott. 1993. Water, water, everywhere. *Disney News* (Spring): 8–10.

Robinett, John W. 1991. In Europe and Japan, the boom is on. *Funworld* (November): 38.

Ruben, Paul. 1993. Batman—Gotham City thrills come to New Jersey. *Park World* (July): 56.

———. 1993. Busch Gardens debuts Kumba. *Park World* (July): 54.

Sherborne, P. 1992. Developers keeping designers busy here and abroad. *Amusement Business* (May 11–17).

Snook, David. 1993. Exploring Asia. *Park World* (May): 52–53.

———. 1992. One step at a time. *Park World* (May): 28.

Steinberg, J. 1993. Foreign parks grow despite economic slump. *Aquatics International* (September/ October): 30.

Taylor, John. 1987. *Storming the Magic Kingdom.* New York: Ballantine Books.

The New York Times. 1993. (19 October): D30.

Turner, Al. Public pool 2000. 1991. *Parks and Recreation* (November): 46.

Walt Disney World 20 magical years The Walt Disney Company.

Additional Resources

AB: Amusement Business—The international live entertainment and amusement industry newsletter. Nashville, TN: BPI Communications.

The Disney magazine. Anaheim, CA: The Walt Disney Company.

Eliot, Marc. 1993. *Walt Disney: Hollywood's dark prince.* New York: Birch Lane Press.

Leisure management: For the leisure professional. Hertfordshire, UK: Dicestar, Ltd.

National Recreation and Park Association. *Parks and recreation.* Arlington, VA: National Recreation and Park Association.

Russo, Doreen, ed. 1992. *The AAA guide to North America's theme parks.* 2nd ed. New York: Collier Books.

Meetings, Conventions, and Special Events

Meetings and Conventions

The recent past has seen the birth of two distinct yet interrelated industries; meeting and convention planning, and the special events industry. Similar in some respects, different in others, both have struggled to emerge from infancy to adulthood. Today they have not only achieved a level of economic power, but are becoming recognized and accepted as vital industries.

The Last Twenty-Five Years

Within the brief time span of twenty-five years, the meeting-planning industry has evolved from doughnuts and handshakes to contracts and liability issues. A quarter of a century ago you would be hard pressed to find anyone who would describe themselves as a professional meeting planner. Today this is no longer true, and professional meeting planners have become essential to the successful planning and delivery of meetings and conventions, no matter what their size. What has happened during this time span to give rise to the industry?

In general, life was simpler and more predictable twenty-five years ago. People tended to finish school, marry, find a job, and settle down. When they traveled, trips were most likely taken by automobile, bus, or train. Although commercial aviation was well established, it was vastly different from the industry that we know today. Airfares were determined by the Civil Aeronautics Board (CAB). The CAB no longer exists, but while it was in force (before the age of deregulation) negotiation of airfares for convention and meeting attendees, or for anyone else for that matter, simply could not happen. Although corporations and businesses might budget funds to pay for employees, usually managers, to attend seminars, meetings, and conventions, air travel was out of the reach of the vast majority of the rest of the population. Small companies, self-employed individuals, and independent members of professional organizations who had to reach into their own pockets to pay their own way, often found the airfare, hotel, and meal expenses prohibitive. The advent of deregulation signaled the age of competitive airfares and routes. Airlines were free to set their own prices and price structures, and planners were able to bargain for reduced airfares for meeting and convention participants. The reduced fares promised the airlines more customers, and at the same time, the lower airfare opened the door for those who had previously been unable to afford the costs. No longer was the meeting industry restricted by geographic convenience. The industry was free to explore alternate sites and venues that were more appropriate to the objectives of the meeting. Business travel could be combined with pleasure, and meeting professionals became increasingly important for the smooth coordination and organization of the diverse needs of the participant.

Twenty-five years ago there were far fewer professional associations. Many associations, like those that represent the meeting-planning industry, or segments of it, were either nonexistent or in their infancy. In fact, there were so few convention centers, conference centers, and convention hotels available that many meeting professionals did not make a site inspection before selecting a site. They did not need to; they had probably visited all available facilities. Today, many cities both in the United States and abroad are realizing the benefits, primarily economic, of hosting meetings and conventions. In an effort to entice the increasing numbers of associations and corporate and incentive groups to their region, convention centers and hotels have undergone explosive growth.

The technology of twenty-five years ago was primitive compared to the technology of today. Audiovisual presentations consisted of such "sophisticated" aids as flip charts; slide, overhead, and opaque projectors; filmstrips; and, if you were really lucky, the use of a 16 mm movie projector. Today's audience would scoff at such unsophisticated technology, and it is unrealistic to expect a population that routinely watches unfolding world occurrences live on television, to sit through the bland audiovisual offerings of past meetings and conventions. We are a media-oriented society, and as such we demand the sophistication associated with computers, video cameras with instant replay, state-of-the-art sound systems, E-mail, fax machines, and other forms of technology. Today's meeting professional needs to be well versed in these areas. Most meeting and conference participants have little tolerance for an experience that fails to incorporate the latest technology.

The changes that have occurred during the past quarter of a century have necessitated the use of professional planners. Could we return to doughnuts and handshakes? It is possible, but highly improbable. The complexity of today's meetings and conventions industry, combined with the litigious nature of our society, argues strongly against such a move. Knowledge, skill, experience, flexibility, communication expertise, and professionalism are the traits needed by today's planner. Who are these people?

Types of Planners

Today's planners are a diversified lot who primarily work in three different capacities: as planners for corporations, for associations, or as independent meeting professionals. Corporations are familiar entities to all Americans. We hear about them on the news, read about them in the newspaper, and encounter them almost daily in our personal lives. Examples of corporations that have in-house meeting professionals are American Telephone and Telegraph (AT&T), International Business Machines (IBM), and Johnson and Johnson. In-house planners (individuals who work for the company) can be either centralized or decentralized. A planner who works for a centralized system works for one department within the corporation. This department is responsible for planning, organizing, and delivering meetings for all segments of the organization. A decentralized system means that there is no central department responsible for these matters; instead, individual units which need to hold meetings are responsible for making their own arrangements.

In case a corporation does not have its own in-house planners, or is too busy for the workload to be handled by its system, it can hire independent planners. Independent planners work on a contractual basis to assist the corporation with individual projects. They may do this part-time or on an "as needed" basis. It all depends upon the arrangements made: the needs of the company, and the availability of the planner.

Besides working for corporations and with individual clients, independent planners may also work for associations. Associations are usually voluntary organizations of people who give of their time to promote a common interest. They may employ paid employees who work full or part-time for the association. While the line is not always clear, we usually distinguish between trade associations and professional associations or societies. Trade associations are made up of individual members of an industry. An example is the National Association of Balloon Artists. This association is comprised of members who work with balloons. They may manufacture balloons, provide balloon decor, or work in any other area that is concerned with balloons. Individual members come from a variety of backgrounds. They may have college degrees in diversified areas, or no degrees at all.

Unlike trade associations, professional societies and associations are made up of individuals who usually share a common educational background, training, and experience. The American Medical Association and the American Bar Association are two examples of professional associations. Both require that members have a degree from an accredited medical or law school. In addition, both stipulate that you must pass an examination before you are allowed to practice in that profession and that members participate in some type of ongoing professional enrichment experience.

When you become a member of an association or a society you share and receive information concerning the specific interest of the organization. This can be done through newsletters, bulletins, trade publications, meetings, conventions, etc. The association will frequently lobby in its behalf both on local and national levels, work to promote its goals, conduct research into items that impact upon its interests, or do any number of things to advance the position of the group as a whole, or of individual members.

Association planners work for non-profit organizations such as The Association of Trial Lawyers of America or The New Jersey School Boards Association. They are hired by the association and are responsible for planning and managing the association's conventions, board meetings, regional meetings, continuing education, etc. The three main hubs for associations are New York City, Chicago, and Washington, D.C.

Examples of associations and societies include:

International Association of Amusement Parks and Attractions—IAAPA

International Special Events Society—ISES

Albert B. Sears, Jr. is the assistant vice president for the National Fire Protection Association (NFPA). Mr. Sears has been with NFPA for twenty-eight years and has been their meeting planner for the past twenty-four years. In 1970 he formed the association's Meetings and Travel Department, and in 1972 he produced the association's first Fire Safety Exhibit. The Fire Safety Exhibit has grown from 41 booths in 1972, to well over 400 booths today.

Mr. Sears was a founding member of the New England Chapter of Meeting Professionals International (MPI) and is a past international president of MPI. He has written numerous articles on hotel fire safety for the meetings industry trade press and has received numerous awards for his contributions to the profession.

Albert B. Sears, Jr.

International Association of Fairs and Expositions—IAFE

Professional Conference Management Association—PCMA

Meeting Professionals International—MPI

Canadian Association of Fairs and Expositions—CAFE

You have probably noticed that MPI does not contain the word association or society in its title. Don't be fooled. An organization may be an association or a society without officially stating those words in their title. In fact, Meeting Professionals International is one of the leading associations for meeting planners.

Meeting Professionals International

Based in Dallas, Texas, MPI was founded in 1972. During the last twenty-two years, membership has grown to include 12,500 members (both planners and suppliers) representing 42 countries. MPI is governed by a voluntary international Board of Directors elected by the membership. A staff of 50 is led by the Executive Vice President/CEO of MPI (table 4.1).

As a professional association, MPI offers continuing education through its annual conference, chapter programs, institutes, international symposia, and professional education conference, and resource center. In addition, MPI publishes *The Meeting Manager* (a monthly magazine), Conference Daily (an on-site conference newspaper), MPI Express (a monthly FAX newspaper), and a membership directory. MPI also operates both a bookstore and a resource center. Finally, MPI has had an instrumental part in development of the Certified Meeting Professional (CMP) designation, administered by the Convention Liaison Council. The letters CMP after a meeting professional's name indicates that they have achieved the highest level of expertise in meetings management. The CMP is attained by the successful completion of a fifteen page application, a check of references, three to five years of experience, and the successful passing of a three hour national examination.

Convention Liaison Committee

In 1949, leaders in the convention industry realized the need for standardization of industry practices and established a body called the Convention Liaison Committee (CLC). The Convention Liaison Committee eventually changed its name to the Convention Liaison Council.

The council is composed of organizations that are involved in all types of meetings. The CLC uses the term *meetings* to include "all events that bring people together in common business, vocational, avocational or educational interest: conventions, conferences, seminars, and expositions" (*The CLC Manual* 1989: 4).

The CLC's basic objectives are:

1. To promote cooperation and understanding among all parties involved in meeting planning.

**Table 4.1   Meeting Professionals International Mission
Statement and Supporting Goals**

MISSION STATEMENT

Meeting Professionals International (MPI) is the pivotal force in positioning meetings as a primary communication vehicle and a critical component of an organization's success. MPI leads the meeting industry by serving the diverse needs of all people with a direct interest in the outcome of meetings, educating and preparing members for their changing roles and validating relevant knowledge and skills as well as demonstrating a commitment to excellence in meetings.

SUPPORTING GOALS

Professionalism   MPI members will demonstrate and be recognized for a consistently high level of professionalism. Professionalism includes understanding and achieving or exceeding the objectives of the meeting people with a direct interest in the outcome of meetings, i.e., displaying industry technical knowledge and behaving in an ethical manner.

Educational Leadership   MPI will be the leading resource and dissemination point for general and specific knowledge and education in the meeting industry.

Globalism   MPI's structure, membership, products, and services will reflect and will be designed for a global marketplace.

Financial Viability   MPI will maintain financial viability which will allow it to achieve its stated goals and respond effectively to strategic opportunities and challenges.

Elevate Meetings as a Strategic Tool   MPI will promote the strategic use of meetings as a powerful communication tool and essential component of an organization's success. MPI will promote identification of models for determining a measurable return on investment for people with a direct interest in the outcome of meetings.

Advocacy   MPI will respond to its leadership role by maintaining an advocacy role in key issues, concerns, and opportunities that directly affect the industry.

Technology   MPI will promote the appropriate use of leading-edge technologies and processes that increase the effectiveness of meetings.

Information provided by the Public Relations Division of Meeting Professionals International's Marketing Department.

2. To promote sound and consistent convention procedures and practices through a program of education for meeting planners.
3. To conduct educational and other activities of mutual interest to sponsoring organizations.
4. To promote publicly the role that conventions perform in industry, in national and regional economy, and in local communities

(*The CLC Manual* 1989: 3).

Essential skills can be practiced and potentially acquired by someone wishing to become a meeting professional. These skills include negotiating, budgeting and handling money, managing others and understanding contract and liability issues. The CMP examination is based upon twenty-five identified meeting-planning functions and twenty-two conditions. Using a test consultant, the CMP board canvased 400 meeting planners to determine these areas. Questions are based upon these applied skills as they can be affected by the twenty-two conditions. The twenty-two conditions are items which planners need to take into consideration when making decisions (see Appendix A).

These are the areas in which you will need to gain competency if you wish to become a professional meeting planner. If these areas excite and appeal to you, then you may have found your career.

Convention and Visitors Bureaus

Most of us know what meetings and conventions are, and we have probably attended them in the past. Denney Rutherford has pointed out that for the professional planner, modern meetings and conventions involve more than just the standard definition accepted by laypeople. He states that such gatherings often:

- Occur at specific places called facilities
- Involve food and beverage service
- Provide for specialized technical support such as audiovisual equipment
- Require transportation
- Require housing
- Involve exhibition of products
- Require convention or meeting delegate entertainment
(Rutherford 1990: 2)

Even the above elaboration does not do justice to the complicated and detailed job that meeting professionals encounter. Housing is an example.

If the meeting is small, or if a property is very large, the host facility may be able to accommodate the number of attendees on site. Larger, more complex meetings may require the use of multiple facilities. Certain information must be supplied by the meeting professional regardless of whether one site or several sites will be used to house people. This information includes the probable number and the type of rooms that will be needed, including the potential number of single, double, triple rooms, etc.; the number of nonsmoking and accessible rooms needed; and the pricing policy for rooms. Arrival and departure dates and times are also important information. Historical information from past events can usually be used as a basis for prediction of needs. Deadlines with favored rates for early registration can spur attendees to make an early commitment.

If only one site is involved, things are less complicated than if multiple sites are required. Negotiation need only occur between the meeting professional and the sales/marketing staff at the site. When there is only one site it is easier to negotiate for items other than sleeping and meeting rooms, such as food and beverage amenities, use of recreational facilities, audiovisual needs, and staffing requirements. But what about a large meeting or convention?

Once the size of the group extends beyond the boundaries of one site, negotiations become more complicated. The planner must locate sleeping rooms at several facilities. When attendees are housed at multiple sites, negotiations must be done separately with each hotel, and transportation to the meeting site(s) becomes an important consideration. A reasonable walk to one participant may not be reasonable to others. Across the street can be a long way to some senior citizens, people with small children, and individuals with disabilities. Planners may have to generate rooming lists, assign roommates, handle special requests, and in general, coordinate the effort to obtain appropriate accommodations for everyone. This is now becoming complicated. Fortunately, many cities have a convention and visitors bureau (CVB) with an effective housing bureau that handles all sleeping room reservation requests.

Areas that rely on conventions and tourism as a local industry may have an active convention and visitors bureau. These bureaus can be independent organizations, a branch of local government, or part of the chamber of commerce. Their function is to promote their destination as a site for meetings, conventions, and tourism. This could be an individual town, county, region, or any other feasible geographic arrangement. The bureau serves as the liaison between the visitors to the area and the member businesses, which will benefit from having them there. Because CVBs are often supported by membership dues, they represent all business members equally and recommend sites based on the information given by the meeting professional. Most bureaus operate by distributing the meeting or convention requirements of potential customers to all suppliers who would be able to meet the specifications.

Having a convention and visitors bureau with a housing bureau will quickly simplify the "housing" aspect of the job. Many bureaus are now equipped with computers, which greatly simplify matters. A centralized source may be available to provide participants with appropriate accommodations. The computer can quickly tell planners which sites are available, the number of rooms that are nonsmoking, the types of room configurations, amenities, etc. At the end of the meeting, the housing bureau may supply a summary of the housing used by attendees. This will help the planner when making decisions and documenting specifications for the next meeting. This also becomes part of the historical information that will be useful when tracking the growth of the meeting. Knowledge and effective use of all the resources of a convention and visitors bureau is essential for meeting professionals.

Attributes of Professional Planners

You should be starting to see some of the required attributes of meeting professionals. Obviously, as in the "housing" example, a planner needs to know what resources are available and must be very organized and detail oriented. It is not enough to see the big picture; you must see, understand, and organize, the little picture as well. This includes all types of details; for example, having water on the podium for speakers, having the appropriate phone numbers readily available when the bulb blows in the slide projector and the spare bulb is also broken, and having a "Plan B" for all possible situations.

Plan B is a course of action to follow when the original plan does not materialize as anticipated. Every organizer quickly learns about Plan B. No matter how well you organize something, no matter how much you anticipate the "what ifs" of organizing a meeting or convention, there is always the unexpected. What if the main speaker doesn't show up because the plane was grounded in Chicago due to inclement weather? What if there is a demonstration by an opposing group at your meeting? What if there is an emergency medical situation? What if the lights go out in the middle of a session? What if? What if. . . .

If you do not like dealing with the "what ifs" of life, then you probably do not want to become a planner. Flexibility and the attribute of staying calm under fire are two very desirable qualities to have.

Along with the ability to be flexible and to remain calm and composed is the necessity of being able to deal with people. Good communication skills are indispensable. Planners need to listen to their clients and to help them clarify their objectives (both overt and covert). They also need to be able to clearly explain options and consequences, to listen for hidden agendas and apprehensions, and to help their clients work through these roadblocks. Finally, anyone who deals with people needs patience and tact. Although the majority of your clientele are reasonable, understanding individuals, there are others who are not.

Today's Planners

Twenty-five years ago a typical planner was part-time and male. Who are the meeting planners of today? This was one of the questions answered in the March 1, 1992, edition of *Meetings and Conventions, (M&C)*. *M&C*, published by The Reed Travel Group, commissioned Market Probe International to conduct this "Meetings Market Report." Based on survey responses from 1,205 corporate and 802 association planners who were members of MPI, the results show that the industry has changed considerably in the last decade.

In 1981, 55 percent of the total membership of MPI was female. Today that figure has risen to 80 percent. Between 1983 and 1991, women gained in terms of numbers, both in the corporate and association sector. In 1983, 15 percent of the corporate planners were women, but by 1991 that figure had changed to 43 percent, an increase of 12 percent. A slightly larger increase of 14 percent was gained by women who identified themselves as association planners. The number of women in this area increased from 34 percent of the total planners in 1983 to 48 percent in 1991 (*M&C* 1992: 134–35).

No one knows for sure why the numbers have changed, and why more women than men are picking careers as professional planners. Speculation includes the rationale that, perhaps, women are more detail oriented than men, and therefore inherently more suited for the industry. More likely is the idea that there has been a shift in the corporate world regarding the delegation of responsibilities. Two decades ago, the planning of meetings and conventions was done on the side, usually by the CEO's secretary or by someone in the advertising, human resources, marketing, or public relations department. Two decades ago, this person was probably male. Today these activities are done by individuals who have administrative or clerical responsibilities. Detail-oriented and competent, these people are usually secretaries and most always women.

Also, we need to remember that women have joined the job market in general during the last two decades. We have more women lawyers, physicians, engineers, etc. The demographics of the population as a whole tell us that women have left more traditional roles to enter the workforce. Unfortunately, although women have gained in numbers, their salary gains have not kept up with the gains of their male counterparts.

Women earn less than men in the meeting-planning industry. A 1991 survey done by MPI of its membership discovered that women earned approximately 20,000 dollars a year less than men for similar positions. Figures for various parts of the county were as follows:

	Women	Men
Northeast	$39,309	$59,166
Midwest	$32,986	$48,055
South	$33,160	$52,000
West	$34,594	$50,500
Canada	$39,399	$55,000

(*M&C* 1992: 136–37)

We need to remember that the meeting and convention industry is not the only field where inequalities of salary exist. Women often face obstacles no matter what field they are in. Other obstacles for women may include excessive travel requirements, which make it extremely difficult to establish a reasonable family life; forms of sexism when dealing with members of the trades and other groups; the "old boys network"; and the infamous "glass ceiling."

The good news for women is that they usually move easily through the ranks to the top of the meeting-planning department. The good news for everyone is that this is an exciting and always challenging profession. Every day is different from the previous one; you meet new people, learn new skills, discover new information, and see new places. In this 65 billion-dollar-a-year, service-oriented business, many meeting professionals find that the satisfaction of a job well done, the challenge of doing that job well, and the appreciation of a satisfied client are the fuel that motivates them to keep on going.

The Special Events Industry

The special events industry has undergone extensive growth in the past two decades, and while there are no precise figures regarding the amount of dollars expended and generated, there is no doubt that it is substantial. Robert Jackson and Steven Schmader (1990: x) feel that this is a 1.8 billion-dollar industry. Whether or not this estimate is correct is unknown. In 1988, the International Special Events Society (ISES) conducted a membership survey to determine the economic effect of the industry. Figures ranged from 65,000 to 25 million dollars. The wide range, which reflected the gross revenue of special events firms, was attributed to variations in companies in terms of size, staff, and type of events handled. Regardless of the accuracy of either of these figures, there is no doubt that the special events industry is here to stay and that it has become an economic force both in North America and around the world. But just what are special events?

Suzanne Bristow is the president of Crossroads Entertainment and Event Corporation and CBD Enterprises. She is chairman of the board, Zoological Society of Metropolitan Toronto, director of the foundation board of The Toronto Hospital, The Toronto General and Western Divisions, and sits on the board of management of the Metropolitan Toronto Zoo, The Arts Foundation of Greater Toronto and the International Special Events Society. She is treasurer of the International Special Events Education Foundation and holds various committee memberships. Suzanne has won many awards for her charity work and industry-related achievements. She is a lecturer at George Brown College and a professor at Ryerson Polytechnic University. As a public speaker and fund-raiser she has been involved with everything from hospitals to movie premiers. Suzanne was the executive producer for "Skate the Dream," a spectacular show featuring the world's largest group of gold medal Olympians. She was recently appointed executive producer of The Tornoto Arts Awards evening. Throughout her career, Suzanne has been associated with numerous performers and special events.

Suzanne Bristow

There have always been events that are special. Weddings, birthdays, graduations, religious holidays, and other important occurrences are examples of special events. People have marked these events with ceremonies, rites, and rituals from the earliest of times. The special events industry, however, is a relatively new phenomena. Jackson believes that "The beginning of the special events industry as we know it today, happened sometime in the mid-1970s, with the exact date and event depending on whom you ask" (Jackson and Schmader 1990: ix).

Defining a Special Event

Special events seem easy to recognize, but they are difficult to define. Don Getz has stated: "Defining *event* is a straightforward matter; determining what makes one special is problematic" (Getz 1991: 43). In his book, *Festivals, Special Events, and Tourism*, Getz defines and explores the meaning of the words *exhibition, gala, festival, jamboree*, etc., and has compiled the most comprehensive and thorough collection of the terms associated with the running of special events. Getz uses the following as a working definition for special events:

> A special event is a onetime or infrequently occurring event outside the normal program or activities of the sponsoring or organizing body.
> To the customer, a special event is an opportunity for a leisure, social, or cultural experience outside the normal range of choices or beyond everyday experience (Getz 1991: 44).

Joe Jeff Goldblatt, a leader and pioneer in the area of special events, has also formulated a definition for the term special events. In his book, *SPECIAL EVENTS The Art and Science of Celebration*, Goldblatt acknowledges that there is a problem arriving at a definition that is agreeable to all. He states that this is because of the uniqueness brought to the definition by the different backgrounds of those in the industry. The caterer, musician, entertainer, and decorator, all define the event from their perspective.

In an effort to help us distinguish between special events and regular occurrences, Goldblatt offers the following clarification.

Daily Events	**Special Events**
Occur spontaneously	Are always planned
Do not arouse expectations	Always arouse expectations
Usually occur without a reason	Are usually motivated by a reason for celebration

(Goldblatt 1990: 1)

Goldblatt goes on to point out that although special events may appear to be spontaneous, they are not. They have been carefully planned and orchestrated and therefore seem to occur effortlessly. Finally, Goldblatt reminds us that the key ingredient in all special events is celebration.

> For most of us, a special event requires a definite reason for celebrating. In daily life you are content to accept routine; in fact, your comfort relies on it.

You rise, wash, and brush your teeth. When you enter the bathroom, you do not expect, nor would you likely appreciate, balloons dropping and fireworks exploding (Goldblatt 1990: 1).

Goldblatt is correct; celebration is the spark plug for special events. In fact, the basis of his definition of a special event is celebration. "A special event recognizes a unique moment in time with ceremony and ritual to satisfy specific needs" (Goldblatt 1990: 2).

For our purposes we are going to take the best of Getz, and of Goldblatt, and expand the definition. We will use the following definition for the term *special event:*

> A special event is an important occurrence that has been purposefully designed and is out of the ordinary. It involves the coordination of people, activities, and services, to ensure the competent and safe delivery of the event.

We have kept the concept of a special event as celebration, and have added the idea that it is purposefully designed. This is important. Special events are not spontaneous, unplanned events. Spontaneous unplanned events are *happenings,* and although they may be fun and interesting, they have little to do with special events. Any "happening" that you may see at a special event has been carefully planned, designed, and rehearsed.

We have also added the idea that the coordination of people, activities, and services occurs during special events. Whether the event is small or large, there is someone orchestrating the show. Even the smallest special event has someone in charge.

Finally, we have said that there is the competent and safe delivery of the event. Special events professionals are knowledgeable concerning the safety aspects of organizing and running special events. They know how to effectively move people from one venue to another. They know how to spot and correct or eliminate potentially dangerous situations. They are concerned with the well-being of everyone who is attending the event and are sensitive to the needs of special populations. Long before there was an Americans with Disabilities Act (ADA), professional event planners were arranging and organizing events so that all could attend and be comfortable.

Special events professionals serve a variety of markets and provide a variety of services. Joe Jeff Goldblatt (1990: 14) has created the special events umbrella. The special events umbrella highlights the areas that comprise the special events industry. Goldblatt has identified seven of these areas.

1. Catering
2. Entertainment
3. Effects
4. Sound
5. Transportation
6. Lighting
7. Decor

They represent the different components utilized in the organizing and delivery of special events, and are used by special events professionals to create a total package. An eighth area, event promotion and marketing, should be added to complete the umbrella.

To most people, event promotion and marketing includes the usual players: advertising agencies, marketing firms, and public relations companies. However, there has been an increase in the demand for special events firms to use their events to market and promote companies and products. We are not easily entertained; many of us feel that we have seen it all. The advantage of using a special events company, as opposed to more traditional sources, lies in the breadth of resources available to them and to their understanding of the appropriateness of fun.

Event promotion and marketing is an important segment of the umbrella. You can create and plan a dynamite event, but if not properly promoted and marketed, you may be left with a wonderful plan and few participants. More than one event has fizzled because the planners got stuck in the planning stage and forgot to promote and market the event. Whether officially acknowledged or not, special events professionals are definitely skilled marketers and promoters.

Under his umbrella, Goldblatt has listed the five major markets served by the industry. The first market is the social events market. Here we find anniversaries, showers, baptisms, bar and bat mitzvahs, and other causes for celebration. Despite what many people think, this area has a significant clientele. Have you attended a wedding, a retirement party, a graduation party? Almost every one of us attends at least one or two of these events a year. Who suggested and arranged for the flowers, entertainment, and food? Was it the usual fare, or was it unique? If it was extraordinary, unusual, and exciting, then you can bet that a special events professional was involved with the project.

Also under the umbrella, we find the areas that we normally think about when discussing special events markets: retail, corporate, government, and meetings and conventions. We have already talked about meetings and conventions, but what about the retail, corporate, and government markets?

Have you ever been driving down the highway and seen a gorilla waving at you from the side of the road? I have. Several years ago while visiting my sister and her family in California, I was amazed to see a gorilla waving at me from the side of the coast highway. I was so intrigued by the experience that I turned my car around to see what was happening. What I found was a special event in progress, the opening of a new retail clothing store. There were balloons, street performers, special discounts, free prizes, and a host of other activities going on to celebrate the opening of the store and, of course, to bring in customers. The gorilla had done its job and drawn attention to the event! The government and corporations may not consider a gorilla a suitable means of launching new ventures, but they use parallel events, perhaps a dignified ribbon-cutting ceremony or a gigantic balloon launch. It all depends on the purpose of the event and the wishes of the client.

Special events may involve small or large numbers of participants. Some have low or no budgets, while others have no limit. They may last a few hours or a few days. In spite of the variations, there are common denominators. Everyone has a budget and a reason for holding their event. What prompts an organization, government, or individual to go through the time, expense, and uncertainties that accompany the creation, organization, and delivery of a special event? There just *has* to be a reason for doing this.

Patricia Nunno Roque is the president of Business Boomers, Inc. Business Boomers is a consulting firm that provides creative marketing solutions through a carefully combined matrix of marketing, public relations, advertising, and sales promotions tactics. She was a founding member of the Northern New Jersey Chapter of the International Special Events Society (ISES).

Ms. Nunno Roque, on the left, is seen posing with Giants football super-star Bart Oates at a 1991 Corbo Jewelers half-million dollar "Diamonds of Distinction Tour" in conjunction with De Beers' Diamond Promotion Service.

Patricia Nunno Roque

Reasons for Organizing Special Events

Obviously there are payoffs for running a special event, and the generation of revenue is usually the first reason that comes to mind. Very few people will intentionally embark on the task of designing a special event in order to lose money. The reality of today's economic climate is such that profit is expected to be an outcome of the event. Even nonprofit organizations will insist that an event at least break even and cover its expenses. Here are some of the reasons why special events are held.

1. Bring revenue to the area
2. Reward or acknowledge individuals or groups
3. Increase membership
4. Unite a group or groups
5. Make a profit
6. Get a tax write-off
7. Provide an outlet or release
8. Entertain
9. Introduce new or different products or concepts
10. Inform, educate, or promote a cause
11. Promote political or nationalistic views
12. Perform a ceremony

In addition, Jim Hilton suggests other reasons for organizing and running special events. Some of Hilton's reasons involve emotional and social motivators.

> Special events ignite or inspire community spirit; they give people a chance to have fun and at the same time, they are a great training ground for potential leaders in the community or organization; and they bring together people of all ages, incomes, shapes, colors, and sizes . . . old friends gather new memories, new friends find other new friends, newcomers meet the locals, oldsters sputter and smile at the whipper-snappers, and everyone shares a satisfying sense of accomplishment in working toward a common goal (Hilton 1990: 5).

First Night is an example of a special event that accomplishes many of these goals. First Night Boston, is an alcohol-free New Year's Eve "Celebration of the Arts." Started by performers who were watching New Year's Eve revelers on television, it has become a way for families, singles, and the old and the young to ring in the new year. (It also became a way for the performers to generate some revenue.) First Night has grown from its original site in Boston to encompass approximately 105 other sites across America and in other countries.

Types of events are limited only by the imagination of the planner. Traditional activities including concerts, specialty meetings, trade shows, and sporting events take on an extra dimension under the control of a special events professional.

On December 31, 1976, the first First Night was held in Boston, MA. A nontraditional public celebration, First Night seeks to unite the community while providing an alternative to traditional New Year's Eve celebrations.

Courtesy of First Night, Boston, MA. Photo of street performer by Sarah Putnam; photo of Theatre on the Boston Common, Rick Hornick.

Special events professionals share many of the same attributes that meeting planners have. They need to be organized, know how to deal with people, and how to make and administer budgets. They also need to know how to utilize the components in Goldblatt's special events umbrella. Meeting planning and special events firms are integrated industries; they utilize the knowledge and expertise of a variety of other industries, and sometimes the line between these areas is difficult to draw.

The International Special Events Society

The International Special Events Society (ISES) was founded in 1987 in response to the phenomenal growth that was happening in the special events industry. ISES was formed to not only promote the personal and

Klaus Inkamp's title is, manager, International Meeting and Hospitality Programs, for the Coca-Cola Company. His duties include the planning and execution of meetings and programs on both the national and international levels.

During the past several years he has been involved with logistics for the Olympic Games. During the 1992 Olympic Summer Games in Barcelona, Mr. Inkamp was responsible for planning, negotiating, budgeting, housing, ground transportation, ticketing, staffing, give-aways and other items, for over eighty international clients. He also managed a local staff of over 300 people.

Mr. Inkamp belongs to several professional organizations, including Meeting Professionals International (MPI), the National Association of Catering Executives (NACE), and the International Special Events Society (ISES). He is on the board of governors and co-chair of the Education Committee for ISES and is the current president of their educational foundation, the International Special Events Education Foundation (ISEF). He holds the distinction of being one of the first twenty-four people to receive the designation of Certified Special Events Professional (CSEP).

Mr. Inkamp grew up in Gemany, where his family ran a "mom and pop" bakery and grocery store. He says, "I was involved in the service industry from a very young age. Our motto was 'the customer is always king.' This holds true for me today."

Klaus Inkamp

professional growth of its members, but to be a centralized source for education, information, networking, professional development, and ethics awareness (table 4.2).

ISES is the only umbrella organization that represents all aspects of the special events industry. Specifically, ISES was founded to do the following:

- Promote the art and science of special event production
- Establish a code of ethics for the special events industry
- Educate members and the public in the advancement, improvements, and uses of special events
- Ensure that valuable services and quality products are provided
- Provide a meeting place and an opportunity for members to exchange views and discuss matters of mutual interest to the profession

Table 4.2 ISES Principles of Professional Conduct and Ethics

Each member of ISES shall agree to adhere to the following:
1. Provide to all persons truthful and accurate information with respect to the professional performance of duties;
2. Maintain the highest standards of personal conduct to bring credit to the special events industry;
3. Promote and encourage the highest level of ethics within the profession;
4. Recognize and discharge by responsibility, to uphold all laws and regulations relating to ISES policies and activities;
5. Strive for excellence in all aspects of the industry;
6. Use only legal and ethical means in all industry activities;
7. Protect the public against fraud and unfair practices, and attempt to eliminate from ISES all practices that bring discredit to the profession;
8. Use a written contract clearly stating all charges, services, products, and other essential information;
9. Demonstrate respect for every professional within the industry by clearly stating and consistently performing at or above the standards acceptable to the industry;
10. Make a commitment to increase professional growth and knowledge by attending educational programs recommended, but not limited to, those prescribed by ISES;
11. Contribute knowledge to professional meetings and journals to raise the consciousness of the industry;
12. Maintain the highest standards of safety, sanitation, and any other responsibilities;
13. When providing services or products, maintain in full force adequate or appropriate insurance;
14. Cooperate with professional colleagues, suppliers, and employees to provide the highest quality service;
15. Extend these same professional commitments to all those persons supervised or employed;
16. Subscribe to the ISES Principles of Professional Conduct and Ethics and abide by the ISES Bylaws.

Courtesy of the International Special Events Society.

ISES is administered by a thirty-member board of governors and has an eleven-member executive committee. It is located in Indianapolis, Indiana, and is a nonprofit corporation.

Currently the 1,101 members of ISES may be found in six countries, thirty-seven states, three provinces, and two territories. There are also seventeen active ISES chapters both in the continental United States and abroad. In 1991, a comprehensive membership survey was taken to determine the composition of the membership. The breakdown of membership by discipline is as follows:

Event planning and coordination was the principle activity cited by 31 percent of the membership, followed by individuals who identified themselves as being involved with technical services and products. Together these two categories account for almost half of the ISES membership. The membership categories for the survey were derived from the choices made on the ISES application form (table 4.3).

In June of 1992, ISES provided initial funding to facilitate the creation of the International Special Events Education Foundation, Inc. (ISEF). Educators and practitioners from the United States and Canada met at the Sheraton North Shore Inn in Northbrook, Illinois, to discuss and formulate the final plans for the first certification program established for the special

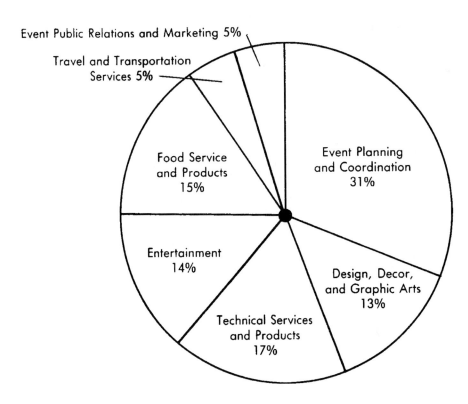

Membership by discipline.
Courtesy of the International Special Events Society.

Table 4.3   International Special Events Membership Categories

1. **Event Planning and Coordination**—Special event planners, producers and coordinators; meeting planners (association, corporate, and government); wedding consultants and party planners, facility venue managers; institutions (educational, cultural, and nonprofit); fund-raisers; producers and managers of parades, festivals, circuses & carnivals, sporting events, and concerts' convention and exposition service managers; and any other entities that provide these types of services for the special events industry.

2. **Design, Decor, and Graphic Arts**—Floral designers; prop and display; balloon artists; invitation designers; printing companies; ad art specialists; and any other entities that provide these types of services for the special events industry.

3. **Technical Services and Products**—Rental; tenting; lasers; lighting; audio visual; photographers; video; film; special effects; pyrotechnics; staging; and any other entities that may provide technical services and products to the special events industry.

4. **Entertainment**—Theme or amusement parks; booking agencies; musicians, vocalists; disc jockeys; magicians; sporting event promoters or managers; carnival, festival or circus performers; concert promoters or managers; speciality acts; performing artists; and any other entities that provide or produce entertainment for the special events industry.

5. **Food Service and Products**—Catering, on and/or off premise; specialty bakeries; restaurants; facility operators; hotels; and any other entities that provide food services and products to the special events industry.

6. **Travel and Transportation Services**—Destination management services; incentive travel companies; valet parking services; ground operators; ground transportation services, bus, van & limousine services; and any other entities that may provide these types of services to the special events industry.

7. **Event Public Relations and Marketing**—Advertising agencies; media companies; public relations firms; marketing companies; awards, novelty, and promotional products companies; professional support services; and any other entities that provide these types of services or products to the special events industry.

Courtesy of the International Special Events Society.

events industry. From June 19 to June 21, these individuals discussed, examined, debated, and explored issues and facets of this program.

Work on the certification process had been started in November of 1990, at Roosevelt University in Chicago, Illinois. The evolution of the process had been long and laborious. Giving birth to a certification process is not an easy task. Resistance may be felt from those who are established in the industry and who perceive certification as a threat. They may fear that they will be ineligible, and therefore excluded, under the new certification requirements. Also, professionals in the industry need to fully understand the advantages of certification and to see how it can benefit them as individuals, as well as benefiting the industry as a whole. What appears to be a simple task can sometimes be more complicated than originally anticipated.

For three days, fourteen individuals with diverse interests and backgrounds worked to tie together the progress made since the 1990 Roosevelt University meeting and to establish a vehicle for the implementation of certification. What emerged was ISEF. The board members discussed the concept of ISEF, reviewed and ultimately accepted bylaws, structured the composition of the board including term of office and membership, and then drafted and adopted a mission statement. The following was unanimously accepted as the mission statement of the International Special Events Education Foundation Board:

1. To direct the certification process for the CSEP designation
2. To foster, implement, and direct educational programs for the special events industry
3. To assume the responsibility of producing the ISES Conference for Professional Development (CPD) and other regional ISES seminars and programs
4. To be fiscally responsible for the activities of ISEF

(*CSEP* adopted June 21, 1992)

The original certification plan had called for two tiers: the certified special events professional (CSEP) and the special events coordinator (SEC). These categories were arrived at as a result of an extensive study, done by the Canadian government, which identified professional competencies. The study issued by the Tourism Standards Consortium of Western Canada, produced several documents, one of which was the "Events Coordinator Standards."

It was this document that became the foundation for the newly adopted professional certification of Certified Special Events Professional (CSEP). After discussion and much consideration, the CSEP definition was accepted as follows:

The Certified Special Events Professional (CSEP) designation is the hallmark of professional achievement in the special events industry. The CSEP is earned through education, performance, experience and service, and reflects a commitment to professional conduct and ethics (*CSEP* adopted June 20, 1992).

The first CSEP examination was conducted in August of 1993, in Toronto, Canada.

In August of 1994, the ISEF board members met in Charlotte, North Carolina, to review the progress made to date by the foundation and to prepare for incorporation. The purpose of this meeting was to adopt a mission and a vision statement and to discuss the proposed Articles of Incorporation and the proposed Bylaws of Incorporation. With minor modifications, both of these documents were unanimously passed and on September 26, 1994, ISEF was issued a Certificate of Incorporation by the Secretary of the State of Indiana.

Meetings/conventions and special events are two areas that are finally coming of age and receiving the recognition that they deserve. The possibilities and opportunities available in either of these disciplines are endless. They are exciting and challenging fields that are ideal for those who love working with people, have good communication and organizational skills, and a creative mind.

Summary

There are similarities and differences between the job responsibilities of meeting professionals and those of special events professionals. One aspect they have in common is that both of these areas have evolved from part-time positions and/or job responsibilities to become full-time, legitimate, recognized careers.

There are corporate, association, and independent meeting professionals. The job responsibilities and descriptions vary for each of these positions and from site to site. But, like special events professionals, the meeting planner needs to have excellent organizational skills, a knack for working with people, adaptability, and the ability to show grace under fire.

Special events professionals may work in corporate settings, or they may be entrepreneurial in nature and have their own business. The special events industry is comprised of many different areas and includes individuals with expertise in the following areas:

1. Event planning and coordination
2. Technical services and products
3. Food service and products
4. Entertainment
5. Design, decor, and graphic arts
6. Event public relations and marketing
7. Travel and transportation

Meeting professionals, or any other individual or group, may call on special events professionals to plan and produce a special activity or portion of an event. Special events professionals may also organize and deliver an entire event on their own.

Both of these professions may occur in retail, corporate, government, social, or professional settings. Members of both areas must keep current concerning the use of sophisticated audiovisual options as well as the latest communication options for facilitating the exchange of information and for providing for the rapid and accurate transmission of contracts, letters of agreement, changes regarding format or venue, and the other details and arrangements involved in the competent delivery of their services.

Discussion Questions

1. In this chapter we have mentioned the glass ceiling and the old boys network. What are these two concepts?
2. What can professional organizations do to enforce proper professional conduct and their code of ethics?

3. Which professions, other than meeting planning and the special events industry, may have unspoken and sometimes unconscious restrictions regarding employment, retention, and promotion? Which populations are more likely to be affected by these attitudes?
4. How would the work environment differ for a corporate meeting planner, an association meeting planner, and a special events professional?

Chapter Exercises

1. Make a site visitation to a facility that holds meetings and/or conventions. What types of meeting services are available at this site? What other general services are available?
2. Attend a special event. What was the stated purpose of the event and was it achieved? What suggestions do you have for making the event run more smoothly, safely, or more profitably?
3. Write to a professional organization to determine the requirements for membership. What benefits would you receive as a member?
4. Contact a CVB and ask them for information about their organization and their services.

References

Adams, D. 1992. *Best festivals: Mid-Atlantic.* Woodstock, VT: The Countryman Press.

Catherwood, Dwight W., and Richard L. Van Kirk. 1992. *The complete guide to special event management.* New York: John Wiley and Sons, Inc.

Cox, Harvey. 1969. *The feast of fools.* Cambridge, MA: Harvard University Press.

Duarte, A. 1992. Women swell the ranks. *Meetings and Conventions* 1 (March): 135–37.

Earles, Zeran. 1993. First Night celebration: Building community through the arts. *Festival Management and Event Tourism* 1: 32–33.

Getz, Donald. 1991. *Festivals, special events, and tourism.* New York: Van Nostrand Reinhold.

Goldblatt, Joe Jeff. 1990. *Special events: The art and science of celebration.* New York: Van Nostrand Reinhold.

Hildreth, Richard A. 1990. *The essentials of meeting management.* Englewood Cliffs, NJ: Prentice Hall.

Hilton, Jack. 1990. *How to meet the press — A survival guide.* Champaign, IL: Sagamore Publishing, Inc.

Hilton, Jim. 1990. *Home grown fun raisers: Special events that make money.* Alexandria, VA: National Recreation and Park Association.

International Special Event Society (ISES) annual report. 1993. Indianapolis, IN: International Special Event Society.

Jackson, Robert, and Steven Wood Schmader. 1990. *Special events: Inside and out.* Champaign, IL: Sagamore Publishing, Inc.

James, Edwin Oliver. 1961. *Seasonal feasts and festivals.* London: Thames and Hudson.

Jedrziewski, David R. 1991. *The complete guide for the meeting planner.* Cincinnati, OH: South-Western Publishing Co.

Maryland National Capital Park and Planning Commission. 1991. *Directory of successful fundraisers.* Alexandria, VA: National Recreation and Park Association.

Meeting Planners International. 1993. *CMP informational package.* Dallas, TX: Meeting Planners International.

———. 1993. *Membership prospectus and application form.* Dallas, TX: Meeting Planners International.

Meetings and Conventions. 1992. *Meetings market report.* Secaucus, NJ: The Reed Travel Group.

Morton, Annie, Angie Prosser, and Sue Spangler. 1991. *Great special events and activities.* State College, PA: Venture Publishing, Inc.

National Recreation and Park Association. 1991. *Directory of festivals and special events.* Alexandria, VA: National Recreation and Park Association.

Professional Convention Management Association. 1989. *Professional meeting management.* 2nd ed. Birmingham, AL: The Professional Convention Management Association.

Rutherford, Denney G. 1990. *Introduction to the conventions, expositions, and meeting industry.* New York: Van Nostrand Reinhold.

Stafford, John. 1993. Standards and certification for event professionals. *Festival management and event tourism* 1: 68–69.

The CLC manual. 1989. 5th ed. Washington, DC: The Convention Liaison Council.

Turner, Victor W., ed. 1982. *Celebration studies in festivity and ritual.* Washington, D.C.: Smithsonian Press.

Urlin, Ethel. 1971. *Festivals, holy days, and saint's days.* Ann Arbor, MI: Gryphon Books,.

Weirich, Marguerite L. 1992. *Meetings and conventions management.* Albany, NY: Delmar Publishers Inc.

Additional Resources

American Society of Association Executives. n.d. *Making your convention more effective.* Washington, D.C.: American Society of Association Executives.

Association meetings: The executive's guide to meeting management. Maynard, MA: The Laux Company.

Chapman, Edward A., Jr. n.d. *Exhibit marketing: A survival guide for managers.* New York: Sextant Communications.

Convene: The journal of professional convention management. Birmingham, AL: The Professional Convention Management Association.

Convention Liaison Council. *Convention Liaison Council glossary.* 1986. Washington, D.C.: Convention Liaison Council.

Drew, Jeannine, and the 3M Meeting Management Team. 1994. *Mastering meetings: Discovering the hidden potential of effective business meetings.* New York: McGraw Hill.

Festival management and event tourism: An international journal. New York: Cognizant Communication Corporation.

Jarrow, Jane, and Ciritta Park. n.d. *Accessible meetings and conventions.* Columbus, OH: Association on Higher Education and Disability (AHEAD).

Meeting news: News, destinations, education. New York: Miller Freeman, Inc./United Newspapers Group.

Meeting Planners International. 1989. *The arranger: A comfort calculator.* Dallas, TX: Meeting Planners International.

Meetings and conventions: The meeting and incentive planner's resource. Secaucus, NJ: The Reed Travel Group.

Meetings today: News and trends for corporate meeting planners and purchasers. A supplement to *Business travel news: The newspaper of the business travel industry.* Manhasset, NY: CMP Publications, Inc.

Murray, Sheila L. 1983. *How to organize and manage a seminar.* Englewood Cliffs, NJ: Prentice Hall, Inc.

Nadler, L., and Z. Nadler. 1987. *The comprehensive guide to succesful conferences and meetings.* San Francisco: Jossey-Bass.

Price, Catherine H. n.d. *The AMA guide for meeting and event planners.* New York: American Management Association.

Special events: The international magazine for special event professionals. Culver City, CA: Miramar Publishing Company.

Successful meetings: The authority on meetings and incentive travel management. New York: Bill Communications, Inc.

Surbeck, Linda. 1991. *Creating special events.* Louisville, KY: Master Publications.

Torrence, Sara R. 1991. *How to run scientific meetings.* New York: Van Nostrand Reinhold.

Wolfson, Stanley M. 1984. *The meeting planners' complete guide to negotiating: You can get what you want.* Washington, D.C.: Institute for Meeting and Conference Management.

————. *The meeting planners' guide to logistics and arrangements.* Washington, D.C.: Institute for Meeting and Conference Management.

————. *The meeting planners' workbook: Write your own hotel contract.* Washington, D.C.: Institute for Meeting and Conference Management.

Event Management

LEARNING OBJECTIVES

1. *To distinguish between the differences in job responsibilities for traditional planners in commercial recreation and tourism and for event managers.*
2. *To demonstrate how the standards developed by the Tourism Standards Consortium of Canada reinforce the emergence of two distinct levels of managerial expertise for commercial recreation and tourism.*
3. *To define event management and to list examples of sites where you will find event managers.*
4. *To cite examples of some of the major events that fall under the purview of event management.*

Introduction

Event management is an emerging term for a series of established and related job titles that span several industries. At the moment there does not seem to be widespread agreement regarding a definition for event management or for the title event manager.

We are all familiar with the term "manager." There are human resources managers, facility managers, convention managers, sports managers, concert managers, trade show managers, exposition managers, and auditorium managers. It seems to be that almost everyone wants to be a manager. Why?

The word "manager" not only carries with it the image of power and prestige, but also the expectations of high remuneration. Along with the above go the perquisites, or perks, of the position. Perks may include a guaranteed parking place, an executive secretary, stock options, and of course, the key to the executive washroom. An interesting definition of a manager is the following:

> Managers [are] quasi-mythical beings, frequently male, who live out their lives in box-like spaces called offices. It is usually easy to differentiate managers from the other beings who also inhabit the office ecosystem. The managers are the ones with the most padding on their chairs and the largest desks (Mescon 1981: 4).

While we could debate the authenticity of this rather cynical description of managers, in reality most managers work long, hard hours for the salaries and the perks that they receive.

Managers

All managers, regardless of their title, are engaged in the same types of activities. Griffin and Van Fleet see the functions of managers as planning and decision making, organizing, leading, and controlling (Griffin 1993: 7 and Van Fleet 1991: 15).

Planning and decision making refer to the responsibility of management for the setting of goals and for the development of a strategy for achieving them. Goals guide an organization from where it is now to where it would like to be later. Without goals, organizations, like people, have no direction. The nature of the goals, and the manner in which they are achieved, depends on the philosophy and purpose of the organization, and on the leadership style of the manager.

Organizing is the process of determining how to group activities and resources for the achievement of goals. For managers this often means making tough decisions regarding the allocation of money, supplies, equipment, and staff. Lean times and a lack of available resources, whether material or human, can make for some stiff competition inside an organization. The manager is responsible for determining how the distribution of resources will occur. Sometimes smaller units or departments must be consolidated, or even eliminated, so that the organization as a whole will be healthier. The manner in which this process happens and is carried out can tell employees, stockholders, consumers, and others, what and who the organization values.

Leading refers to motivating the members of an organization toward an understanding of goals. This is often a difficult task, especially if resources or staff are being cut or eliminated. Leading people so that they recognize and understand goals is an extremely important part of a manager's job. To do this requires an understanding of human nature so that you can get everyone pulling in the same direction. Most employees look to managers for clues regarding the health of their organization. They also look to managers for guidance and for a sense of stability and purpose. Managers are often "the keepers of the flame." They keep everyone on task and reiterate the vision of just exactly where the organization is going.

Finally, controlling is the process of observing and adjusting the activities and resources of the organization so that goals are either reached or redefined. No plan, no matter how well formulated, comes off exactly as projected. Variables both inside and outside the organization cause managers and employees to adjust their expectations. The fall of the Berlin Wall and the dissolving of the Soviet Union were two major external factors that caused many organizations to readjust their goals, change their activities, and reexamine the allocation of their resources.

Managers must perform each of these functions simultaneously. Although they may be stronger in some, they need to be able to carry out each of these functions effectively and in concert with one another.

Managers are not born, they are made. What potential managers need is the desire and the determination to acquire the skills needed for success. These skills include

Conceptual skill: thinking abstractly and seeing relationships between and among issues.

Diagnostic skill: analyzing problems and conditions that may interfere with achieving goals.

Interpersonal skill: communicating the vision and mission of the organization to workers and motivating them to strive to achieve those goals.

Technical skill: understanding and having knowledge of the industry.

First-line managers get their name from the fact that they occupy the first level of management that occurs between employees and management. As you would expect, first-line managers spend a large amount of time supervising employees. Many of them are company employees who have risen through the ranks by demonstrating that they know their job and that they have managerial potential, which means that in addition to conceptual and diagnostic skills, they have very strong interpersonal and technical skills. First-line managers may also be individuals who are hired from outside of the company. Many college graduates look to first-line management

Different management levels require a different mixture of these skills. Management levels include first-line, middle, and top management.

TOP MANAGERS	CONCEPTUAL	DIAGNOSTIC	INTERPERSONAL	TECHNICAL
MIDDLE MANAGERS	CONCEPTUAL	DIAGNOSTIC	INTERPERSONAL	TECHNICAL
FIRST-LINE MANAGERS	CONCEPTUAL	DIAGNOSTIC	INTERPERSONAL	TECHNICAL

positions as a way to gain entry into their area of professional interest and to put their feet on the first rung of the career ladder.

Whether you rise through the company ranks or are hired from outside of the organization, having strong interpersonal and technical skills are essential for successful first-line managers. Technical skill is the ability to demonstrate to employees just exactly how something should be done. It's a "show me" type of situation. Interpersonal skills, which include the ability to explain, repeat information, be patient, motivate, arbitrate, and discipline if necessary, are also required traits for a first-line manager.

A first-line management position is sometimes difficult to occupy. As you rise above the rank of "employee" and enter the realm of management, you may suddenly find yourself in the position of being the shock absorber between two worlds.

Middle managers used to comprise the largest group of managers in many companies. Their name aptly describes exactly where they fall in the organizational chart—directly above the first-line manager and directly below top management. Many people see middle managers as having an equal distribution of conceptual, diagnostic, interpersonal, and technical skills. Some see the middle manager as an endangered species. Indeed, if there is going to be a management cut, it is usually the middle manager who goes first. Organizations and companies, in an effort to become cost-effective and efficient, have been changing their organizational structures. The traditional pyramid shape is rapidly changing to the leaner, meaner, pancake version. The flattening of management levels has meant the reduction of middle managers.

Top managers comprise a relatively small and select group. Although there are many first-line managers, the competition to become a middle and eventually a top manager narrows the field considerably.

Many dedicated and extremely talented athletes attend the Olympics and compete, but in the end only three people stand on the risers to receive the gold, silver, and bronze medals. The same holds true in management.

Top managers need strong conceptual and diagnostic skills. They need to know the other players in the industry, and to be knowledgeable about current and projected trends, technology, and developing conditions that could affect the organization. Top managers determine organizational strategy and establish operating policy. In addition, they are expected to represent the organization to internal and external entities. The prestige and remuneration are high for many top managers, but the demands of the position often consume most, if not all, of the manager's time and energies.

All managers must contend with forces both inside and outside of their organization. Like the conductor of an orchestra, they must make sure that everyone understands what tune is being played, that all instruments are present and tuned, and that everyone is playing together. Unlike orchestra conductors, the event manager has different forces to contend with if the event is to be successful. Some of these forces are inside the organization and include the goals and objectives of the organization, the influence of unions, the standard operating procedures (SOPs) of the agency, and the motives and actions of employees, volunteers, and other managers. Other forces are outside the organization and include suppliers, the media, contractors, and consumers. Whether the force is inside or outside the organization, the event manager must work to coordinate all activity so that the outcome is the smooth delivery of an event.

Event Managers

Event managers do not differ significantly from other types of managers. The same functions, skills, and levels of management expertise required for any other industry are required of event managers. Yet, although conceptual, diagnostic, and interpersonal skills are transferable from one job or position to another, technical skill is not. Technical skill is industry specific.

Event Managers and Special Events Professionals

Some people have not recognized any difference between the job responsibilities of someone who is in the special events industry and someone who is in event management. These terms have often been used interchangeably and, to date, there has been no agreement regarding the distinction, if any, between these two titles. But this is changing.

The Tourism Standards Consortium

Established in 1991, the Tourism Standards Consortium (TSC) is a partnership formed by the Pacific Rim Institute of Tourism and the Tourism Education Councils of Saskatchewan, Manitoba, and Alberta. The mandate to TSC was to improve the image, service, and professionalism of the tourism industry by identifying standards and establishing a certification process for the tourism industry.

Two occupational areas were identified under the heading of Events and Conferences—Special Events Coordinator and Special Events Manager. The standards for both of these areas were identified and developed by special events professionals in the province of Saskatchewan. TSC asked for permission to use the original standards developed by Saskatchewan for the purpose of validating them in western Canada. Special events professionals from this area met to review the original standards. They then amended and endorsed a revision of the Saskatchewan standards. A document was produced by the Saskatchewan Tourism Education Council detailing the final competencies required for the two occupational titles and outlining the process for certification.

TSC developed a challenge-model certification program for the occupational title of Special Events Coordinator. Individuals wishing to be certified have to pass a written examination, successfully complete an on-the-job performance review, and successfully pass an industry-designed evaluation conducted by a trained industry professional. Candidates for the certification process know what areas will be tested and can challenge certification when they feel that they are ready to do so.

The job skills and responsibilities for the two areas are:

Special Events Coordinator.   The Special Events Coordinator is responsible for coordinating an event by:

- creating and executing a detailed plan from established objectives and strategies
- implementing policies and procedures
- training, motivating and leading staff and volunteers
- monitoring and evaluating event and making necessary adjustments

Special Events Manager.   The Special Events Manager is responsible for:

- determining the parameters, policies and procedures of the event
- planning and designing the event
- overseeing the coordination of the event
- developing and implementing the marketing plan for the event
- preparing financial and business reports related to the event
- developing risk management plan

(Saskatchewan Tourism Education Council 1993)

There is clearly a difference in the amount of expertise and experience required to succeed as a Special Events Coordinator as opposed to a Special Events Manager. These positions **are** different and it is interesting to note that while the TSC mandate did not specify that two different levels had to emerge—they did.

The question of what distinguishes an event manager from a special events professional is an interesting one. The tendency is to put these two positions on opposite ends of a continuum. But, somewhere in the middle things get muddy, and we can no longer make a judgment regarding the function of the individual who is right in the middle of the scale. When do you cease being a special events coordinator and become an event manager?

The continuum analogy is further complicated by the problem of positioning. Who goes on the low end of the continuum? Is the position of special events coordinator the starting point for sliding up the scale to the ultimate position of event manager? Many who believe in the continuum believe that is so. They reinforce this position by looking to the description of the levels of management discussed earlier in this chapter and equating the functions and skills of the first-line manager to those of the special events coordinator and the functions and skills of the top manager to those of the event manager.

There is, of course, another option which states that neither of these positions are related nor are they part of any continuum—they are two distinct and separate fields. The rationale for this position comes from the belief that those in the special events industry are highly creative, oriented toward the arts and entertainment, knowledgeable concerning event design, and generalists in nature. In other words, they are the *ultimate* program planner. Event managers, on the other hand, do not have the flair, daring, and love of inventing, nurturing, and delivering individual programs. They are "big picture" people who truly fit the description of those who are top managers.

A third option is that, while at some point in time these two areas were the same, they are in the process of diverging. Rather than being one tree or two completely independent trees, they are really two divergent branches on the same tree.

Perhaps the most creative approach to answering the question of how we can distinguish a special events coordinator from a special events manager is the suggestion that the latter manage to draw *major media interest* for their events. But regardless of which, if any, of these scenarios is correct, it has become apparent that special events professionals and event managers are different and have different job descriptions.

While special events professionals design and deliver diverse events at different sites, event managers may be employed by a single facility or employer and are responsible for managing the events that take place at their site.

Examples of Sites Where Event Managers May Be Found

Concert halls	Convention centers
Theme parks	Fairs
Expositions	Sport arenas and facilities
Destination resorts	Environmental centers
Public recreation departments	Museums
Zoos	Corporations
Cultural centers	Educational centers
Not-for-profit organizations	Living history attractions
Arts centers	Foundations

The use of several different titles to describe event managers further complicates identifying who is an event manager and who is not. Title alone does not tell us the function of an individual; however, event managers may use any of the following descriptive titles: president, vice president, general manager, director, executive director, chairperson, producer, and coordinator.

For our purposes, we will use the following definition of an event manager:

> An event manager is an individual who is responsible for the total *delivery* of an event. While they participate in event planning, their primary purpose is to coordinate and manage the various parties involved in the event (both internal and external) so that the end result is the competent, safe delivery of the event.

It is important to understand that one of the primary functions of an event manager is facilitation. A facilitator is an individual who makes it easier for things to get done. They know how and where to find the resources needed to make tasks easier, as well as understanding the process for completing the assignment. They understand the unwritten rules of how to function in a system to get things done, as well as the written standard operating procedures (SOPs) of the organization.

Event managers see the big picture while keeping their finger on the pulse of what is happening in the remotest part of the operation. Much of what they know comes to them through the eyes and ears of the individuals they employ. These employees are highly competent, trusted, goal-oriented, and share the vision of the organization.

Multipurpose Facilities

Multipurpose facilities are just what they sound like. They are buildings, arenas, convention centers, stadiums, or sites that change configuration to accommodate different events. They are multidimensional and adaptable. The primary purpose of the construction of a stadium may be to house a professional sports team, but today's economics dictate that, whenever possible, the facility must accommodate other functions. The people who are responsible for the smooth transition from one event to another with minimal interruption to the business of the site are event managers.

Madison Square Garden

Madison Square Garden is neither square nor a garden. Located in New York City, it was the site, in July of 1992, for the Democratic National Convention. Originally designed to stage indoor sporting events, the Garden, as it is affectionately called, has become a multipurpose facility. Two of New York's professional sports teams, the New York Knickerbockers (basketball) and the New York Rangers (ice hockey), use the 20,000-seat arena as their home. In addition to sports, the Garden also hosts the Ringling Brothers and Barnum and Bailey Circus, Walt Disney's World on Ice, World Federation Wrestling, Nickelodeon, and major concerts. The Garden is also a meetings and conventions host site and has space to accommodate from 20 to 20,000 individuals in state-of-the-art meeting and reception facilities.

The 1992 Democratic National Convention was one of the more media-intensive events held in the Garden in recent years. Covered by 205 television stations in the United States, a 200-million-dollar renovation completed in September of 1991 not only rejuvenated the Garden but provided 16,099 seats with an unobstructed view of the podium.

Over 13,000 credentialed reporters, 4,928 delegates and alternates, 380 dignitaries from 87 countries, and 5,000 others that included family members, VIPs, and elected officials who were not delegates, descended on the city.

New York City assigned 2,500 police officers to the convention site and budgeted 20 million dollars for convention security and services. In return for this investment, the city expected the convention to generate 188 million dollars in direct spending, based on spending estimates of 353 dollars a day per visitor. Hundreds of millions of dollars more in indirect spending were expected to spin off from convention-related activities. City tax revenues totaling 27 million dollars were expected to be generated to offset the 20 million spent for security and services.

Rental of the Garden for the convention was a mere 4 million dollars. Six hundred miles of electric and phone cables were laid under the convention floor. The estimated cost for the 6,000 new phone lines alone was 3.6 million dollars.

In addition to the money spent inside the Garden, convention suppliers and other businesses were benefiting economically from the convention. Posters, flags, banners, bunting, and 60,000 helium-filled balloons all helped to "dress" the Garden and create a festive atmosphere. Retailers, museums, attractions, theaters, and hotels and restaurants all benefited from the spin-off generated by the convention.

Once a center of indoor sports attractions, the Garden has adapted itself to the times by capitalizing on its ability to be flexible and to host a variety of different events.

The Domed Stadium

The world's first domed stadium was the Astrodome. Built in Houston, Texas, and opened in 1964, it was the harbinger of things to come. Before the Astrodome, stadiums and game schedules were at the mercy of the elements. Rain, snow, or excessive heat or cold could alter or curtail the use of the stadium. Interruption in the use of the stadium meant two things, disappointed fans and lost profits.

In 1976, Toronto, Canada was awarded an American League baseball franchise. The plans for the new team, dubbed the Toronto Blue Jays, called for the upgrading of an old stadium to become their home field. The first game in the renovated stadium was played on April 7, 1977. Eventually, the necessity for a domed stadium was discussed. Site selection and preparation began in April of 1986 and by June 3, 1989, the new stadium opened.

SkyDome is a stadium with the world's first fully retractable roof—the "convertible" of stadiums. SkyDome is really three venues in one—an open-air stadium for the summer months, a domed stadium for the fall and the winter, and SkyBowl, an intimate seating area for smaller audiences. The roof of SkyDome is made out of four panels. Three of these panels are retractable. One panel rotates 180 degrees, while the other two panels slide forward and retract. It takes twenty minutes to open SkyDome.

Conversion of the field inside SkyDome from football to baseball takes approximately twelve to fourteen hours. Seating capacity for concerts (full mode, not SkyBowl) is 67,000. When configured for football, the facility seats 53,000, and the baseball configuration allows seating for 50,600. The baseball field has a unique feature, a hydraulic pitcher's mound. An 18-foot fiberglass dish is located beneath the field in a holding chamber that is filled

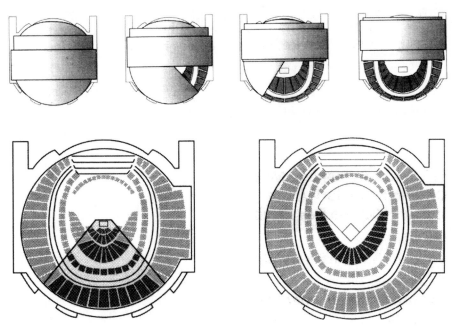

The roof of SkyDome (top) moves at a rate of 71 feet (21 m) per minute and takes 20 minutes to open or close. SkyDome (bottom) can be transformed into a variety of configurations.
Courtesy of SkyDome, Inc.

Sky Tent

Baseball Mode

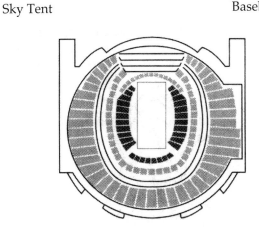

Football and Soccer Mode

with water. As the chamber is filled, the mound rises to field level. Once it reaches the proper height, it is locked into place.

SkyDome also has the ability to convert itself into SkyBowl. SkyBowl is created by SkyTent, a large acoustical curtain that is suspended from the ceiling by metal trusses. SkyTent divides the stadium into a smaller setting for audiences of 10,000 to 26,000.

SkyDome also has the first hotel built into a domed sports and entertainment facility. There are seven restaurants and bars (including a Hard Rock Cafe), a fitness club, and in excess of 4 million dollars in Canadian

Table 5.1   Estimated Benefits from Operations—SkyDome (per annum in millions)

	Metro Toronto	Ontario*	Canada**
Value added to Gross Domestic Product	$326	$371	$385
Number of jobs	12,000	14,500	16,000
Taxes (excluding property taxes)	$0.2	$40.1	$75.8
Property taxes	$4.2	—	—

Source: Stadium Corporation estimates. Information courtesy of SkyDome, Inc.
*Includes Metro Toronto
**Includes Ontario

artwork. The Rolling Stones, Wrestlemania VI, and the New Kids on the Block are just some of the entertainers who have performed in this domed facility.

The total cost of SkyDome through June of 1992, was 600 million dollars. Its estimated economic benefits per year for Metro Toronto, Ontario, and Canada can be seen in table 5.1.

The list of SkyDome features and amenities goes on and on. The uniqueness, versatility, and consistent quality of Skydome earned it the *Performance Magazine* award of "Stadium of the Year" for three consecutive years.

Sports Events

Americans are not the only people who love their sports. Sports effect not only the economy of many nations, but also help to shape popular culture. Sports items become collectibles, and athletes are elevated to superstar status based on their ability to slam, ram, or jam a ball or a puck into a net, over a net, or through a net. Popular clothing reflects sports loyalty as both children and adults pledge allegiance to their team or to their favorite player.

The half-time show at the 1993 Super Bowl drew an audience of 133 million viewers. Produced by Radio City Music Hall Productions, the half-time show featured superstar Michael Jackson. A 30-second commercial spot cost advertisers 850,000 dollars. Obviously the reason why an advertiser would spend 850,000 dollars for a 30-second spot is exposure. While this was the same price as the charge for the previous Super Bowl, it was twenty times the advertisement rate per second of the first Super Bowl when a 60-second spot cost a mere 85,000 dollars.

The Olympic Games

There is no sporting event that is celebrated by more people than the modern-day Olympic Games. The opening night of the 1992 Summer Games in

Barcelona, Spain saw 65,000 people in the stands. They were joined by an estimated additional 3.5 billion television viewers. Even the tiny nation of Vanuatu saw the Olympic Games.

Vanuatu is a tiny Pacific Island nation that was formerly New Hebrides. The population of Vanuatu consists of 165,000 people who live on eighty-three different islands. Vanuatu had six athletes competing in the Barcelona Games. The state-owned television station, which is called "Our Television Station," televised the Olympics to the citizens of Vanuatu on 500 television sets that were especially flown in for this occasion by Air Vanuatu. There were television sets in this tiny nation prior to the Barcelona Olympic Games, but they were mainly used to view videotapes. This was the first time that the tiny nation had seen the Games live. To them this event must have been awesome. After all, the Barcelona Games took more than three years to produce and cost 1.5 billion dollars. The opening ceremonies included 20,000 participants, 317 musicians, and 64 tons of powder for the fireworks. This window into the global village catapulted the citizens of Vanuatu into the midst of a gigantic modern-day event and sparked debate over the effect of television on this tiny island nation. Some individuals sat and watched the event unfold with astonishment, others saw the unwrapping of a peaceful island existence. Although the six athletes from Vanuatu did not bring back the gold, they did bring back tales and stories of Barcelona and of the people that they had met. Either way, the citizens of Vanuatu had met the outside world—and we had met them as well.

The Olympic Games were originally established for competition and to promote peace and friendship among athletes and nations. Today the Games also promise the rewards of remuneration and corporate sponsorship. This issue has been controversial to some extent, but the huge success of the 1984 Games in Los Angeles turned many a skeptic into a convert. Michael Payne, the marketing chief of the International Olympic Committee (IOC), has stated that without corporate sponsorship there would be no Games. The financial burden of organizing such an event has become too large for a city or a government to host, without additional funding from outside sources. Even the first modern Olympic Games held in Athens in 1896 had stadium advertising. The official program for these Games had an advertisement for Kodak—a sponsor of the 1994 Winter Games.

The Lillehammer Winter Games held in 1994 cost the Norwegian government and private investors over 1 billion dollars. Capital improvements included the boring of a tunnel under the city to facilitate traffic flow, and new water and sewer lines. There was no McDonald's built in Lillehammer to accommodate the fast-food crowd, but there was one in Oslo. The featured sandwich was a "Norsk McLaks Meny," which translates into a "Norwegian McSalmon Meal." The advertising gained from being a sponsor, or from having your product or service seen on television or reported in print, has led to conflict and rivalries between competing sponsors.

In Lillehammer, competition for sponsorship became so intense that the IOC ordered that a Swiss bobsled be repainted to wipe out the name of a Swiss bank. They also stationed monitors at the top of ski runs to place masking tape over the name of goggle manufacturers if they felt that the lettering was excessive. The IOC does not allow advertising at Olympic venues, and there would be no free advertising at Lillehammer.

Sponsorship is sold on several levels and includes various benefits. Becoming an exclusive Olympic sponsor for the 1994 Winter and the 1996 Summer Games cost 40 million dollars in cash, goods, and/or services. For this investment the sponsor received either worldwide or U.S. marketing rights to both of the events. Competition for sponsorship can be fierce and has led to ongoing battles between official sponsors and companies who have become adept at walking the fine line of truth in advertising.

The 1996 Summer Olympic Games will be held in Atlanta, Georgia. Getting the games to Atlanta took three years and included the submission of a bid to host the Games, site inspections, numerous meetings, the formation of the Atlanta Organizing Committee (AOC), and the submission of a five-volume bid document. Competition to host the Summer Games drew formal bids from five additional cities—Athens, Belgrade, Manchester, Melbourne, and Toronto.

The official body that is organizing the Atlanta Games is the Atlanta Committee for the Olympic Games (ACOG). ACOG is a private, nonprofit organization and was incorporated in January of 1991. ACOG will be working with the International Olympic Committee (IOC), the United States Olympic Committee (USOC), the City of Atlanta, and the Metropolitan Atlanta Olympic Games Authority (MAOGA). MAOGA is a public authority whose role is to review financial statements, budgets, and construction contracts. In addition MAOGA will approve of venue changes and the construction of the Olympic stadium.

The board of directors of ACOG oversee the decisions made by the organization and coordinates the activities of the officers. They have also established an executive committee and four standing committees—Audit, Compensation and Executive Resources, Equal Economic Opportunity, and Finance and Administration.

The process of staging an event of this size can be overwhelming, and in September of 1993, ACOG already had 461 full-time employees. Two of the main reasons for undertaking such a task are civic pride and the economic impact on the host city and the surrounding areas (table 5.2).

The 1994 financial forecast projected by ACOG indicated that revenues minus expenses would result in breaking even. While there would not be positive cash flow, the real prize for the staging of the event is not the expected net, but the economic impact expected for the state of Georgia during the organization and delivery of the Games.

> Hosting the 1996 Atlanta Centennial Olympic Games will have a $5.1 billion impact on Georgia's economy over the 1991 to 1997 period, according to an economic impact study released in October, 1992 . . . Olympic-related sporting events, visiting media, athletes, officials and spectators will have an impact of $2.7 billion. A significant temporary boost in employment is anticipated, particularly in the year leading up to and

Atlanta Committee for the Olympic Games.
Source: ACOG.

Board of Directors

ACOG President & CEO — W. P. Payne

ACOP Marketing — W. H. McCahan

Senior Policy Advisor External Relations — S. C. Franklin

Local Government/ Community Relations — D. K. Getachew-Smith

Equal Economic Opportunity Program — G. S. Walker

Physical Legacy — S. R. Day

Olympic Programs — L. P. Stephenson

Senior Executive Assistant — D. B. Bowles

Communications — C. R. Yarbrough

State Government Relations — R. L. Thomas

Corporate Secretary & Corporate Services — V. T. Watkins

Opening and Closing Ceremonies — K. L. Dollar

COO — A. D. Frazier, Jr.

Executive Assistant to Co-Chair of Board — D. W. Gatin

Deputy COO — K. Y. Wallace

Sports — D. L. Maggard

Venues — D. B. Arnot

Special Projects & Technology — R. Knowles, III

Games Services — S. W. Anderson

Atlanta Olympic Broadcasting — M. C. Romero

International Relations — C. H. Battle, Jr.

Operations — M. J. Dillard

Finance & Management Services — P. C. Glisson

Administration — C. C. Isaacs-Stallworth

Construction — W. J. Moss

Table 5.2   1994 Atlanta Committee for the Olympic Games Financial Forecast

REVENUES

Broadcast rights	$555,500,000	
Joint venture	513,390,000	
ACOG share of TOPIII	114,380,000	
Ticket sales	261,230,000	
Merchandising	28,700,000	
Other income	107,471,000	
Total Revenue Forecast		**$1,580,671,000**

EXPENDITURES

Executive Administration:

Administration and human resources	$38,118,000	
Executive operations	24,523,000	
Financial and management services	120,277,000	
Total Executive Administration	**$182,219,000**	

Construction:

Venues	$469,628,000	
Village	47,000,000	
Total Construction	**$516,628,000**	

Functional Operations:

Communications and government relations	$13,719,000	
Corporate services	44,778,000	
Host broadcasting	106,329,000	
Merchandising	16,647,000	
Sports and intl. organizations	147,625,000	
Olympic ceremonies	24,180,000	
Olympic programs and physical legacy	52,481,000	
Operations	405,350,000	
Sr. policy advisor and ext. relations	10,015,000	
Total Functional Operations	**$821,125,000**	
Contingency/Net Funds Flow	**$60,000,000**	
Total Expenditure Forecast		**$1,580,671,000**

Information provided by the ACOG.

including the Games. The state of Georgia will also receive incremental tax revenues estimated at $198.7 million from personal and corporate income taxes, sales and use taxes, and motor fuel taxes (*ACOG Press Guide* 1993: 27).

In addition to hosting the Summer Games, Atlanta will also hold the Paralympic Games. Like the Olympics, they will be privately financed. The Paralympic Games attract world-class athletes who have either physical or visual impairments. First held in Rome in 1960, they will be held in Atlanta following the Olympic Games. Approximately one-third the size of the Olympics, it is expected that 4,000 athletes from 102 nations will attend.

While the XXVI Olympiad at Atlanta will mark the celebration of the Centennial Olympic Games, the XVIII Olympic Winter Games at Nagano, Japan is a link to the arrival of the next century.

> The Nagano Olympic Games are a link to the 21st century, inspiring our search for wisdom for the new era, respect for the beauty and bounty of nature, furtherance of peace and goodwill. Friends worldwide are heartily welcome to share, in the spirit of competition and fair play, the joys and glory of the XVIII Olympic Winter Games (Vision for the 1998 Nagano Olympic Winter Games 1992).

Nagano City was awarded the XVIII Olympic Winter Games on June 15, 1991. From then until February 7–16, 1998, the Nagano Olympic Games Organizing Committee (NAOC) will be engaged in the process of creating, organizing, coordinating, and delivering this event. Like Atlanta and the other modern-day Olympic cities, Nagano has needed to establish a relationship with the other parties involved with this event.

NAOC needs to work with the Japanese government and the Nagano Prefecture (which is the equivalent of a state or a province). Event sites, the IOC, and the Japan Olympic Committee (JOC) as well as national federations representing the various Olympic sports must also be included in the discussions and plans for the Winter Games.

In order to facilitate communications and to ensure that work is divided into manageable parcels, NAOC established an executive board and a

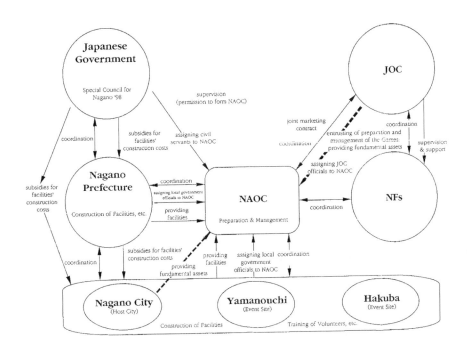

Relationship between Nagano Olympic Games Organizing Committee (NAOC) and Connected Organizations.
Courtesy Nagano Olympic Organizing Committee.

steering committee to oversee the project. In addition, seven commissions were created and given areas of responsibility (see Appendix D).

There will be approximately sixty countries and 3,000 athletes in Nagano in 1998. A total of sixty-four events in seven sports: 29 in skiing, 20 in skating, 6 in biathlon, 3 in luge, 2 in ice hockey, 2 in bobsleigh, and 2 in curling will be held at the XVIII Winter Olympic Games.

There are other major sporting events besides the Olympic Games that draw large crowds, warrant major media attention, and have a social and an economic impact on the host site and the surrounding area. The Friendship Games, Commonwealth Games, Wimbledon, and the World Cup are a few of these events.

Festivals, Feasts, Fairs, and Fiestas

In addition to events related to and revolving around sports, another category of events for the nonsports-minded among us exists. Besides being called festivals, feasts, fairs, and fiestas, they may also be referred to as galas, jamborees, jubilees, pageants, parades, and processions. Or, how about commemorations, celebrations, carnivals, or attractions? For definitions of all of these titles see the glossary of the book *Festivals, Special Events, and Tourism,* by Donald Getz.

Each year thousands of festivals and events are held around the world. They attract all kinds of people who are looking to relax and have a good time with family and friends. While the main theme of sporting events is competition, the theme of festivals is one of celebration. The marking of the changing of the seasons, the cycle of birth, life, and death, the reminder of fallen heroes, or the commemoration of a religious event binds participants together.

Festivals around the World

Calgary Winter Festival	Calgary, Alberta
Musikfest	Bethlehem, Pennsylvania
Folklorama	Winnipeg, Manitoba
Kentucky Derby Festival	Louisville, Kentucky
Carnaval	Rio de Janeiro, Brazil
Gilroy Garlic Festival	Gilroy, California
Macon Cherry Blossom Festival	Macon, Georgia
Le Festival Du Voyageur	Winnipeg, Manitoba
Mardi Gras	New Orleans, Louisiana
Boston Early Music Festival	Boston, Massachusetts
Carnavals sans Frontieres	Nice, France
Jacksonville Jazz Festival	Jacksonville, Florida
Naantali Music Festival	Naantali, Finland
Colorado State Fair	Pueblo, Colorado
Edmonton Klondike Days	Edmonton, Alberta

Bayfest	Green Bay, Wisconsin
Oktoberfest	Munich, Germany
Boise River Festival	Boise, Idaho
Macy's Parade and Events	New York, New York
Fiestas de Octoubre	Guadalajara, Mexico
Riverbend Festival	Chattanooga, Tennessee
Tournament of Roses	Pasadena, California
Wexford Festival Opera	Wexford, Ireland

These events are not related to conventionally recognized sports, although it could be argued that some of them represent some exclusive nontraditional sports.

The Albuquerque International Balloon Fiesta

The Albuquerque International Balloon Fiesta started in 1972 with thirteen hot air balloons. Today, the fiesta has 626 balloons, is governed by a thirty-member board of directors, has a year-round paid staff of seven and mobilizes 1,000 volunteers to successfully execute this event.

International media coverage of the fiesta, which is held for nine days starting on the first weekend in October, is done by fifty countries who have live satellite broadcasts. In 1993 there were balloons from eighty-one countries outside of the United States. Kodak has become the major sponsor of the fiesta, with other corporate sponsors participating on various levels.

The event itself is spectacular. The balloons stand fifty to eighty feet tall. New balloons cost an average of 10,000 dollars. Customizing a balloon can push that cost to over 200,000 dollars. The fiesta attracts some of the most spectacular balloons from all over the world. Specially shaped balloons include Suleyman the Magnificent, the flying saucer, the Harley Davidson balloon, Miss Piggy, and the shopping cart.

In 1992, an on-site marketing study was conducted by ABT International to determine the audience profile, assess the event, and determine the economic impact of the fiesta. Results of the study found that 1.482 million spectators attended the event in spite of strong winds. Most of the attendees were from out of town (62 percent) with 84 percent coming from the southwest region of the United States. The economic impact for 1992 for the nine-day event totaled 94.8 million dollars of direct and indirect spending.

Direct-impact spending included 23.4 million in on-site spending, 4.8 million in organizer and sponsor spending, and 3.9 million in direct spending by attendees. Most of this last category was generated by out-of-town visitors who spent money for lodging, transportation, and food. The indirect impact of 62.6 million dollars resulted from the respending of primary income in the local economy. The fiscal impact from state and local taxes was almost 1.4 million dollars.

The Edinburgh Festivals

If ever there was a town that loved its festivals, it is Edinburgh, Scotland. Edinburgh hosts nine different festivals each year (table 5.3).

Each year the nine festivals produce over 2,000 events at 238 venues and draw an audience of 1.3 million people. The International Festival is the oldest festival in Edinburgh. It is also the largest international festival in the world.

Each year, for three weeks, the International Festival produces musical and theatrical events. Although many of the events are expensive and require formal dress, there are also more casual events for the sneaker crowd. The Fringe Festival occurs concurrently with the International Festival, draws twice the crowd, and produces nine times the number of events.

Fringe festivals often accompany large events. Fringe events in general are composed of individuals and groups who did not become participants in the main festival. They organize themselves into an accompanying festival that is structured, but is more flexible and spontaneous. The Fringe includes hundreds of performances each day, including Shakespeare, jazz, comedy, musicals, and the bizarre. The fun of attending the Fringe is that events are more diverse, less predictable, and a whole lot cheaper.

The economic impact for Edinburgh and the Lothians (the area to the south of the city) was 44 million pounds of direct expenditure, which resulted in 9 million pounds of local income and 1,300 equivalent full-time jobs. If you add the benefits to Scotland, these figures rise to 72 million pounds and 3,000 equivalent full-time jobs (Scottish Tourist Board 1993: 72–73).

Table 5.3 Edinburgh Overall Festivals Profile

Festival	Number of Events	Number of Venues	Total Audience
International Festival	110	25	245,000
Fringe Festival	990	140	500,000
Jazz Festival	421	20	65,000
Film Festival	153	3	15,000
Military Tattoo	1	1	200,000
Book Festival	170	1	62,000
Folk Festival	50	6	8,000
Science Festival	290	41	201,000
Children's Festival	12	1	30,000

Source: Festival Management & Event Tourism Vol 1 No. 2, 1993. *Edinburgh Festivals Study: Visitor Survey and Economic Impact Assessment Summary Report*, February 1992—Scottish Tourist Board, p. 72.

Note: The above table excludes attendance at the Glenlivet Fireworks Display, estimated to attract up to half a million people.

Management Corporations

The British Columbia Pavilion Corporation (BCPC) of Vancouver, British Columbia is an example of a company that manages and markets several diverse event venues. BCPC operates five facilities: Fraser Valley Trade and Exhibition Centre (Tradex), Robson Square Conference Centre, B.C. Place Stadium (B.C. Place), Vancouver Trade and Convention Centre (VTCC), and The Bridge Film Studios.

The two largest facilities are B.C. Place and the Vancouver Trade and Convention Centre. Both of these sites are located in close proximity to one another in downtown Vancouver. B.C. Place was built in 1982 and was used for Expo '86. It is Canada's first and the world's largest air-supported domed stadium and multipurpose facility. B.C. Place's roof is made of a fiberglass woven fabric, coated with Teflon. Although only 1/30 of an inch thick, the roof is stronger than steel and allows 20 percent of the natural light to penetrate through the fabric. The building of the air-supported roof as opposed to a traditional roof saved 20 million dollars and a year of construction time.

B.C. Place employs 60 full-time and as many as 1,000 part-time employees. Although it cost 111.4 million dollars to build, additional costs including architect fees, bonding, insurance, start-up costs, and an owner's contingency fund brought the total price tag to 126 million dollars. In return for this investment, B.C. Place contributes over 90 million dollars to the economy each year.

The Canada Pavilion at Expo '86 was reborn as the Vancouver Trade and Convention Centre (VTCC). The VTCC is located on the waterfront on the site of the largest pier restoration in the world. Five thousand pilings remaining from the year 1928 were joined by 908 new pilings to create the current site. VTCC has twenty-one meeting rooms, 94,000 square feet of column-free exhibition space, and can cater banquets of 6,000 or receptions of 10,000. This facility is already taking bookings through the year 2015. It served in 1993 as the site for the April 3–4 meeting between President Clinton and Russian President Boris Yeltsin. It will be the site of the '96 International Conference on AIDS (adding an estimated 30 million dollars to the city's economy), and the Seventeenth World Congress of Gerontology from July 1–6 in 2001.

Professional Organizations

Two of the professional organizations that represent event managers are the International Association of Auditorium Managers (IAAM) and the International Festivals Association (IFA).

IAAM is the world's largest association devoted exclusively to the management of arenas, stadiums, convention centers, performing arts theaters, and amphitheaters that are open to the public. IAAM represents

B.C. Pavilion Corporation Organization Chart Management Committee December 14, 1994
Courtesy British Columbia Pavilion Corporation.

				Warren Buckley				
				President and C. E. O.				
				631-3008				

Barry Smith — Senior Vice President and C. F. O. — 631-3009

Pat Brand — Director Human Resources, and Corporate Services — 631-3038

Brenda Sandes — Director Marketing — 631-3041

Lorne Cochrane — Manager, Information Services — 631-3035

Walt Judas — Communications Manager — 631-3022

John Harding — Director of Finance — 631-3026

Neil Campbell — General Manager B. C. Place Stadium — 661-3445

Susan Croome — General Manager Bridge Studios — 291-0650

Tim Leclair — General Manager TRADEX — 857-1263

Dan London — General Manager VTCC — 641-1405

Tracey Short — Facility Manager RSCC — 660-2831

approximately 1,800 managers and companies who provide goods and/or services to these types of facilities. Members of IAAM can attend seminars, educational programs, and district meetings. In addition, they have on-line access to industry data and can attend the Public Assembly Facility Management School run by IAAM.

The International Festivals Association is a professional association dedicated to the festivals and special events industry. With worldwide membership totaling over 1,400 members, it sponsors three annual seminars at various festival cities. The quarterly magazine *Festivals* is free to members along with the monthly newsletter *IFA Today*. The IFA and Purdue University offer the Certified Festival Executive (CFE) program for professional development.

Summary

At the moment there is not agreement regarding the definition for event management. This is an emerging area that may be practiced under a variety of job descriptions, including facility manager, convention manager, trade show manager, exposition manager, or auditorium manager.

Event managers may be first-line, middle, or top managers. Like all managers, they possess conceptual, diagnostic, interpersonal, and technical skills. The event manager differs from the meeting professional and the special events professional. Both meeting and special event professionals have managerial responsibilities, but they are more heavily involved in programmatic considerations than the event manager.

The following definition of an event manager is used in this chapter:

> An event manager is an individual who is responsible for the total *delivery* of an event. While they participate in event planning, their primary purpose is to coordinate and manage the various parties involved in the event (both internal and external) so that the end result is the competent, safe delivery of the event.

Event managers may be found in a variety of places. Some of these sites include the following:

Concert halls	Convention centers
Theme parks	Fairs
Arts centers	Corporations
Zoos	Sport arenas and facilities

It is interesting to note that when the Tourism Standards Consortium of Canada was charged with the mission of identifying competencies and establishing standards under the heading of Events and Conferences, two occupational areas emerged. These two areas were the Special Events Coordinator and the Special Events Manager. The main difference between these levels was the programming and supervisory responsibilities of the coordinator as opposed to the policy, procedural, and other managerial responsibilities of the events manager.

Discussion Questions

1. Examine the responsibilities of the Special Events Coordinator and the Special Events Manager. What are the major differences between these two positions? How do they parallel the skill levels for lower, middle, and top managers that were discussed in this chapter?
2. How do we know when a Special Events Coordinator crosses the line and enters the realm of event management?
3. What effect if any do you believe that multipurpose facilities might have on smaller venues? What might happen to these sites? What populations and which kinds of events might be suitable for smaller sites?

Chapter Exercises

1. Visit a site near you that is responsible for the production of multiple events. Who is the person who is responsible for the delivery of these events? What is his/her job title and job description?
2. Locate a major event that is held in your area. Contact the individual(s) responsible for the delivery of this event to see if you can determine the economic impact that the event has on your area.
3. Divide a piece of paper into four blocks. Label the blocks technical, interpersonal, diagnostic, and conceptual. Evaluate yourself in these four areas. Which are your strong areas? What area needs to be improved? How could you improve this area?
4. Write or visit a major event site and obtain a copy of their program schedule. Analyze the schedule to see how quickly events are turned over. Is an ice hockey game immediately followed by a concert? Do you see any pattern to the way that events are held?

References

Atlanta Committee for the Olympic Games. 1993. *ACOG Press Guide*. Atlanta.

Bhada, Neville, et al. 1993. Research report: Firm specific beliefs of tourism suppliers of the 1996 summer Olympics. *Festival Management and Event Tourism*: 121–24.

Cox, James. 1994. Visa, American Express Spar at Olympics. *USA Today*, 21 February.

———. 1994. Olympics strategy has its rewards. *USA Today*, 21 February.

Crompton, John L. 1993. Understanding a business organization's approach to entering a sponsorship partnership. *Festival Management and Event Tourism*: 98–109.

Democratic National Committee. 1992. Convention guide. *The New York Times*. 13 July.

Getz, Donald. 1991. *Festivals, special events, and tourism*. New York: Van Nostrand Reinhold.

Getz, Donald. 1993. Case study: Marketing the calgary exhibition and stampede. *Festival Management and Event Tourism*: 147–56.

Goldman, J. David. 1993. Atlanta counts down the days. *Aquatics International* (November/December): 13.

Griffin, Ricky W. 1993. *Management*. 4th ed. Boston: Houghton Mifflin Company.

Hughes, Howard L. 1993. Olympic tourism and urban regeneration. *Festival Management and Event Tourism*: 157–62.

International Festivals Association. 1993. Profile. *Festival Management and Event Tourism*: 132–33.

Jackson, Eden. 1992. Atlanta gears up for 1996. *Aquatics International* (May/June): 14.

Kraus, Richard G., and Joseph E. Curtis. 1990. *Creative management in recreation, parks, and leisure services.* 5th ed. St. Louis: Times Mirror/Mosby College Publishing.

Mercer, G. William. 1993. Public event planning and security in British Columbia: An overview. *Festival Management and Event Tourism*: 137–42.

Mescon, Michael H., Albert, Michael and Khedouri, Franklin. 1981. *Management: Individual and Organizational Effectiveness.* New York: Harper & Row.

Purdum, Todd S. 1992. New York: The good, the bad and the political. *The New York Times.* 13 July.

The Saskatchewan Tourism Education Council. 1993. *Events and Conferences: Special events coordinator & special events manager occupational standards.* Saskatchewan.

Schmidt, William E. 1994. Lillehammer's moment in the twilight. *The New York Times.* 16 January.

Scottish Tourist Board. 1993. Edinburgh festivals study: Visitor survey and economic impact assessment summary report, February, 1992. *Festival Management and Event Tourism*: 71–78.

Sunday Star Ledger 1994. (Newark, New Jersey). Preview Edition: World Cup 1994 (Advertising Supplement), 12 June.

Shelton, Peter. 1993. Winter games. *Sunday Star Ledger* (Newark, New Jersey), 17 October.

Swanson, Kathy. 1993. NFL scores with radio city and Michael Jackson. *Special Events* (July): 14–17.

Van Fleet, David D. 1991. *Contemporary Management.* 2nd ed. Boston: Houghton Mifflin Company.

Walsh-Heron, John, and Terry Stevens. 1990. *The management of visitor attractions and events.* Englewood Cliffs, NJ: Prentice Hall.

Weston, Susan A. 1994. Festivals—A celebration of life. In *ISES Gold: An anthology of expertise from members of the International Special Events Society,* edited by Joe Jeff Goldblatt et al., 67–73. Louisville, KY: Master Publications.

Wilkinson, David G. 1988. *The Event Management and Marketing Institute.* Toronto: The Event Management and Marketing Institute.

Additional Resources

Agent and manager—The bible for facilities: Expositions, sports, and entertainment. New York: Bedrock Communications, Inc.

Albrecht, Karl. 1988. *At America's service: How corporations can revolutionize the way they treat their customers.* Homewood, IL: Dow Jones-Irwin.

Berlonghi, Alexander. 1990. *The special event risk management manual.* Dana Point, CA: Alexander Berlonghi.

Blanchard, Kenneth, and Norman Vincent Peale. 1988. *The power of ethical management.* New York: Fawcett Crest Books.

Casino player: The magazine for gaming enthusiasts. Atlantic City, NJ: ACE Marketing.

Doyle, Michael, and David Straus. 1982. *How to make meetings work.* New York: Jove Books.

Hilton, Jack. 1990. *How to meet the press: A survival guide.* Revised ed. Champaign, IL: Sagamore Publishing, Inc.

Rowland, Diana. 1993. *Japanese business etiquette: A practical guide to success with the Japanese.* 2nd ed. New York: Warner Books.

Sletten, Eric. 1994. *How to succeed in exploring and doing business internationally.* New York: John Wiley and Sons.

Travel and Tourism

LEARNING OBJECTIVES

1. *To understand the economic impact that tourism has on the national, regional, and local levels of a country.*
2. *To explore models of tourism evolution.*
3. *To discuss the types of agents, agencies, and tours that exist in the industry.*
4. *To examine some of the reasons why people travel.*
5. *To introduce the World Tourism Organization and its work concerning recommendations on tourism statistics.*
6. *To examine the potential for sustainable development and the use of tourism as a force for peace.*

Introduction

The world has become a very small planet. The ability to travel to different places via instantaneously beamed television transmission has made it so. Different customs, cultures, and rituals wander freely through the air waiting to pop out of the television sets of sophisticated city dwellers and rural villagers all over the world. This shared window to the world has broadened our collective consciousness.

Familiarization with others has made it less intimidating to get out of our easy chairs and to go and see for ourselves what exactly is going on "over there." "They" are just as interested in us. This curiosity, plus safer and more economical travel systems, has spawned a huge industry. No longer the sole purview of established nations, emerging countries are awakening to the realization that there is revenue to be produced by plugging into the industry. Tourists bring with them dollars, which support local industries, allow for the construction or renovation of infrastructures, and stimulate economic development far beyond their initial spending point.

The Economic Importance of Tourism

There is no doubt that tourism generates revenue. World tourism receipts and arrivals for 1992 were up from the figures recorded for the previous year. International tourist receipts totaled an impressive (US $) 279 billion dollars, an increase of 6.8 percent. International tourist arrivals were also up 4.5 percent to 476 million (*World Travel and Tourism Review* 1993: 8). All of this happened in spite of political instability and economic recession that affected many parts of the world.

During 1992, countries outside of the United States spent (US $) 1.14 billion dollars on tourism advertising in the United States alone. The purpose of all this advertising was to attract Americans. Canada's contribution was approximately 27 million dollars. This included expenditures by the federal government, the provinces, Air Canada, and large cities. In addition, Royal Caribbean Cruise Line spent more than 35 million dollars in media advertising in 1992. This was only one cruise line—all together the cruise industry spent a total of 208 million dollars (*Exclusive* 1993: 6).

Tourism Revenue in North America

In North America (Canada, Bermuda, and the United States of America) people were busy traveling during 1992. Accounting for just 5.2 percent of the world's population, North America's share was 19.6 percent of the total receipts for world tourism. While the region as a whole did well, the benefits were not distributed equally.

Tourist arrivals in Bermuda and Canada declined in 1992 but increased by 7 percent in the United States; the sixth annual increase in a row. While 45 million Americans traveled internationally in 1992 and spent (US $) 58 billion dollars, 46 million visitors came to the United States and spent (US $) 76 billion dollars. The net result for the United States was a travel surplus (*World Travel and Tourism Review* 1993: 70). All this travel took place in spite of two major hurricanes and a major earthquake, all of which occurred in popular tourism locations.

These figures are impressive, but most of us still want to know how this affects us on a regional or local level. Revenue was not distributed equally, and there were winners and losers in the (US $) 279 billion dollar figure cited earlier. Tourist arrivals and receipts for the Middle East in 1991 did not do well because of the Gulf War, and needless to say, tourism in what once was Yugoslavia ceased to exist.

Tourism in Canada

Canada occupies 3,851,809 square miles and covers a larger portion of North America than the United States. Like the United States, the topography of Canada is varied. Unlike the United States, which is organized into states, Canada contains ten provinces and two territories. The province of British

Columbia is located on the west coast and shares its border with the states of Washington, Idaho, and Montana.

Tourism Canada is the branch of the federal government that is responsible for nurturing and supporting the tourism industry in Canada. Founded in 1934 and originally called the Canadian Travel Bureau, the bureau underwent several name changes before becoming Tourism Canada in 1983. The mandate to Tourism Canada is to oversee the orderly growth of tourism in Canada on both the domestic and international levels. This is accomplished by gathering data regarding the state of the travel industry in Canada and by giving guidance to the other tourism delivery agencies across the country.

The Province of British Columbia

British Columbia recognizes the importance of travel and tourism to the economy and has taken a proactive stance regarding the gathering and analysis of tourism information and marketing for tourism. In British Columbia, the Ministry of Small Business, Tourism, and Culture is responsible for working with those involved in the tourism industry. Together with suppliers, communities, the federal government, and other agencies, the Ministry works to ensure sustainable development for British Columbia.

The province knows that tourism generates over (CN $) 5.4 billion dollars in revenue, employs over 180,000 people annually, and adds (CN $) 2.7 billion dollars to the provincial Gross Domestic Product (*A Vision for Tourism* 1993: 3). Gross Domestic Product (GDP) is how the province measures the "value-added" from tourism activity to the economy of British Columbia.

> For example, if a restaurant uses $11 worth of food and other inputs for a $20 meal, it has created $9 of 'value-added' or GDP in producing this meal. GDP consists of the wages and salaries paid to workers, other costs such as interest payments and depreciation, and the profit earned by owners. Because GDP measures the value that each industry has added during its production of products and services, GDP is a better indicator of economic impact than receipts or revenues (*Tourism Gross Domestic Product* 1993: 4).

In order to arrive at an accurate GDP it was necessary for British Columbia to determine what portion of industry revenue was attributable to tourism activity. This was done for 150 service industries. Some of the broad general categories included were transportation and storage, retail trade, accommodation and food, and other services. The other services category included leisure, recreation, and many other subcategories related to commercial recreation.

British Columbia recognizes that the tourism industry entails the interaction between and among visitors, suppliers, and host communities. "Visitors represent the demand side as consumers of goods and services; the supply side is made up of the businesses, associations, government agencies and communities which provide the tourism-related products" (*Tourism Gross Domestic Product* 1993: 1). This approach to recognizing the importance of the industry and the supply and demand side of tourism,

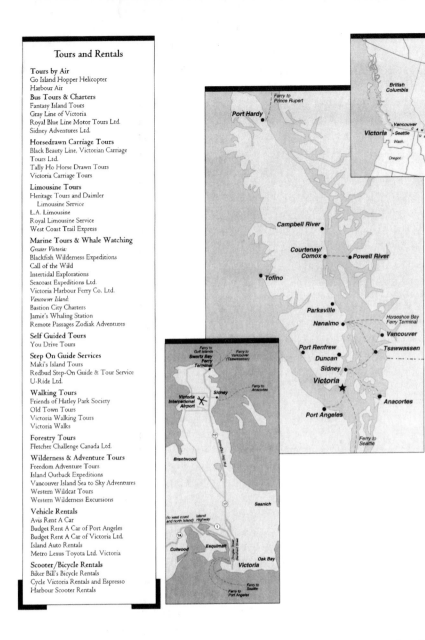

Tours and Rentals

Tours by Air
Go Island Hopper Helicopter
Harbour Air

Bus Tours & Charters
Fantasy Island Tours
Gray Line of Victoria
Royal Blue Line Motor Tours Ltd.
Sidney Adventures Ltd.

Horsedrawn Carriage Tours
Black Beauty Line, Victorian Carriage
Tours Ltd.
Tally Ho Horse Drawn Tours
Victoria Carriage Tours

Limousine Tours
Heritage Tours and Daimler
Limousine Service
L.A. Limousine
Royal Limousine Service
West Coast Trail Express

Marine Tours & Whale Watching
Greater Victoria:
Blackfish Wilderness Expeditions
Call of the Wild
Intertidal Explorations
Seacoast Expeditions Ltd.
Victoria Harbour Ferry Co. Ltd.
Vancouver Island:
Bastion City Charters
Jamie's Whaling Station
Remote Passages Zodiak Adventures

Self Guided Tours
You Drive Tours

Step On Guide Services
Maki's Island Tours
Redbud Step-On Guide & Tour Service
U-Ride Ltd.

Walking Tours
Friends of Hatley Park Society
Old Town Tours
Victoria Walking Tours
Victoria Walks

Forestry Tours
Fletcher Challenge Canada Ltd.

Wilderness & Adventure Tours
Freedom Adventure Tours
Island Outback Expeditions
Vancouver Island Sea to Sky Adventures
Western Wildcat Tours
Western Wilderness Excursions

Vehicle Rentals
Avis Rent A Car
Budget Rent A Car of Port Angeles
Budget Rent A Car of Victoria Ltd.
Island Auto Rentals
Metro Lexus Toyota Ltd. Victoria

Scooter/Bicycle Rentals
Biker Bill's Bicycle Rentals
Cycle Victoria Rentals and Espresso
Harbour Scooter Rentals

Travel information from British Columbia.
The Greater Victoria Visitors and Convention Bureau/Tourism Victoria.

has enabled the province to gather important information about the distribution of the GDP derived from tourism. It has also allowed British Columbia to strategically position itself for the upcoming worldwide competition for tourist revenue.

Tourism on the Local Level—Vancouver Island and Victoria

Vancouver Island is located off the coast of southern British Columbia and is accessible by air and by sea. Victoria, the island's major city, is located on its southern tip and is part of an area known as Greater Victoria. Greater Victoria has a total population of approximately 290,000 people and encompasses three other municipalities besides Victoria: Oak Bay, Saanich, and Esquimalt.

The Greater Victoria Visitors and Convention Bureau/Tourism Victoria, and The Greater Victoria Visitors and Convention Bureau/Destination Marketing Commission have aggressively promoted and marketed their area as "Victoria and the Island—Imagine it in Living Colour." In 1992, the area attracted 3.25 million visitors who spent (CN $) 750 million dollars, (CN $) 97.4 million of which was hotel revenue (*Winter 1992 Exit Survey* 1993: insert).

The concerted effort by British Columbia and by Vancouver Island to understand their consumers and to strategically plan for the future has made a difference. They have taken the time to lay the proper foundations for the further expansion of their total share of tourism revenues.

Tourism in the United States of America

The United States of America is comprised of forty-eight contiguous states, the states of Alaska and Hawaii, and several territories and trusts. The fifty states cover 3,536,278 square miles. Much of the promoting of tourism for the United States has not been done by the federal government but is done on the state, regional, or local levels of government. Convention and Visitors Bureaus and state Departments of Travel and Tourism (or their equivalents) promote their constituency to both domestic and international travelers. Professional and industry organizations and associations as well as individual business entities also try to promote and market their specific interests and areas. Support and funding from the federal level for promotion and marketing have been minimal.

In 1940, the federal government passed the Domestic Travel Act. This act authorized the National Park Service (NPS), as part of the Department of the Interior, to manage and promote domestic tourism. The occurrence of World War II curtailed the involvement of the park service with this mission. Coping with restrictions of budget, expanding parks and facilities, and increased visitation after World War II, the NPS did not have much time for promoting travel and tourism.

Tourism promotion and marketing remained basically ignored until President Dwight D. Eisenhower proclaimed 1960 as the year for all peoples to visit the United States. The invitation applied equally to domestic and international visitation. However, although he acknowledged the importance of tourism, Eisenhower felt that it was not the responsibility of the government to advertise and promote travel and tourism. It was not until 1961 when the International Travel Act was passed by Congress that a serious attempt was made to promote the United States as a destination for international travelers. The International Travel Act established the United States Travel Service (USTS), which came under the auspices of the Department of Commerce. The USTS was authorized to establish offices overseas for the purpose of promoting the United States as a destination for international travelers. One of the motives for the passing of this act was to try to help reverse the travel deficit that the nation was experiencing. After World War II many Americans returned to visit the places where they had been stationed and had fought during the war. Those countries that had been devastated by the war were rebuilding and were not sending any travelers over here. The result was an imbalance of too many American tourism dollars going abroad and the lack of tourism dollars coming to America.

It was not until 1975 that the original power given to the NPS to promote domestic tourism was transferred to the USTS. Eventually the USTS became the U.S. Travel and Tourism Administration (USTTA) through the passing of the National Tourism Policy Act of 1981. The USTTA is the American equivalent of Tourism Canada, is still a part of the Department of Commerce, and is headed by an Under Secretary of Commerce.

The next important act to be passed was the Tourism Policy and Export Promotion Act of 1992. The purpose of this act was to make federal grants available to states and cities for the purpose of promoting their regions outside of the United States. The act also included the establishment of a Rural Tourism Development Foundation to attract visitors from abroad to rural areas.

In spite of all of this legislation and the USTTA, many feel that the federal government has no clear mission or vision regarding the direction and future of the travel industry. Much of the involvement by government has dealt with issues of regulation and not with promotion or strategic planning. Individual commissions and administrations such as the Interstate Commerce Commission, the Federal Aviation Administration, and the Federal Highway Administration regulate their individual interests without seeing the whole.

Tourism on the Local Level—Washington, D.C.

The nation's capitol, Washington, D.C., is a primary destination for both domestic and international visitors. In 1992, the capitol was host to 19.2 million visitors. The majority, 17.6 million, were domestic visitors. Besides its past and current interest as the place where the business of governing one of the oldest and largest democracies in the world occurs, historical monuments and museums make Washington one of the nation's most interesting sites.

Three organizations, the National Park Service, the Smithsonian Institution, and the Washington, D.C. Convention and Visitors Association represent the city's tourism interests. The Washington, D.C. Convention and Visitors Association (WCVA) is the parallel organization of The Greater Victoria Visitors and Convention Bureau. WCVA has been in existence since 1931 and is a voluntary organization that represents all segments of the Washington tourism industry.

> WCVA's major goal is to enhance the city's economy by continually
> increasing the number of overnight visitors to the Washington area. To
> accomplish this task, the Association works in conjunction with the city

government and subscribing companies to collectively market the Washington area to prospective meeting and convention clients, tour organizers, business and vacation travelers (*Annual Report and Travel Trends* 1992: 1).

WCVA represents local commercial recreation and tourism industries, while the mission of the National Park Service is to preserve and protect some of the nation's most revered historic sites and monuments.

There are twenty National Park Service sites within the heart of the District of Columbia. These sites include the Washington Monument and the Lincoln and Jefferson Memorials. One of the more recent memorials is the Vietnam Memorial, which is located in a forty-acre site known as Constitutional Garden. Other sites include Ford's Theatre, the Frederick Douglass Home, the National Mall, and the White House. In addition to preserving and protecting our heritage, National Park Service rangers conduct educational, interpretive, and living history programs.

The Smithsonian Institution was founded when James Smithson, a British scientist, bequeathed his entire fortune of a half million dollars to the United States. Smithson stipulated that an establishment to increase and diffuse knowledge be founded at Washington under the name of the Smithsonian Institution. Interestingly enough, Smithson had never been to America.

Today the Smithsonian Institution consists of thirteen museums and the National Zoo. Supported privately and federally, there is no admission charge. Often referred to as the "Nation's Attic" because of its huge collection covering almost every facet of the human struggle, the Smithsonian has become the keeper of our past and our present. It houses our collective history and our popular culture. It is the Smithsonian that is the keeper of Howdy Doody, the chairs used by Archie and Edith Bunker, the Hope Diamond, the ruby red slippers from the *Wizard of Oz*, the Apollo 11 command module, Benjamin Franklin's printing press, the "swamp" from *MASH*, the original Star-Spangled Banner, and the Enola Gay.

It is not surprising that the power of the sites preserved by the National Park Service and the splendor of the Smithsonian draw people to Washington. For most domestic visitors who visited in 1992 (13.2 million), the purpose was pleasure. Only 3.4 million came for business or as convention delegates (*Annual Report and Travel Trends* 1992: 11).

Total international visitors to Washington in 1992 numbered 1,634,000 individuals. From 1990 to 1992, the top four overseas countries to lead in visitation to the capital were:

Country	1990	1991	1992
1. Japan	136,000	133,000	210,000
2. United Kingdom	171,000	105,000	164,000
3. Germany	113,000	119,000	112,000
4. France	77,000	92,000	78,000

(*Annual Report and Travel Trends* 1992: 16)

Visits by international tourists from Canada and Mexico were 149,000 and 30,000, respectively, for 1992.

During this time period, tourist revenue for lodging, food, transportation, entertainment, gifts, and other incidentals totaled (US $) 4 billion dollars. All of this activity produced 516 million dollars in tax revenues, of which 235 million remained with the District of Columbia (*Annual Report and Travel Trends* 1992: 10).

The World Tourism Organization

Any viable industry needs to keep records. Questions to be asked include How did we do this year, compared to last year? Who are our customers? What factors influenced the choices made by customers? Having this information allows us to categorize information for statistical purposes, know our market, and follow trends. We have seen the different ways that industry terms and concepts have been explained and defined. This approach helps individual interest groups understand and analyze what was happening in their area, but it does not allow for a broad-based analysis of the industry as a whole.

The World Tourism Organization (WTO) is the organization that is accepted as representing all national and official tourist interests. Located in Madrid, Spain, the WTO acts as a consultant to the United Nations in matters that concern travel and tourism. The WTO is recognized as the voice of world tourism.

In June of 1992, the World Tourism Organization and the Canadian government organized a conference in Ottawa. Dubbed the Ottawa International Conference on Travel and Tourism Statistics, the purpose of this meeting was to see if there could be some agreement regarding the language used to report information that related to tourism. Not only would this allow for the unification of tourism information, but it would lend some credibility to this important industry.

The outcome of the Ottawa Conference was the adoption of a set of recommendations on Tourism Statistics, in March of 1993, by the United Nations Statistical Commission. No country is bound by the recommendations, however, their existence signals a major achievement, a suggested standardized manner in which international tourism statistics can be kept and reported.

The WTO has offered the following definition of tourism: "Tourism comprises 'the activities of persons traveling to and staying in places outside their usual environment for not more than one consecutive year for leisure, business, and other purposes'" (*Recommendations on Tourism Statistics*—short report 1992: 2).

Travelers are classified as either visitors or other travelers. Visitors are either domestic or international and are broken down into two groups: tourists (people who stay overnight) and same-day visitors. Individuals in the other travelers category can be seen in the WTO diagram of the classification of international visitors.

Most of the people in the last category (i.e., the border workers) would hardly categorize themselves as tourists or same-day visitors. Appropriately they are not included in tourism statistics.

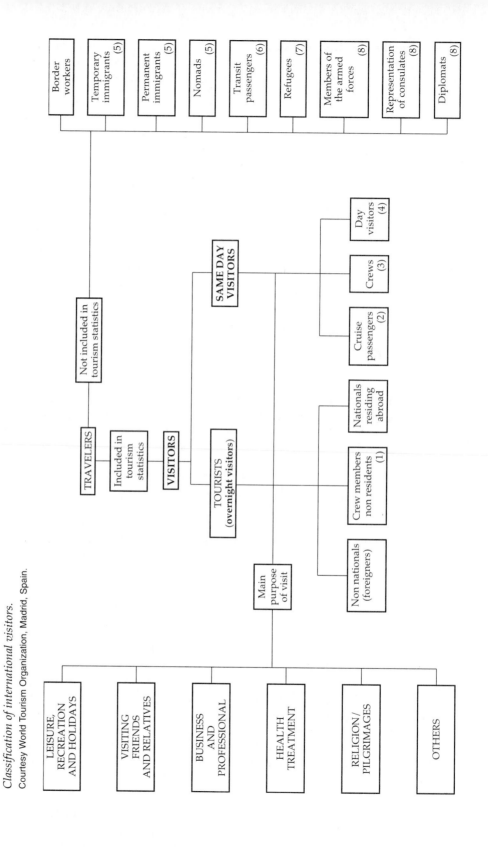

Classification of international visitors.
Courtesy World Tourism Organization, Madrid, Spain.

Tourism from the Demand Side

The WTO discusses both the supply and the demand aspects of tourism. In its simplest form, the demand side of tourism refers to the desire and/or necessity of individuals to travel both in their own country and internationally.

Forms of tourism from the demand side are distinguished by the WTO as domestic tourism, inbound tourism, and outbound tourism. Domestic tourism includes residents of a country traveling only in their country of residence. Inbound tourism includes "nonresidents traveling in the given country; outbound tourism, involving residents traveling in another country" (*Recommendations on Tourism Statistics*—short report 1992: 2).

The exciting aspect of this schematic is that it presents a clear and comprehensive picture of tourism on three levels: internal, national, and international. It also eliminates the concept of foreign visitors/tourists. The word foreign is a word that is loaded with negative connotations and encourages a we/them mentality. In an age of increased multicultural awareness, perhaps it is time that we shed the word foreign from our vocabulary.

Tourism from the Supply Side

Recognizing that travel and tourism is controlled and distributed by a number of sources, the WTO set out to provide a classification of tourism activities as they relate to economic activity. "Statistics on tourism expenditure are one of the most important indicators required by policy makers, planning officials, marketers and researchers. They are used for monitoring and assessing the impact of tourism on the national economy and on the various sectors of the industry" (*Recommendations on Tourism Statistics*—full report 1992: 25).

In an effort to provide a more comprehensive statistical picture of the supply side of tourism the WTO developed the Standard International Classification of Tourism Activities (SICTA). In order to conform to world standards already in existence, SICTA was modeled after the structure of the International Standard Industrial Classification (ISIC). This model consists of the categorization of suppliers under major groupings and then keeps breaking down these units into smaller ones.

While SICTA is most useful to researchers and analysts, it is a reminder of the magnitude and complexity of the supply side of tourism.

Travel Distributors

When most of us think of travel distributors we think of travel agencies. After all, the travel agency is the first line of defense for most of us when we are planning a trip or a vacation. Travel agencies provide us with one-stop shopping for our transportation, recreation, lodging, food, and beverage needs. But travel agencies and travel agents vary. Although most agencies are multiservice operations, some agencies service specialized markets.

A travel agency is run by a manager who should be knowledgeable about the industry and be able to handle any type of business that comes into the agency. This would include international travel, specialized markets, and even corporate travel. The manager is responsible for planning and implementing a promotional and marketing campaign and should be able to sell and operate group tours. Managers also represent the agency by speaking to outside groups such as senior citizen clubs, students at school career days, and local churches and synagogues.

If an agency is large enough, there may be agents who specialize in different types of accounts. A commercial counselor will handle travel arrangements for corporate clients, a domestic counselor will help with vacation and travel plans for the general public, and an international counselor will specialize in international trips. The agency will probably have some commissioned sales representatives as well. These individuals are hired to generate new business, and their salaries are based on the amount of business that they generate.

All of these individuals must know about tour programs, hotels, car rentals, and travel restrictions. One of the most important skills that all these people can possess is to know where to find the answers to the myriad questions that clients ask.

Top Travel Agencies for 1991
(Based on Gross Sales)

1. American Express
2. Carlson Travel Network
3. Thomas Cook Travel
4. Rosenbluth Travel
5. US Travel
6. Liberty Travel

(*Tourism's Top Twenty* 1992: 99)

In addition to travel agencies there are also organized tour operators such as Trafalger, Tauk, and Cosmo. Tour operators package and sell programmed tour packages. The type of package varies, but the concept is the same; travel arrangements, lodging, and usually at least some of your meals are preplanned, prepaid, and highly scheduled. Individuals traveling to countries where another language is spoken or to another part of the world for the first time may find that a tour is a good first introduction to their destination. Tours vary in length from a two-hour trip around London to see the sites, to a lengthy grand tour of the continent. What these tours have in common is that they are structured and led by a tour guide who is knowledgeable about history, demographics, and the must-see aspects of the area.

As travelers become more sophisticated, they seek out novel and unusual experiences. There are travel professionals who specialize in packaging adventure tours and holidays. Examples of these tours include the following:

Climbing and mountaineering in Nepal

White-water rafting in Zimbabwe

Canoeing in Greenland among icebergs and seals

Walking through the Peruvian Andes

Pony trekking in the Scottish Borders

Sailing on Lough Erne in Ireland

Scuba diving and underwater photography in Sri Lanka

Windsurfing in Greece, Turkey, and Sardinia

Looking for elephants in northern India

Cycling in China

These experiences are arranged by tour operators who specialize. Because of the adventuresome nature of their tour packages, they need to hire guides and tour conductors with specialized skills. If you choose to go canoeing in Greenland among icebergs and seals, those responsible for conducting the group need to be well-trained professionals who can handle the extraordinary as well as the everyday agenda.

Most of the people choosing to take this type of tour have some interest and experience in the specific skill needed (cycling, climbing, scuba diving, etc.) to make this a unique and happy experience as opposed to the Bataan death march.

The tour company knows their target markets and may contact clubs and interest groups directly to market their tours, or the clubs may contact the tour company and request that a specialty tour be arranged solely for their group. The tour company may also advertise directly in the magazines and publications read by the target group. Most competent travel agents should be able to help you locate this type of tour by being able to identify companies that have consistently demonstrated good service and have excellent safety procedures and records.

Alternative Travel Arrangements

There are as many types of alternative travel arrangements as there are creative people. Experienced travelers often look for interesting ways to visit new places. One of these alternatives is vacation home exchange.

Vacation home exchanges occur when people or families swap living spaces. People exchange homes by using directories, newsletters, and other types of lists compiled by vacation home exchange clubs. Although they are called clubs, they really are bulletin boards for helping people locate one another. The club charges for a listing in their directory. Correspondence and negotiations occur between the parties involved and do not involve the club.

Home exchange is not for everyone. Some of the positive aspects are reduced costs for living expenses, being in the midst of the culture rather than insulated by a hotel, having the option to cook meals, and escaping from a sterile tourist environment. Objects other than living spaces, such as automobiles, theater tickets, or pets can become part of the exchange.

The negative aspects of home exchange include the reluctance to have strangers occupying your space, having inconsiderate guests who leave your house dirty, and being unclear about who is responsible for repairs to the car, appliances, and other objects.

Home exchangers need to be flexible and adaptable. In spite of the best arranged and researched swaps, horror tales can occur:

> Arriving at our exchanger's holiday home in New England, we found no washing machine/dryer, no pressing iron, no stereo/video, portable TV only of poorest quality, cycles rusted, fleas in furniture, poor, unclean car (*Trading Places* 1991: 167).

In spite of the potential problems, most individuals find their swap satisfactory and trade again and again. It's part of the adventure.

While vacation home exchange definitely falls outside the traditional boundaries of conventional travel arrangements, it is recognized by the WTO in SICTA as part of the industry, and it does contribute to the tourism economy of the host site.

Destination Travel

Destination travel has become popular with individuals who want to travel to one place that provides on-site services and activities. This arrangement works particularly well for families with young children, for older travelers, and for those who like to have a base of operation for their adventure. While you may not get out to meet the locals and to become immersed in the culture of the area, this choice is a great way to relax, unwind, and receive one-stop shopping for all your vacation needs.

Destination travel usually involves visiting sites and attractions that are either natural or manufactured. Natural attractions include places like the coast of Alaska, the Everglades, the beaches of Martha's Vineyard, and the Canadian Rocky Mountains. It is the natural surroundings which draw the people. Many natural attractions have been protected by being declared a national park, reservation, preserve, or wilderness. They are protected and managed by the National Park Service.

Manufactured attractions include places like Las Vegas, the Edmonton Mall, theme parks, and clubs such as Club Med. At these sites you can usually find at least one destination resort. A destination resort is usually a large property which is self-contained. The resort provides such a wide variety of services and activities that there is no need to leave the property. Walt Disney World is an excellent example of a huge destination resort. Las Vegas is an excellent example of a travel destination with several destination resorts.

Understanding Tourism

People travel for many reasons. Your reason for traveling to a specific destination today may not be the same as your reason for traveling there next week, month, or year. If we look at the "visiting friends and relatives" category of the Classification of International Visitors (CIV), it tells us who went where. What it doesn't tell us is why. Did they go to visit these individuals because there was an important event and their presence was *required?* Was their reason to rejuvenate themselves by retreating to a warm nurturing environment where they could gain perspective? Did they go because they wanted to ask to borrow money?

On one level, knowing why does not matter; on another, it does. On the international level, knowing that a certain number of people each year had as their main purpose for traveling the visitation of friends and relatives, as opposed to business and professional travel, is helpful. We can track the categories each year to see if they remain constant or change.

Some Reasons Why People Travel

Romance/sex	Shop
Support a person or team	Relax
Become part of a shared experience	Escape
Experience the unique	Self discovery
Reduce boredom	Be entertained
Cultural enrichment	Have an adventure
Be challenged	Promote a cause
Immersion in another culture	Fulfill an obligation

We might even postulate the reasons for such occurrences and maybe break the categories down into smaller units to generate more specific information. This could help us make future predictions. On the other level, this information does not help us if we are a health-related spa or a hotel that concentrates on arranging business meetings. Although the industry as a whole may be doing well, this information does not tell us why people have stopped coming to our particular facility or why the industry is doing poorly, yet we are having to turn people away. Information of a different kind is needed to answer this question.

Models of Tourism Evolution

The tourism industry is a complicated and intertwined business. The interaction between the host community and the tourist is symbiotic in nature. Models have been designed to explain the economics of this relationship and to forecast future trends. Two models show the evolution and impact of tourism on the local community. Both models show the evolution of tourism from its initial welcoming stage to the realization of its impact on the quality of life of local residents and its perceived quality of being undesirable.

In 1979, George Doxey described the evolution of the relationship between tourist and host community. The initial contact shows the welcoming of the tourist by the community. Tourist revenue stimulates the local economy and is seen as being a good deal for everyone. The second stage shows an apathetic attitude with tourists starting to be held responsible for changes in quality of life and for additional burdens on old infrastructures. The third stage indicates saturation of the site as it gains in popularity. This leads to increasing pressures between tourist and community and eventually to change. In stage four the honeymoon is definitely over as tourists are blamed for the changes and for the problems caused by too many people and clashing cultures. The final stage indicates that the original attitudes towards tourism development are ignored, changed, or violated. The attributes that attracted the original tourist population have ceased to exist, and a new visitor population may emerge. Doxey's model was followed in 1991 by Stanley Plog's description of the life cycle of tourist destination. Like Doxey, Plog sees the initial destination going from desirable to overpopulated, to ultimate decline and decay. But we have learned that the relationship between tourists and sites does not have to be this way.

The Greening of the Industry

For a long time we have been a consumptive society. The prosperity that followed World War II convinced us that there was no end to our resources. Energy was cheap, clean water was plentiful, and disposing of garbage was as easy as opening another landfill or sending another barge load of garbage out to sea. It was hard to conceive of a time when a land as vast as ours could neither continue to absorb our trash nor supply our raw materials and energy. While a vocal few spoke in behalf of the land and the environment, most of us knew that although there might be a problem, it just couldn't be as bad or as urgent as they were saying.

The gas pump crises of the 1970s caught many of us by surprise. A new acronym OPEC (Organization of Petroleum Exporting Countries) entered our vocabulary. We became acutely aware that what happened "over there" could have consequences over here. For many of us this was a new revelation.

Not once but twice we had to line up at gas stations to buy gasoline. Red and green flags flew to indicate the availability of gas. Cars with license plates ending in odd numbers were allowed to purchase gas only on specific days. Even-numbered plates had the alternate days. Line disputes led to violence in some cases, as the gas guzzling, heavy chromed, massive automobiles of the '70s sucked up fuel at an alarming rate. We had been hit where it hurt us the most—the rationing of fuel for our automobiles.

Fuel surcharges began to be levied against the cost of taking a cruise. Airfares rose to compensate for rising prices for aviation fuel, and prices of petroleum-based products such as photographic film also increased. Tourist destinations that relied heavily on local people for their business wondered how all of this would affect them. With higher prices and long lines at those stations lucky enough to have gas, would people choose to travel or would they stay home?

In response to the 1973 energy crisis, Congress overrode the National Environmental Policy Act to allow for the building of the Alaskan oil pipeline. Eventually the petroleum problem eased, and as we entered the

'80s we forgot the gas pump crises of the '70s. We reverted to our old habits and our familiar consumptive ideology.

In the summer of 1987, we received a wakeup call as garbage and dead fish washed up on America's shores. In 1988, syringes, rubber gloves, and other medical waste hit the beaches of the East Coast. Dirty medical waste, coupled with an increased awareness of the arrival of AIDS, made going to the beach a very unattractive choice. Neighboring states pointed fingers at one another while environmental voices reminded us that what we dump at sea doesn't necessarily stay there. Meanwhile, shore industries were calculating their losses as business dropped dramatically.

U.S. environmental policy has been inconsistent, and there is no national vision or plan. At the national level, each new president has proclaimed that he is committed to helping the environment. The Environmental Protection Agency (EPA) is the branch of the federal government that is concerned with environmental issues, but much of the responsibility for regulation and enforcement has been left to the individual states. They are subject to the pressures of interest groups who argue in favor of their position. Meanwhile "band-aid" measures are used to stop the ecological hemorrhaging that was and is happening.

Efforts to educate and change the habits of citizens are carried out through schools, interest groups, and other service-oriented agencies. Some change in habits has occurred as a result of local recycling programs. Most of these programs were initiated in an effort to cut taxes for solid waste services. The recycling of glass, aluminum, and newspapers rose along with the consciousness of many to the plight of the environment.

Environmental Types

A 1990 Roper Organization study of Americans classified individuals into five environmental types: True-Blue Greens, Greenback Greens, Basic Browns, Grousers, and Sprouts. True-Blue Greens are individuals whose behavior is consistent with strong environmental views; they are willing to lobby to make their views known. Greenback Greens also have strong views. They are

Calvin and Hobbes   by **Bill Watterson**

willing to pay substantially higher prices for products that are green (environmentally compatible), but are not as proactive as the True-Blue Greens.

Basic Browns do not believe that they can make a difference. They are not likely to follow environmental practices but may recycle bottles and cans. They comprise the largest segment of Americans—50 million people or 28 percent. Grousers may make some attempt at following basic environmental practices, but defend their poor practices by criticizing others and offering excuses. Sprouts have demonstrated green tendencies but have not yet taken a clear environmental position (*Discover America: Tourism and the Environment* 1992: 37). But why do we care about True-Blue Greens and Basic Browns? After all, this is a chapter on travel and tourism.

The travel and tourism industry was quick to realize that site desirability is directly related to the quality of its surroundings (remember the medical waste?) and that profit is maximized by making smart choices. Knowing the demographics of your market, including how they stand on environmental issues, can affect the choices that you make and the types of experiences that you offer. Smart choices include the protection of the site and the area around the site from harmful chemicals and other hazards. It also includes energy conservation that leads to reduced operating costs and the careful use of water and other finite resources. Those who do not care about the environment because of altruistic reasons quickly learn that saving money is a good motivator.

We began to see that if everyone removed a souvenir rock from the canyon, eventually there would be no more rocks. If there were no more rocks, then erosion would occur more easily. If erosion occurs the trail may disappear. If the trail disappeared, there would be no way to get down into the canyon, and if the canyon is compromised then tourists would not come. If tourists would not come, then we would be out of business. The same scenario holds true for the displacement of wildlife and for the littering of areas with garbage. When we go to visit the Alps we expect to see beautiful scenery and magnificent mountains, not trash and graffiti.

Slowly many people started to wake up and realize that acid rain does not respect borders and that the decimation of rain forests and wetlands affects more than the immediate area. We learned that the floors of Canterbury Cathedral could be worn down by the passing of too many feet and that our breathing could damage fragile paintings, frescoes, and walls. We learned that people are not likely to support and protect areas that they are not allowed to visit, and that they need to appreciate and have an understanding of the importance of different sites. How can we promote responsible travel and tourism knowing all these things?

What has emerged is a concept that is known by different names. Some of these titles include ecotourism, green travel, green tourism, environmental tourism, and sustainable development.

Sustainable Development

In October of 1991, the Travel and Tourism Research Association of Canada held a conference in Quebec. The topic of the conference was tourism, the environment, and sustainable development. The Keynote Address was given by Dr. R. W. Slater, the Assistant Deputy Minister, Corporate Policy Group, Environment, Canada.

In his address, Dr. Slater stated that "sustainable development is premised on the notion that the economy and the environment are but two sides of the same coin; in other words, the two are intimately linked" (Slater 1992: 10). This marked a change in belief systems. While many had viewed economic development and environmental concerns as mutually exclusive, sustainable development saw them as mutually supportive. This change in thinking was reflected in the Green Plan.

On December 11, 1990, Canada made public the Green Plan. This plan outlined Canada's commitment to promoting sustainable development. Realizing that economic development and the environment are interlinked, the Green Plan outlined the measures that Canada would take for the next six years to promote sustainable development. Not all of these 100 initiatives dealt specifically with tourism, but many of them will effect and shape the future of the industry.

The significance of the Green Plan was that it was a national vision acknowledging the interdependence of economic development and environmental protection. Coupled with the vision was a comprehensive plan funded by the federal government. Over the next six years, 3 billion Canadian dollars will be added to the existing funds designated for federal environmental expenditures.

Industry Response

Industry response to the ideas championed by the Green Plan and in support of the concept of sustainable development has been encouraging. Canadian Airlines developed a program to reduce waste and to recycle and reduce disposable waste. Even before the announcement of the Green Plan, individual interest groups were looking for ways to institute environmental programs.

> In the fall of 1990 Canadian Pacific Hotels and Resorts (CPH&R) undertook the development of an environmental program for all of its hotels in Canada. The objective was to institute the highest possible standards of environmental responsibility throughout the chain. The program also aims to identify areas where environmental improvements can result in lower operating costs (Checkley 1992: 34).

CPH&R was also initiating an environmental program at their U.S. hotel chain—Doubletree Hotels.

Along with efforts to recycle and reduce, some of the members of the tourism industry realized that responsible actions regarding conduct also needed to be explored.

Brian Falconer, the president of Maple Leaf Adventures, Inc. is a wilderness tour operator. Sailing aboard his 92-foot schooner, the *Maple Leaf*, Falconer offers tours that focus on interpreting the natural history and native culture of the North Pacific coast, the wilderness areas of southeast Alaska, and the Queen Charlotte Islands, known as Gwaii Haanas, or place of wonder. Gwaii Haanas has recently become one of Canada's newest national parks. Prior to becoming a national park, a small group of tour operators had offered almost all of the opportunities to see this area, which was accessible only by boat or seaplane. The designation of national park increased the numbers of people who wanted to see this area as well as the number of tour operators.

Before designating this area as a national park, the indigenous people (the Haida), and the Canadian Park Service had to agree on how Gwaii Haanas would be managed. Meetings were held so that all interested parties would be able to contribute to the final outcome. What emerged was a code of conduct for commercial tour operators. Falconer stated:

> It was agreed that we would concern ourselves only with issues which we could address by our own actions and that, although we hoped others would follow our example, the guidelines were not intended to tell others what they should or should not do. Hence each clause was prefaced with "We will" and not "Thou shalt" (Falconer 1992: 22).

Known as the Code of Conduct For Commercial Tour Operations, this document covered such areas as etiquette, wildlife, food gathering, and archaeological, cultural, and historic sites. This was industry gently trying to regulate itself through cooperation (see Appendix B).

The First "Green" Olympic Games

The 1994 Winter Olympic Games in Lillehammer, Norway was the first green Olympics ever planned. The environmental theme of the Lillehammer Olympics was awareness. Pictograms on trash cans encouraged visitors to separate glass and paper into appropriate cans, and plates used to serve food were made of a potato-based starch that could either be fed to animals or composted.

Whenever possible, sites served multiple purposes. The ice hockey arena, Hakon Hall, also doubled as a concert hall and had a climbing wall installed. Energy was recycled whenever possible, and builders were threatened with heavy fines for cutting trees unnecessarily. Even the bullets used at the biathlon stadium were retrieved to keep them from going into the river beyond the stadium. Eventually, they were remelted and used again.

An environmental monitoring system was developed and installed to gather information on air and water pollution, wind direction, temperature, and waste control. This information was used to help make decisions regarding pollution control. Finally, Hakon and Kristin, the two Olympic mascots, were used to promote the green theme by appealing to Norwegian children and taking part in environmental events.

Tourism as a Force for Peace

It is much easier to generalize about people than it is to know them as individuals. Stereotypes are easily perpetuated, and generalization leads to the belief that most members of a group are the same. While our mouths say what is politically correct, a small voice in our head whispers something else. You know what these stereotypes are. . . .

For a long time the image of someone from the United States of America was that of "the ugly American." The ugly American was a loud, boorish individual who had no tolerance of the culture and customs of others. The ugly American could not understand why English was not spoken wherever he went, why other cultures have differing tastes in foods, and why a country that struggled with starvation would refuse to slaughter and eat cows.

Consider the following true story which occurred in a Chinese cemetery. While watching a Chinese person reverently placing fresh fruit on a grave, an American visitor asked, "When do you expect your ancestors to get up and eat the fruit?" The Chinese person replied, "As soon as your ancestors get up and smell the flowers" (Axtell 1990: 6).

The satirist H. L. Mencken further defined the mind set of the ugly American. He did this by commenting on the ethnocentric attitude of Americans toward language and attributing the following statement to them: "If English was good enough for Jesus Christ, it's good enough for me" (Axtell 1989: 163). How is it that Americans traveling abroad earned the reputation of being such obnoxious travelers?

Contact theory holds that exposure to individuals who are different from ourselves will help us gain a deeper appreciation for their customs and culture, but let's face it, before the advent of economical jet planes, most Americans were exposed to only other Americans.

By European standards, the United States of America and Canada are huge countries which would encompass several European nations. Geographically separated from much of the world, the isolation of the United States was vividly brought to my attention by some Dutch friends of mine. When they first came to America, Marion and Leonie were amazed at the size of the country—the fact that you could travel for weeks speaking one language, and that there was one form of money. Malls, highways, supermarkets, and wooden houses positively amazed them. They spoke several languages and regularly visited other countries for vacation. Neither one knew how to drive a car and traveled by public transportation or bicycle at home.

I hadn't really thought about any of this before. A trip to Holland dramatized for me exactly what they were talking about. I was humbled by my lack of ability to communicate in Dutch (which to me resembled Klingon). I was totally dependent on the good will of people to help me get around and to understand Dutch money (which looked a lot like Monopoly money). Everyday tasks became mysteries to be solved. Why did the bathroom contain only a sink and a shower? Where was the toilet? How do I order coffee that isn't so strong that I won't sleep for the next two weeks, or for that matter, how do I order coffee? I hated to admit it, but for all my education and training I was decidedly at a disadvantage. This was not a good feeling. I could see how the title of ugly American might be correct. Fortunately for me, I was among warm and loving friends who empathized with my situation. It was the same one that they had encountered when they came to America.

While the image of the ugly American is changing, there is good news and bad news. The good news is that many Americans have become more sophisticated and sensitive travelers and that cultural tourism is on the rise. Cultural tourism occurs when people travel from where they live to other places. The purpose of their trip is to experience different cultures by having direct contact with those in that culture. They may do this by meeting those who live there or by sampling other dimensions of the culture such as art, food, architecture, music, or whatever. The fact that the demographics of the United States has changed to make us more culturally diverse has increased our awareness of the customs and culture of others right here. This coupled with the technological advances made in video and audio transmissions has served to help reverse our narrow view of the world.

The bad news is that although Americans have become better travelers and their image has changed, in at least one respect, it has not changed for the better. The ugly American image is fading, but a new image is emerging—that of Americans as a brutal and aggressive people. Our recent history has led many of us, and much of the rest of the world, to this conclusion. The shooting of a Japanese student who did not understand English sufficiently to comply with the instructions of a homeowner who thought that he was being threatened, and the indiscriminate killing of German and American tourists in New York, Florida, and other American cities has alarmed the tourist as well as the citizen. In 1993, a Vacation Travel Intentions Survey conducted by the Canadian Tourism Research Institute showed that fewer Canadians were choosing to travel to Florida. The reason for this was twofold: the result of the low exchange rate for the Canadian dollar and the media reports of attacks against tourists (*Exclusive* 1993: 8).

The difference between perception and reality can be light-years apart. In spite of the perceptions that are held about individual groups and nations, most people share the same basic tenets: a love of family and friends, the longing for a better life for their children, and a desire for peace. It is easy to hate what you don't understand. Tourism encompasses more than "doing" twenty countries in thirty days while seeing everything and experiencing nothing. Tourism can and should be a force for peace. It can change our lives and make us broader-minded and better people.

Summary

Travel and tourism has a discernable impact on many parts of the world and is a major economic force. The effect of this industry is felt on the national, regional, and local levels, and in some cases it is the major revenue producer for an area.

The World Tourism Organization (WTO) acts as a consultant to the United Nations in matters that pertain to travel and tourism and is recognized as the voice of world tourism. In an effort to fully understand the impact of the industry, the WTO and the Canadian government organized a conference in Ottawa in 1992. The result of the Ottawa Conference was the adoption of a set of recommendations on tourism statistics by the United Nations Statistical Commission. This signaled a major achievement—a suggested standardized manner in which international tourism statistics can be kept and reported.

Careers in travel and tourism, including the types of travel agents, agencies, and tour options that exist, are examined. In addition, the reasons why people travel are explored. These reasons are varied, and the effect that the travelers have on host communities is not always positive. Doxey and Plog both described models demonstrating the symbiotic relationship of visitor and host community. Both models indicate the final disenchantment of the host community with the visitor and the dissolving of the relationship. The suggestion is made that the negative cycle of tourism need not occur and that perhaps the role of tourism is the role of being a force for peace.

Finally, in order for the industry to continue to endure, travel professionals have become involved with the promotion and delivery of services and programs that support environmental concerns. Under the titles of ecotourism, green travel, and sustainable development, industry professionals are marketing trips and hotels that are ecologically friendly.

Discussion Questions

1. What conditions must exist on the national, regional, and local level in order for a program of sustainable development to succeed?
2. Do you believe that contact theory can work and that exposure to individuals who are different from us can increase our understanding of one another?
3. Do you feel that the inevitable outcome of tourism development will result in the endings predicted by Doxey and Plog?
4. At what cost does a region benefit from the economic rewards of tourism?

Chapter Exercises

1. Can you list at least three alternative travel arrangements other than home exchange?

2. See if there is an organization for international students on your campus. If there is, go and meet one of these visitors. If there is no formal organization, see if you can meet a visiting student anyway.
3. Locate a tourist attraction near your campus and visit this site. Who are the people who are visiting the attraction? Have you been to this site before? Why or why not?

References

1992 annual report tourism Victoria. 1993. Victoria, BC: Greater Victoria Visitors and Convention Bureau.

A vision for tourism. 1993. Province of British Columbia, Canada: Ministry of Tourism.

Annual report and travel trends 1992. 1992. Washington, D.C.: Convention and Visitors Association.

Axtell, Roger E., ed. 1990. *Do's and taboos around the world.* New York: John Wiley and Sons, Inc.

———. 1989. *Do's and taboos of hosting international visitors.* New York: John Wiley and Sons, Inc.

Barbour, Bill, and Mary Barbour. 1991. *Trading places—The wonderful world of vacation home exchange.* Nashville, TN: Rutledge Hill Press.

Checkley, Ann. 1992. Canadian Pacific hotels and resorts update. In *Tourism—Environment—Sustainable development,* edited by Laurel J. Reid. Canada: Travel and Tourism Research Association.

Conference Board of Canada. 1993. *Canadian Tourism Research Institute Exclusive.*

Doxey, George V. 1979. When enough's enough: The natives are restless in Old Niagara! *Recreation Land Use in Southern Ontario* (G. Wall, ed.). Waterloo, Ontario: Department of Geography, University of Waterloo.

Falconer, Brian. 1992. Tourism and sustainability. In *Tourism—Environment—Sustainable development,* edited by Laurel J. Reid. Canada: Travel and Tourism Research Association.

Okrant, Mark. 1992. A skeptic's view of sustainability and tourism. In *Tourism—Environment—Sustainable development,* edited by Laurel J. Reid. Canada: Travel and Tourism Research Association.

Plog, Stanley. 1991. *Leisure Travel.* New York: John Wiley and Sons.

Reid, Laurel J., ed. 1992. *Tourism—Environment—Sustainable development: Conference proceedings.* Canada, Travel and Tourism Research Association.

———. 1993. *Community and cultural tourism.* Canada: Travel and Tourism Research Association.

Slater, R. W. 1992. Understanding the relationship between tourism environment and sustainable development. *Tourism—Environment—Sustainable development,* edited by Laurel J. Reid. Canada: Travel and Tourism Research Association.

Tourism Gross Domestic Product. 1993. Province of British Columbia, Canada: Ministry of Tourism and Ministry Responsible for Culture.

Tourism highlights 1992. 1992. British Columbia, Canada: Ministry of Small Business, Tourism and Culture.

U.S. Travel Data Center. 1992. *Tourism's top twenty.* Washington, D.C.: Business Research Division, University of Colorado and the U.S. Travel Data Center.

U.S. Travel Data Center. 1992. *Discover America: Tourism and the environment.* Washington, D.C.: Travel Industry Association of America.

Winter 1992 exit survey. 1993. Victoria, BC: Tourism Victoria.

World Tourism Organization. 1992. *Recommendations on tourism statistics.* Madrid, Spain: World Tourism Organization (short and long versions).

World travel and tourism review. 1993. Wallingford, UK: CAB International.

Additional Resources

Airliners: The world's airline magazine. Miami, FL: World Transport Press, Inc.

ASTA agency managment: Official publication of the American Society of Travel Agents. Greensboro, NC: American Society of Travel Agents.

Bernstein, Peter W. 1993. *1993 great vacation drives plus fabulous festivals, theme parks, and new museums.* Washington, D.C.: U.S. News and World Report.

Birnbaum, Alexandra Mayes, ed. *Stephen Birnbaum travel guides.* New York: Harper Perennial.

Blank, Uel. 1989. *The community tourism industry imperative: The necessity, the opportunity, its potentials.* State College, PA: Venture Publishing, Inc.

Braganti, Nancy L., and Elizabeth Devine. 1984. *The travelers' companion to European customs and manners.* New York: Meadowbrook.

Brannen, Christalyn, and BLC Intercultural. 1991. *Going to Japan on business: A quick guide to protocol, travel, and language.* Berkeley, CA: Stone Bridge Press.

Bryant, Page. 1991. *Terravision: A traveler's guide to the living planet Earth.* New York: Ballantine Books.

Business travel news: The newspaper of the busines travel industry. Manhasset, NY: CMP Publications, Inc.

Coltman, Michael M. 1989. *Introduction to travel and tourism: An international approach.* New York: Van Nostrand Reinhold.

Corporate travel. New York: Miller Freeman, Inc./United Newspapers Group.

Cummings, Jack. 1991. *The business travel survival guide.* New York: John Wiley and Sons.

Davidoff, Philip G., and Doris S. Davidoff. 1990. *Worldwide tours: A travel agent's guide to selling tours.* Englewood Cliffs, NJ: Prentice Hall, Inc.

Devine, Elizabeth, and Nancy L. Braganti. 1988. *The travelers' guide to Latin American customs and manners.* New York: St. Martin's Press.

Fillinger, Louis. 1992. *The group travel handbook: How to organize and conduct group travel programs for any group.* Saratoga, CA: R and E Publishers.

Finch, Christopher. 1992. *Highways to heaven: The auto biography of America.* New York: Harper Collins Publishers.

Fridgen, Joseph D. 1991. *Dimensions of tourism.* East Lansing, MI: The Educational Institute of the American Hotel and Motel Association.

Friedheim, Eric. 1992. *Travel agents: From caravans and clippers to the Concorde.* New York: Travel Agent Magazine Books.

Funnell, Charles E. 1983. *By the beautiful sea: The rise and high times of that great American resort, Atlantic City.* New Brunswick, NJ: Rutgers University Press.

Gilford, Judith. 1994. *The packing book: Secrets of the carry-on traveler.* Berkeley, CA: Ten Speed Press.

Graber, Eden, and Paula M. Siegel. 1990. *Fielding's traveler's medical companion.* New York: Fielding Travel Books.

Griffin, Al. 1974. *"Step Right Up, Folks!"* Chicago: Henry Regnery Company.

Grotta, Daniel, and Sally Weiner Grotta. 1992. *The Green travel sourcebook: A guide for the physically active, the intellectually curious, or the socially aware.* New York: John Wiley and Sons, Inc.

Groves, Clinton H. 1993. *Jetliners: The world's great jetliners, 1950s to today.* Enthusiast Color Series. 1993. Osceola, WI: Motorbooks International Publishers and Wholesalers.

Gunston, Bill, ed. 1989. *The air traveler's handbook: The complete guide to air travel, airplanes, and airports.* New York: St. Martin's Press.

Hardesty, Von, and Dominick Pisano. 1984. *Black wings: The American Black in aviation.* Washington, D.C.: Smithsonian Institution Press.

Hill, Deborah J. 1990. *A guide for the practical traveler: Travel tips international.* Worthington, OH: Renaissance Publications.

Hoffman, Ellen. 1988. *How to plan a succesful trip.* Washington, D.C.: Farragut Publishing Company.

Howell, David W. 1989. *Passport: An introduction to the travel and tourism industry.* Cincinnati, OH: South-Western Publishing, Inc.

Jacobs, Timothy. 1988. *The history of the Pennsylvania Railroad.* Greenwich, CT: Bonanza Books.

Jansz, Natania, and Miranda Davies, ed. 1990. *Women travel: The real guides.* New York: Prentice Hall Trade Division.

Jenkins, Darryl. 1993. *Savvy business travel: Management tips from the pros.* Homewood, IL: Business One Irwin.

Journal of travel and tourism marketing. Binghampton, NY: The Haworth Press.

Kataoka, Hiroko C., and Tetsuya Kusumoto. 1991. *Japanese cultural encounters and how to handle them.* Lincolnwood, IL: Passport Books.

Khan, Mahmood, Michael Olsen, and Turgut Var, eds. 1993. *VNR's encyclopedia of hospitality and tourism.* New York: Van Nostrand Reinhold.

Ledray, Linda E. 1988. *The single woman's vacation guide.* New York: Fawcett Columbine.

Lisella, Julia, and Gloria McDarrah, eds. 1991. *The Wall Street Journal guides to business and travel: USA and Canada.* New York: Fodor's Travel Publications, Inc.

Lundberg, Donald E. 1990. *The tourist business.* 6th ed. New York: Van Nostrand Reinhold.

McIntosh, Robert W., and Charles R. Goeldner. 1990. *Tourism: principles, practices, philosophies.* 6th ed. New York: John Wiley and Sons, Inc.

Metelka, Charles J. 1990. *The dictionary of hospitality, travel, and tourism.* 3rd ed. The Travel Management Library Series. Albany, NY: Delmar Publishers, Inc.

Morris, Mary, ed. 1993. *Maiden voyages: Writings of women travelers.* New York: Vintage Departures.

Morris, Mary. 1988. *Nothing to declare: Memoirs of a woman traveling alone.* Penguin Travel Library. New York: Penguin Books.

Multinational Executive, Inc. 1990. *Multinational executive travel companion: Travel tips worldwide.* 21st ed. Stamford: Suburban Publishing of Connecticut, Inc.

National Geographic: Official journal of the National Geographic Society. Washingon, D.C.: Natonal Geographic Society.

Newby, Eric, ed. 1985. *A book of travellers' tales.* New York: Penguin Books.

Oakes, Claudia M. 1978. *United States women in aviation through World War I.* Smithsonian Studies in Air and Space, No. 2. Washington, D.C.: Smithsonian Institution Press.

O'Brien, Tim. 1991. *The amusement park guide: Fun for the whole family at more than 250 amusement parks from coast to coast.* Chester, CT: The Globe Pequot Press.

Orlebar, Christopher. 1986. *British Airways: The Concorde story.* London: Temple Press.

Platt, Richard. 1992. *Stephen Biesty's incredible cross sections.* New York: Alfred A. Knopf.

Pybus, Victoria, ed. *Adventure holidays.* (Series) Princeton, NJ: Peterson's Guides.

Ross, Victoria Jennings. 1988. *Official guide to the National Air and Space Museum.* Washington, D.C.: Smithsonian Institution Press.

Shelley, Rex. 1993. *Culture shock! Japan: A guide to culture and etiquette.* Portland, OR: Graphic Arts Center Publishing Company.

Simmons, James C. 1990. *The big books of adventure travel: 500 great escapes.* New American Library. New York: Plume.

Starr, Nona, and Karen Silva. 1990. *Travel career development.* 4th ed. Boston: Houghton Mifflin Company; Wellesley, MA: Institute of Certified Travel Agents.

Sternstein, Ed, and Todd Gold. 1991. *From takeoff to landing: Everything you wanted to know about airplanes but had no one to ask.* New York: Pocket Books.

Sutton, Horace. 1980. *Travelers: The American tourist from stagecoach to space shuttle.* New York: William Morrow and Company, Inc.

Swinglehurst, Edmund. 1982. *Cook's tours: The story of popular travel.* Poole, Dorset, England: Blandford Press.

Taylor, Sally Adamson. 1990. *Culture shock! France.* Portland, OR: Graphic Arts Center Publishing Company.

Tour and travel news: The newspaper for the retail travel industry. Manhasset, NY: CMP Publications, Inc.

Travel Holiday. New York: Travel Holiday.

Travel USA. A supplement of *Tour and travel: The newspaper for the retail travel industry.* Manhasset, NY: CMP Publications, Inc.

Vann, Frank. 1988. *How they work: Civil airliner—Boeing 747 jumbo jet.* New York: Exeter Books.

Weissman, Arnie, ed. 1991. *Travel geography and destinations.* 3rd ed. Austin, TX: Weissman Travel Reports.

Wilkins, Mike, Ken Smith, and Doug Kirby. 1992. *The new roadside America: The modern traveler's guide to the wild and wonderful world of America's tourist attractions.* New York: Fireside.

Yeager, Jeana, and Dick Rutan. 1987. *Voyager.* Boston: G. K. Hall and Company.

Lodging, Food, and Beverage

LEARNING OBJECTIVES

1. *To introduce the different classification systems and rating systems for hotels and resorts.*
2. *To discuss the distribution channels available for owning and managing businesses in the lodging, food, and beverage industry.*
3. *To explore the duties, responsibilities, and interaction between those working in the front of the house and employees in the back of the house.*
4. *To introduce some of the professional organizations in the lodging, food, and beverage industry.*

Lodging

There is a vast system of hotels, motels, resorts, and motor inns in North America and around the world. These businesses provide for the needs and wants of individuals and groups who are away from home, regardless of their reason for traveling. The diversity of the industry is overwhelming. Properties range from tiny bed and breakfast (B&B) operations that offer a clean, comfortable place to stay, to huge destination resorts that are self-contained cities with hundreds of rooms. Collectively these operations cater to every imaginable type of customer and offer every type of experience from the rustic to the radically creative.

Introduction

Hotels, motels, resorts, and motor inns can be categorized by a number of factors. Amenities, room rates, and types of services available are all variables used to help determine whether the hotel is designated as an economy, midprice, or luxury property. Other classification terms used to describe properties are budget, full-service, upscale, limited-service, first class, or all-suite.

Travelers choose where to stay based on their needs and their budgets. Price and types of services are usually two pieces of information that most of us want to know before making a reservation. Location is also important. Is the property easy to get to? Is it in an area that is perceived to be safe? Is it close to the attractions and places that we want to visit? For individuals traveling with children, the range of services offered may be extremely important, and they may be willing to pay a higher rate in exchange for a pool, game room, washer/dryer, or suite-style accommodation.

Business travelers might look for a property that has a business center, which is complete with photocopier, fax machine, secretarial service, health club, message center, and other amenities to help them complete their business transactions.

Amenities may be important to some and not to others. Their purpose is to enhance the image of the property and to make life as pleasant as possible so that customers will want to return. The surprise of a mint on a turned-down bed, or a morning paper left outside of a guest's room can do much to make a stay pleasant and memorable.

There is wide variety not only in the types and sizes of properties, but in the varieties of services offered. The availability of amenities is directly related to the type of property and to the price that is charged for the experience. This is a highly competitive business, and guests expect to receive value for their money. In some hotels, amenities and services range from having your hair cut to having your own private butler assigned to your suite.

There is a song that states, "Be it ever so humble, there's no place like home." Personally, I am willing to give up some of this "humility" for the hotel pool, hot tub, night club, and maid service. I want people to make my bed, pick up my wet towels, make my meals, tidy up my room, and leave a little piece of chocolate on my pillow when they turn down my bed. After all, one of the greatest aspects of a hotel, resort, or other alternative sleeping space is that it is a sanctuary from everyday life. I know that I am willing to sacrifice, at least for a couple of weeks, to live like the rich and famous, sleep among trees and lions, or live beneath the sea. (I don't know about your community, but none of these experiences is available to me in my present habitat. The lions pose a particular problem and are not allowed within city limits.)

This is a rewarding yet demanding industry that is open at all hours, year-round, and relies on repeat business in order to compete and survive. Customers expect a certain level of treatment and will take their money elsewhere if they are not treated appropriately.

Distribution Channels

A single property may be owned by an individual or a group of investors. A B&B is a good example of the type of entry-level operation that someone

Key Largo Undersea Park is the home of Jules' Undersea Lodge. Because guests must scuba dive in order to reach the undersea hotel they must either be certified divers or take an introductory scuba course with one of the park instructors. Guests must be at least 12 years of age and in good medical health.
Courtesy Jules' Undersea Lodge.

JULES' UNDERSEA LODGE

JULES' UNDERSEA LODGE, the world's first and only underwater hotel, invites you to experience an incredible adventure you will never forget . . . a voyage to our Lodge, five fathoms beneath the luminescent water of a tropical lagoon in Key Largo, adjacent to John Pennekamp Park.

Dine as exotic fish drift by your window. Explore the sunken wrecks just a short dive away from your undersea home. The "HOOKAH" tethered breathing lines eliminate bulky scuba tanks and cumbersome equipment. As a result, diving is effortless, with a limitless air supply. To live beneath the sea was once just the dream of science-fiction writers . . . Now it is reality.

The Lodge is designed to accommodate up to six divers in luxury — the air conditioned suites look out to the sea through spectacular 42-inch windows, and include a stereo, VCR, television, refrigerator and global communications. There are separate galley and dining areas, and separate bathroom and shower.

with an entrepreneurial spirit might open. Capital investment is relatively low, the potential for profit from sweat equity is good, and the reward of working for yourself appeals to many. But, like the amusement parks of today, many lodging operations are being consolidated and bought by large companies and corporations.

The sole focus of the corporation may be the building and management of hotels, or the hotel aspect of the corporation may be a strategic business unit (SBU), which is one of many business interests that the company owns. Either way, if a company decides to increase its number of property holdings, then it must determine how this expansion will occur. Options are that the company will own all or part of each property and manage it, not own the property but manage it, or they will franchise their product.

Organizational Structure

Organizational structures for lodging and for food and beverage differ greatly. The simplest structure is comprised of a single owner who is also the manager of the site. The owner may be the sole employee or may supervise one or more additional employees. An example of this type of structure is a lodging site where there are limited sleeping rooms, such as a B&B.

As the business becomes larger, responsibilities may be divided by function (marketing, finance, operations, etc.) in order to make the division of work more manageable. As growth occurs and more properties are acquired, a divisional system of organization may be instituted. In this type of arrangement, different subgroups with the same structure are set up to respond to the markets in their geographic area. Finally, the company may become part of a larger, diversified unit that has many interests. The company then becomes an SBU in an organization that has many interests.

Owning and Managing

One question is whether to keep the business in the family or to make other arrangements to ensure that name recognition into other areas and markets occurs through expansion. If the corporation chooses to own and manage the property, they are not only choosing the hardest but also the slowest way for the company to expand. This type of expansion involves commitment of monies and other resources. Assigning capital and company resources to expansion means that these resources are not available for other projects or opportunities that might arise.

The advantage of choosing this option is that the integrity of the brand name is protected, because the corporation controls all properties directly. In addition, consistency concerning quality of product delivered is more easily controlled and monitored than other options. In a company-owned-and-managed chain, customers know that they will find the same amenities, services, policies, and procedures. They may even find the same wallpaper and furniture in their sleeping rooms. To frequent travelers familiar surroundings and routines allow for an easier transition as they travel from property to property.

Managing

The second-best choice for maintaining product integrity and consistency is to have the property owned by investors but managed, for a fee, by the company. This option frees up corporate monies, because the investors are the ones who are financing the venture. The company is responsible for management operations.

The potential downside of this arrangement is that the property may not be profitable. In addition, tax breaks for investors are not as lucrative as they used to be. The investors may not want to pump more money into a marginally producing or profit-losing venture. They may choose not to do needed renovations, or they may be financially unable to keep the property up to company standards. The company then must decide whether it will be responsible for the needed renovations or if it will relinquish this facility and forfeit the marketplace.

Franchising

A third and common method of increasing the distribution network for all types of companies is to offer franchises. When you purchase a franchise, you purchase the use of the company name for the purpose of selling their product or service. Franchise agreements vary from company to company. The amount of control exerted by the parent company is different from franchiser to franchiser. Also, in some agreements you can buy the rights to be the sole franchisee to do business in a certain area or even in an entire country.

There have been examples of franchising throughout history. In the Middle Ages, the Catholic Church and local governments granted tax franchises to tax collectors. These individuals made the rounds and collected taxes, keeping a percentage of the amount collected for themselves and sending the rest to the Church. In the United States, examples of early companies involved in franchising included the McCormick Harvesting Machine Company, which started to franchise its products circa 1850, the Singer Sewing Machine Company circa 1860, General Motors (1890), Coca-Cola (1899), Rexall Drugs (1902), and Western Auto (1909) (Khan et al. 1993: 251).

In 1919, Roy Allen and Frank Wright opened a root beer stand. That one stand grew and became 2,500 A & W stands, most of which were franchised. San Bernardino, California was the initial site of one of the most famous and prolific franchises to date. In the 1940s Maurice and Richard McDonald opened a restaurant. The McDonalds developed and instituted a system of producing hamburgers and french fries quickly enough to keep up with customer demand. Ray Kroc, a salesman, was impressed by the efficiency of the McDonald's operation and convinced them to franchise their business. Kroc then sold the franchises and split the profits with the McDonalds. He also worked on refining the system established by Maurice and Richard and emphasized fast service, cleanliness, and a uniform product. Today, McDonald's Hamburger University ensures that a universal product is produced. The McDonald's hamburger served in Boise is the same as the McDonald's hamburger served in Schenectady or Paris. McDonald's was a primary catalyst in adding the word fast-food into the vocabularies of millions of people. In fact, the National Restaurant Association (NRA) forecasted that in 1994 fast-food would surpass full-service establishments based on volume sold.

Today's fast-food franchise hamburger leaders include McDonald's, Burger King, and Wendy's. Hotel leaders have been Holiday Corporation,

Days Inn, and Quality International. Restaurants and fast-food franchises are usually controlled more by the parent company (franchiser) than hotels are.

Franchising is not exclusive to the lodging and food and beverage industries but is found in all types of businesses (e.g., car rental agencies, travel agencies, muffler repair shops, convenience stores, and family entertainment centers). There is an International Franchise Association, which represents the various franchise opportunities available, and trade shows for people to explore franchise opportunities.

One advantage to franchisers is that they buy a position in the marketplace by having the right to use a name recognizable to the public. Most travelers would rather stop at a Holiday Inn than at Elsie's Hotel. Franchisees also benefit by receiving support from the parent company. They may obtain technical knowledge in the form of the generic components of the business so that they do not have to spend time reinventing the wheel. Managerial assistance and training may be available, marketing will be aimed at a broader audience on a much larger scale, and hotels may benefit from an established reservation system that includes an 800 number. Other benefits might include development services, advertising, quality assurance, training, and education.

Classification of Distribution Channels

Sophisticated distribution channels have been set up to help chains and franchises achieve better name recognition and market share. Distribution channels for hotels, motels, and resorts include strategic placement in primary, secondary, and tertiary markets. The ranking of a city or town in one of these categories is determined by the size of its market and its buying power. This principle applies nationally and internationally. Primary markets in North America include cities like Boston, Los Angeles, Toronto, Calgary, and Quebec. Secondary markets are Hartford, Salt Lake City, Portland, and San Antonio. Tertiary markets are smaller, less powerful markets. In the United States these markets include places like Des Moines, Iowa; Boise, Idaho; and Spokane, Washington.

International Channels by Level

Primary	Secondary	Tertiary
Paris	Brussels	Cologne
London	Amsterdam	Marseilles
Tokyo	Stockholm	Dusseldorf

Upscale hotel chains strive to be in primary markets first and then move into the other levels (restaurants may do it the other way around). The goal of this strategy is to distribute the product to the customer, first by being where there are customers, and second by positioning yourself in other locations where the customer is most likely to be.

A case in point is the Marriott Marquis Hotel in New York City. As an entity in itself, the hotel will probably never be a major profit producer because of the cost of land and construction. Why, then, would Marriott have engaged in the project? Because of the importance of New York City in the company's channel of distribution for major conventions (Lewis and Chambers 1989: 470).

In order to be a major player in the convention circuit in the United States, a company needs to have a hotel in New York City. The contribution made by the Marriott Marquis Hotel in New York City was not its profit or loss, but its contribution to the Marriott convention network.

There are resort destinations from the Rocky Mountains and Honolulu to Cote d'Azur in France and Costa del Sol in Spain. Having a property in one of these locations may be as important to a hotel company as it is for a fast-food chain to have a location on Route I-95.

Rating Systems

Today there are two formal systems that indicate to travelers the level of service and degree of comfort and amenities that they may expect to encounter. The first and newer system has been made possible by the consolidation of properties into large chains. Staying at a recognized chain such as Days Inn of America, Holiday Inn, or Omni is a predictable experience. Travelers know what to expect, and the chain knows that it needs the repeat business of customers in order to compete; this is the perfect symbiotic relationship.

Before franchises and large chains, a rating system was used to measure quality. This type of system still exists and it is still important. In North America, the American Automobile Association (AAA) and Mobil Oil, publisher of the Mobile Travel Guides, still rate the quality of hotels, motels, and other properties. Both use a rating of 1 to 5, with 1 signifying a good basic facility and 5 an exceptional facility. Properties must meet minimum standards to be listed in these quides, and guides are revised annually.

Guides are used to rate properties in approximately half of the countries in Europe. Fewer chains and more independent properties mean that name recognition cannot be relied on to the extent that it is in North America. Guides for North Americans traveling abroad will often list information about the hotel, eating establishments, surrounding attractions, weather, medical considerations, and local customs. Where to shop, how to use local transportation, and other kinds of "insider" information are frequently included. The proliferation of guide books in the last ten years has been amazing. There are books written for every target population imaginable: singles, the ecology-minded, women, adventure seekers, the disabled, families, and the budget-minded. A visit to any local bookstore will quickly convince you that if there is a specialized population seeking to travel, someone has written a travel book directed at this market.

The Front and Back of the House

Both hotels and restaurants are divided into areas referred to as the front and the back of the house. The back of the house includes those operations that guests rarely see, such as laundry, food preparation, housekeeping, and areas that control, maintain, and repair the systems that run the hotel (electrical, plumbing, HVAC, water, and energy). The back of the house usually coordinates its activities through the back office. The front and back of the house work in concert with one another. Check-out of a guest in the front of the house results in a message to housekeeping, in the back of the house, that an occupied room is now vacant and must be cleaned.

The front of the house is comprised of common areas and those areas where guests come into direct contact with hotel employees. The heart of the front of the house is the front office. The job of the front office is to carry out the activities that occur in this part of the hotel. While most of us do not see the inside of the front office, we do see the front desk. Located in a highly visible, well-trafficked area, the front desk is usually our first and last contact with the hotel. It is here that we register and check out. These two simple functions say volumes about the efficiency and courtesy of the property. Our experience with the hotel employees at the front desk can set in granite our opinion of the hotel.

Other responsibilities of the front of the house include selling rooms (which includes taking reservations and assigning rooms for preregistered and walk-in customers), providing information regarding hotel services and external events, settling customer accounts by preparing the final statement, handling complaints, and coordinating activities that occur in the front of the house with the activities that occur in the back of the house.

Career Realities

Career disadvantages in the industry are long work hours—ten to twelve hour days, changing schedules, six day weeks, and the need to work holidays and weekends (remember that hotels are always open). Larger chains probably require that you be willing to relocate in order to gain experience and to advance within the organization. It may be difficult to find and keep friends because of the hours and the relocation requirements, and the lifestyle is hard on families as well as on singles. In all fairness, it should be mentioned that these problems are not the sole province of this industry. Many of the careers in the service industry occur outside the normal nine-to-five workday and most entry-level employees who are salaried quickly find out that you cannot get ahead in a forty-hour week. The good news is that this industry has exciting career opportunities with the possibility for rapid advancement. It is never boring, and young employees are often given responsibility and decision-making opportunities.

Professional Associations

There are several professional associations to choose from in this part of the industry. The Hotel Sales and Marketing Association International (HSMAI) is the leading organization for hotel sales personnel. HSMAI has over 6,500 members from all over the world and is one of oldest and largest organizations in the hospitality industry. HSMAI offers professional certification as a Certified Hotel Sales Executive (CHSE).

The American Hotel and Motel Association (AH&MA) represents managers of hotels and motels both in the United States and all over the world, as well as over 675 allied companies of the industry. The AH&MA was founded in 1910 with the prime objectives of holding conferences and seminars, providing educational programs, and keeping members updated regarding legislation that affected the industry. The association has an educational institute that offers instructional materials, and it holds courses that lead to the designation of Certified Hotel Administration (CHA). The AH&MA is the primary sponsor of the International Hotel/Motel and Restaurant Show (IH/M&RS), which is held annually in New York City. The 78th Annual IH/M&RS held at the Jacob K. Javits Convention Center had an attendance of approximately 62,000 individuals.

Food and Beverage

The range of choices for ways to eat and drink is as diverse as the options for sleeping when traveling. The food and beverage industry consists of institutional services (schools, hospitals/health care facilities, employee cafeterias/dining rooms, prisons, and the military) as well as commercial and private facilities. Options that are not open to the public-at-large are comprised mainly of private clubs, which have snack bars, dining rooms, or other types of food service available for members and their guests. The industry also includes vending machines, food courts, and food carts.

Introduction

Like hotels, restaurants have become part of the franchise and chain phenomena. During the '60s and through the early '80s, the trend was for larger firms to acquire restaurant chains. The reasons for this happening are the same ones that fueled the hotel consolidation and franchise movement. General Foods bought Burger Chef, Pillsbury purchased Burger King, and Ralston Purina acquired Jack-in-the-Box. All of this "acquiring" resulted in only a few of the top restaurant chains remaining independent.

Many chains expanded nationally in an effort to corner market share. Then they looked for opportunities in other nations in a race to establish themselves in world markets. Burger King, Pizza Hut, McDonald's, and Denny's are just a few of the chains that established themselves abroad. American chains, especially fast-food, have been accepted in other countries because people are already familiar with the concept and the experience. They have been made ready through television and movies and by their own personal travel or the travel of others who relate their experiences.

Chains do make some cultural adaptations, and American chains, especially fast-food, have adapted to the Japanese culture. Squid pizza, curry donuts, bean-paste danish, rice and kim-chee burgers, tempura hot dogs, green tea milk shakes, sashimi submarines, and the BST (bacon, seaweed, and tomato) sandwich, can be found in Japanese fast-food establishments. Ice cream has undergone some changes as Baskin-Robbins offers the standard vanilla and chocolate flavors plus green tea, pumpkin, and honeydew melon. Even the Colonel has compromised his southernly behavior to establish his marketing niche in Japan.

> To see real marketing talent at work, go in mid-December to any Japanese outlet of Kentucky Fried Chicken (there are 1,017 of them, each with a life-sized fiberglass Col. Sanders out front, and wearing a Santa-style red cap in season).
> The KFC folks have successfully sold Japan on the notion that fried chicken is the classic American fare for Christmas dinner. (Two of our own kids have seen the commercials so often that they seem to believe this.) The idea has gone over so well that you have to make a reservation a week or two in advance just to get a carry-out box of chicken—served with the obligatory fried rice balls—on Dec. 24 or 25. KFC puts up giant signs outside of each store in December telling how many reservations are still available (Reid 1993: 18).

The Front and Back of the House

A restaurant, just like a hotel, has a front and back of the house. The front of the house includes the wait staff, counter people, bartenders, dining-room attendants, and other service personnel who deal with customers. The maitre d' or hostess is the manager of the front of the house. This position can also he held by a service manager, banquet manager, or service supervisor. The manager of the front of the house is responsible for supervising the entire operation of the dining room, training the service staff, organizing seating, and working cooperatively with the executive chef in formulating menus. There are also common areas that customers will see and use that are considered "front of the house." These areas include restrooms, meeting and banquet rooms, corridors, lobbies, restaurants, and other dining areas. It should be mentioned that in some restaurants, such as Spago's in Los Angeles, an open kitchen is considered part of the "entertainment." Just as the general attitude of employees who work in the front of the house is important regarding customer perception of service and quality, the condition of the areas in the front of the house is equally important.

The back of the house in a restaurant, like that of a hotel, consists of areas and people that customers usually do not see. Storage areas, closets, supply areas, and receiving and waste removal sites would do little to increase the dining pleasure of customers and neither would watching or hearing the activities of dish washers, janitors, cooks, and other food preparers. The manager of the back of the house is usually the executive chef.

The executive chef is responsible for the development of menus. The executive chef also makes the work schedules, organizes supplies, and oversees the quality of both the food and the service. If the menu is large and the restaurant is busy, there may be several chefs de partie (station or line chefs).

Chefs de partie include the vegetable, pastry, grill, and soup chefs, each responsible for his/her own part of the menu. If there is a sous chef, that person is next in command after the executive chef and may create schedules, assist different food preparation stations as needed, and cover for the executive chef when needed.

Classification

We tend to classify food and beverage establishments just as we do hotels. The simplest system is a three-tiered structure that divides the industry into budget/fast-food, replacement/casual dining, and fine dining/haute cuisine.

Replacement Dining

Replacement dining is also referred to as family or sit-down dining and is meant to replace what and how we are supposed to be eating when we are eating at home. Replacement dining offers full service, is moderately priced, and usually has a reasonably comprehensive menu so that everyone, including the kids, finds something that appeals to them.

This type of restaurant may also do catering and banquets. They may be independently owned, part of a chain, or franchised. They may be themed and also specialize in regional or specialty menus. Examples of this type of restaurant include places that serve Mexican, vegetarian, Italian, southwestern, or Asian cuisine.

Fine Dining

Fine dining or haute cuisine is usually reserved by many of us for special occasions. It is a reward for a job well done or a chance to celebrate a special occasion. There is considerable preparation involved in the making of our meal and the goal is not to mass produce a product and slide it across the counter to us. We are supposed to sit, have meaningful leisurely conversation, and savor both the moment and the food, as opposed to quickly satisfying our hunger. This is not a place for small children unless they are extremely well managed and behaved.

Unfortunately most of us rarely have a chance to experience fine dining or haute cuisine, and many of us choose not to do so. Budget constrictions limit the number of times that we can afford this luxury, and besides, we are in a **hurry.**

Fast-Food

Being in a hurry and eating on the run have established the third category, fast-food, as the primary choice for Americans.

> Food is 'fast' when it is immediately ready to be eaten, and can also be downed quickly. There must be either a puritanical renunciation of the pleasure to be found in savoring food, or a jadedness arising from too many competing calls for our attention—or both—for us to prefer eating fast; we have to want to settle for less. There was a time when having to eat food fast

Located in West Orange, New Jersey, The Manor typifies the finest example of an elegant dining experience. Pictured here is a view of The Manor gardens as seen from the Terrace Lounge.
The Terrance Lounge at The Manor, West Orange, NJ.

was considered to be a misfortune; the ideal state for a diner was that in which speed and food never had to coincide, except in the serving of it. Nowadays, 'fast food' is a phrase that has become so common that a good deal of the disapproval it used to express has disappeared; another paradoxical expression, 'junk food,' was invented, but even it has acquired intimations of pleasurable naughtiness—of daring the unhealthy for the sake of speed and the assuaging of an addiction (Visser 1991: 354–55).

Fast-food consists of pizza, chicken, seafood, and hot dog and hamburger establishments that provide over-the-counter service with the option to either eat in or take out. Many of these businesses cater to families with small children and offer on-site playgrounds, soft play areas, and kid-sized meal packages complete with toys and prizes (an interesting variation on the cereal box prizes of years ago). They use coupons, special meal deals, and budget prices to attract customers. Those businesses with an appropriate area may also sell children's birthday party packages.

Fast-food is comforting because we know what to expect and our menu options are limited.

> When a huge modern business conglomerate offers fast food to travellers on the highway, it knows that its customers are likely to desire No Surprises. They are hungry, tired, and not in a celebratory mood; they are happy to pay—provided that the price looks easily manageable—for the safely predictable, the convenient, the fast and ordinary (Visser 1991: 346).

Fast-food is also readily available at restaurant sites along every highway and road. No one yells when the kids spill their french fries under the table and when little Kerri decides that she'd rather not eat after we've ordered her meal, we are not out ten dollars. It is the perfect place for people with babies, toddlers, and two-year-olds.

Off-Beat Experiences

Unique restaurants, bars, clubs, and other food and beverage enterprises are always springing up. Those who are tired of the mundane look for these places to supplant the predictability and "sameness" of the chain operations. What is interesting is that chains sometimes start out as single-unit businesses that become so popular that they evolve into multi-unit operations. When this happens there is the possibility that they will join the ranks of the common and be replaced by a new and interesting concept or theme. The Hard Rock Cafe, 94th Squadron, and Planet Hollywood will all lose their appeal if we find one on every corner both here and abroad.

Eastern Europe has become an entrepreneur's gold mine for the development of new lodging and food and beverage business. Marxim's is a uniquely themed restaurant in Budapest, Hungary. The inside of the restaurant is decorated in the red and white colors of communism and has portraits of Lenin and Stalin hung on the walls. There is Russian soldier memorabilia and plain wooden booths separated by barbed wire entwined with white doves. Hammer-and-sickle decor is seen everywhere—even on the menu, which features pizzas named after well-known Russian leaders.

Most of the music played at Marxim's is from the '60s and '70s, although a few new groups can also be heard. Young customers see all of this as a joke, but older patrons do not think that it is funny. Owner Zoltan Czvitko feels that there is no political message in all of this, just something that once was and that we are free of now. In the true capitalistic spirit, Czvitko has also started "Pizz" a pizza delivery service. Pizz is open from 10:00 A.M. to 10:00 P.M. (Kazella 1993).

The National Restaurant Association

The National Restaurant Association (NRA) was founded on March 13, 1919, in Kansas City, Missouri. The NRA originated from two different groups, the National Association of Rotary Clubs and the Kansas City Restaurant Association. The former provided the professional principles, the latter the organizational structure. The goals of the NRA are to provide a forum for the common problems faced by restaurant owners, provide guidelines for the safe and sanitary handling and storing of food, and to represent the opinions of the industry to the federal government.

The NRA has an educational foundation that is responsible for arranging seminars and conferences. The foundation also provides educational materials and scholarships for people in the industry and for students seeking careers in the industry.

Recently the Foundation has joined with on-premise retailers and suppliers who have formed the Licensed Beverage Education Consortium (LBEC), to develop a certification program for licensed beverage managers. The Miller Brewing Company provided over 200,000 dollars in start-up grants and professional expertise to advance this cause. The certification program is designed to produce a better-trained and motivated staff who understand beverage products (beverage-alcohol) and who feel more comfortable in selling and promoting these products.

Industry Issues

The use and selling of beverage-alcohol is a current topic of discussion in the industry. The Promotion Information Bureau is a research firm for the beverage-alcohol industry. Based in Norwalk, Connecticut, the Bureau surveyed 75 key chain-restaurant executives who represent over 4,000 outlets. The executives were asked about current and future industry trends including the percentage change in the amount of food as opposed to beverage served. The current sales mix in bars is approximately 54 percent food and 46 percent beverage. The change in percentage of alcoholic as opposed to nonalcoholic beverages served during the last four years was also examined. Beverage-alcohol sales decreased 3 percent during that time, with the 3 percent difference going to nonalcoholic beverage sales. By 1997, those surveyed predicted that the mix would change again to 59 percent food and 41 percent beverage. This would mean that the profit margin made on beverage-alcohol would further decrease (F&B Magazine 1994: 10).

The use of beverage-alcohol is further complicated by the increase in microbreweries. The 1980s saw a resurgence in interest in local breweries called microbreweries that specialize in high-quality, distinctive-tasting beers. If the microbrewery is operated with a bar or a restaurant, it is known as a brewpub. The advantage of the microbreweries is the freshness of the product. Brewing by small companies is both quick and cost effective. It takes two weeks to brew regular beer and four to eight weeks to produce lager. The romance of walking up to the tap at a brewpub and tasting fresh, uniquely produced beer is an idea that has really caught on in the United States and Canada. The number of microbreweries and brewpubs in both countries increased dramatically from 1985 to 1992. Canada went from 17 to 67 properties, while the United States increase was even more dramatic—from 29 properties to 286 (*Hotel & Motel Management* 1993: 20).

Microbreweries have become so popular that Marriott Hotels, Resorts, and Suites has established its own exclusive microbrewed beer in its bars, lounges, and restaurants. Called Champions Clubhouse Classic, it is brewed in Dubuque, Iowa, at Dubuque Brewing and Bottling Company and is the result of a cooperative venture between Marriott, and Brandevor USA, Champions Sports, Inc. (*F&B* 1993: 34).

Along with the beverage-alcohol issue, is the concern over rejuvenating the image of the hotel restaurant. "Hotel food and beverage has fallen into two categories, haughty, normal-people-can't-afford-it food, and oh-my-god, you're-not-going-to-eat-at-the-hotel-restaurant food" (*Lodging Hospitality* 1993: 69). Surveys have further indicated that guests call out frequently for pizza and that the hotel restaurant is often seen as less than adequate. If used at all, it is primarily frequented for breakfast.

As this perception of the hotel restaurant pervades, more hotels are going to outside providers to handle food and beverage functions. Timothy Jeffrey the vice president of *F&B* has stated, "We're in the hotel business, and we as most hotel organizations are not expert foodservice operators. We'd rather hire someone who specializes in that" (*Lodging Hospitality* 1993: 67). Echoing this sentiment, plus acknowledging the power of recognition of a brand name, Disney has added a 400-seat, 20,000 square foot Planet Hollywood restaurant to its Pleasure Island entertainment center. This is the first chain restaurant to be developed at the Disney properties.

Quality of life issues also continue to be debated as smokers and nonsmokers square off regarding the place of smoking in the food and beverage industry. There are advantages (at least to the business) for allowing smoking to continue as opposed to banning it outright. Smokers are more likely to stay longer, order dessert, have an after dinner drink, and tip more generously than nonsmokers. This increases the amount of the check, which increases the profit for the business and boosts the tip for the server.

The environmental impact of both restaurants and hotels on our world is another issue. Hotels have engaged in an amenities war to attract guests. Little thought has been given to the impact from all those little plastic bottles of shampoo, hair conditioner, and hand and body lotion found in hotel bathrooms. Now the development of shatterproof refillable acrylic jars has allowed businesses to replace glass and plastic. Also energy-efficient lighting, appliances, systems, and recycling bins programs have been instituted by many companies in the lodging, food, and beverage industry as a way to cut costs and demonstrate social consciousness. The Swan Environmental Fund instituted by Boston's Park Plaza Hotel and Towers (A Saunders Hotel Group property), is a good example of this type of program. The hotel is proactive on environmental issues and as a result has drawn large numbers of environmental groups as customers. In an effort to help cover their initiatives, the hotel established the Fund. "At check-out, a 50-cent line item marked 'Enviro-Fund' is automatically added to your hotel folio. If you do not want to participate, you simply tell the desk clerk and it is removed" (*Lodging Hospitality* 1993: 14). All donations are matched by the hotel and help to support local and national environmental causes.

Hotels and resorts are also adding family programs and packages in an effort to compete with the cruise industry. Short all-inclusive cruise experiences are winning away the resort crowd. Food and beverage, entertainment, reasonably priced drinks, and optional excursions that are made available and announced beforehand are viewed positively by families and other travelers. Hotels and resorts have hidden taxes and charges. Room/resort taxes, recreation charges, telephone access charges, constant tipping, and a management attitude that views everything as a profit center, are sending many people down to the docks.

But this is a rapidly changing and adaptable industry. Hotels and resorts have instituted all-inclusive packages, kid's clubs, and other programs to keep and gain market share. This is also a somewhat fragile industry with consumers reacting instantly to negative and adverse situations. The presence of Legionnaires disease on the vessel *Horizon* in July of 1994, had many travelers changing their plans.

Finally, the industry needs to come to grips with the condition of its underpaid service personnel. Rapid industry turnover and the abundance of workers with language and cultural barriers has made it difficult to retain a constant workforce. It has been estimated that 70 percent of those in the industry are among the working poor. These individuals are vital to the success of the industry and are the unseen workers in both the back and the front of the house who make everything possible. Often they are undervalued, undercompensated, and forced to rely on tips and gratuities in order to bring their earnings up to acceptable levels.

Summary

There are an enormous number of hotels, motels, resorts, and restaurants around the world. People who travel make their choice concerning where to stay, and how and what to eat, based on many factors. Some of the considerations include purpose for traveling, amenities required, and budget.

The distribution channels for entry into the industry and for conducting business are extremely diverse. There are single-owner establishments, partnerships, and corporate ownership. In some instances a corporation's sole business may be the lodging, food, and beverage industry. In other cases, the corporation may have several business interests with lodging, food, and beverage being one of several strategic business units within the corporation and only one of several corporate holdings.

Franchising is a method that may be used to enter the market. Both individuals and corporations may take advantage of franchise opportunities. The management of the franchise, or of any other business, may be done by the owner or may be handled by a management company. There are advantages and disadvantages to the type of distribution channel used and to management options.

Lodging, food, and beverage businesses are divided into two halves called the front of the house and the back of the house. The front of the house is the visible part. This is comprised of common areas such as lobbies and gift shops and includes all areas where guests come into contact with hotel employees. The back of the house includes those areas that guests rarely see. Areas like the laundry room, kitchen, and the location that houses the heating, ventilating, and air-conditioning systems, as well as any other systems, are considered back of the house.

Much of the budget for the operation of lodging, food, and beverage businesses is dedicated to the use of purchasing energy to run the systems that are needed to keep guests comfortable and happy. The skyrocketing costs in this area have raised the consciousness of many corporations and individual companies to explore ways to reduce consumption and to recycle whenever possible.

Discussion Questions

1. Do you think that the concern over eating healthy foods has had an effect on the fast-food industry? How about an effect on the industry as a whole? Support your answer.
2. What measures in addition to the ones mentioned in the chapter, could lodging, food, and beverage establishments take to reduce waste, recycle, and conserve energy and resources?
3. When considering the purchase of a franchise, what types of information would you ask for before making a decision?

Chapter Exercises

1. Visit your local commercial bookstore and find at least five different books or publications that provide listings for specialized accommodations (i.e., campgrounds, B&B's).
2. Informally survey the area around your school to determine the approximate number and types of lodging, food, and beverage establishments in close proximity to your campus. How would you classify these businesses?
3. Interview two employees—one who works in the front of the house and one who works in the back of the house. Ask each of them what

they think the other person's job responsibilities are. Find out what their job responsibilities are. How much discrepancy is there between what they think the other person does and what that person actually does?

References

Bic Lodging and Travel Division. 1992. More Bic custom hotel amenities. *Lodging Hospitality* (October) 74–75.

Borsenik, Frank D. 1993. Hospitality technology in the 21st century. *Hospitality Research Journal* 17: 259–269.

Brymer, Robert A. 1991. *Hospitality management: An introduction to the industry.* 6th ed. Dubuque, IA: Kendall/Hunt Publishing Company.

Career Information Center. 1987. *Hospitality and recreation/8.* 3rd ed. Mission Hills, CA: Glencoe Publishing Company.

Carlino, Bill. 1993. Fast food tops '94 forecast. *Nation's Restaurant News.* 6 December.

Casual-dining segment grows steadily in 1992, study shows. 1993. *F&B: The Magazine for Involved Food and Beverage Professionals* (May/June): 20.

Choice Hotels International. 1993. How Sleep Inn owner Robert Bland turns walk-in business into a run-away success. *Lodging Hospitality* (August): 23.

Chon, Kye-Sung (Kaye), and Raymond T. Sparrow. 1995. *Welcome to hospitality: An introduction.* Cincinnati, OH: South-Western Publishing Co.

College booking. 1993. *Agent and Manager* (June): 54.

Council on Hotel, Restaurant and Institutional Education (CHRIE). 1993. CHRIE tribune. *F&B: The Magazine for Involved Food and Beverage Professionals* (May/June): 16.

Darzin, Daina. 1993. On expositions: Anatomy of an exposition. Canadian exhibition offers diverse options. *Agent and Manager* (June): 48.

Denefe, Janet. Issues update. 1993. *F&B: The Magazine for Involved Food and Beverage Professionals* (May/June): 6–8.

Drummond, Karen Eich. 1991. *Staffing your foodservice operation.* New York: Van Nostrand Reinhold.

F&B roundup. 1993. *F&B: The Magazine for Involved Food and Beverage Professionals* (May/June): 34.

Gatty, Bob. 1993. Higher taxes may take toll on lodging industry. *Hotel and Motel Management* (8 March): 13.

Gaynor, Mark. 1993. Fighting for the future. *F&B: The Magazine for Involved Food and Beverage Professionals* (May/June): 38–42.

Guests want high-touch tech. 1992. *Lodging Hospitality,* (October): 70.

Hayes, Jack. 1993. Rediscovering the fountain of youth: Chains court kids' market with meal deals. *Nation's Restaurant News* 8 November.

Henry, Vickie. 1994. Making customers feel pampered. *F&B: The Magazine for Involved Food and Beverage Professionals* (May/June): 50.

Industry steps up lobbying against Clinton health plan (under issues update) by Alison Kittrell. 1994. *F&B: The Magazine for Involved Food and Beverage Professionals* (May/June): 67.

Kapner, Suzanne. 1993. Dancing over dollars at NY's 78th annual hotel show. *Nation's Restaurant News* 8 November.

Kazella, Stephen. 1993. Faxed communication from Budapest 24 February.

Keegan, Peter O. 1993. Regional chains pick up growth pace. *Nation's Restaurant News* 25 October.

Khan, Mahmood, Michael Olsen, and Turgut Var, eds. 1993. *VNR's encyclopedia of hospitality and tourism.* New York: Van Nostrand Reinhold.

Kittrell, Alison. 1994. Study projects future of bars. *F&B: The Magazine for Involved Food and Beverage Professionals* (May/June): 10–13.

Lago, Dan, and James Kipp Poffley. 1993. The aging population and the hospitality industry in 2010: Important trends and probable sevices. *Hospitality Research Journal* 17: 29–47.

Lewis, Robert C., and Richard E. Chambers. 1989. *Marketing leadership in hospitality.* New York: Van Nostrand Reinhold.

Lyke, Rick. 1993. Beer: Leader of the pack. *Hotel & Motel Management* (5 July): 20–21.

Martin, Richard. 1993. Disney revs up growth despite French park woes. *Nation's Restaurant News* 6 December.

McDonald's. 1993. As the world shrinks, international franchising looms. *Nation's Restaurant News* (25 October): 48.

Mischitelli, Vincent. 1990. *Your new restaurant.* Holbrook, MA: Bob Adams, Inc.

Morrison, Alastair M. 1989. *Hospitality and travel marketing.* Albany, NY: Delmar Publishers, Inc.

Nozar, Robert A., ed. 1992. *'92 directory of hotel/motel management companies.* Cleveland, OH: *Hotel and Motel Management* (the newspaper of the lodging industry).

Olsen, Glenn W., and Ken Myers. 1992. Hotels and resorts: Family programs and their potential impact. *Hospitality and Tourism Educator* (November): 85–88.

Oshurst, Jim. 1993. Profits in foodstuffs. *Agent and Manager* (June): 46–47.

Reid, T. R. 1993. Welcome to the land of squid pizza, curry donuts and sashimi subs. *The Star-Ledger* 10 October.

Row, Megan. 1993. If you can't beat 'em, join 'em: more hotels are bailing out of foodservice and turning to outside providers, with good results. *Lodging Hospitality* (August): 67–69.

Rushmore, Stephen. 1993. Beyond recycling: the ecotel. *Lodging Hospitality* (August): 10.

Steadman, David. 1991. *Restaurant biz is showbiz: Why marketing is the key to your success.* Greenlawn, NY: Whittier Green Publishing Co., Inc.

Thomas, R. David, Ron Beyma, and Mary Maroon Gelpi. 1992. *Dave's way.* New York: Berkley Books.

Troy, Timothy N., and Laura Koss. 1993. Evaluating unified Europe. *Hotel and Motel Management* (8 March): 15–16.

Van Warner, Rick. 1993. Keeping employees in the dark does nothing to brighten profits. *Nation's Restaurant News* (6 December): 21.

Visser, Margaret. 1991. *The rituals of dinner.* New York: Penguin Books.

Wagner, Grace. 1993. Lodging today. Park Plaza invites guests to give. *Lodging Hospitality* (August): 14.

———. 1992. Strategies/A hotel-within-a-hotel opens in London. *Lodging Hospitality* (October): 32.

Wolff, Carlo. 1992. Roomservice blues: Travelers cite erratic execution and high prices. *Lodging Hospitality* (October): 61–62.

Additional Resources

Ableman, Michael. 1993. *From the good earth: A celebration of growing food around the world.* New York: Harry N. Abrams, Inc.

Anderson, Kenneth N., and Lois E. Anderson. 1993. *The international dictionary of food and nutrition.* New York: John Wiley and Sons, Inc.

Axler, Bruce H., and Carol A. Litrides. 1990. *Food and beverage service. Wiley professional restaurateur guides.* New York: John Wiley and Sons, Inc.

Benning, Lee Edwards. 1992. *The cook's tale: Origins of famous foods and recipes.* Old Saybrook, CT: Globe Pequot Press.

Bernstein, Charles, and Ronald N. Paul. 1994. *Winning the chain restaurant game: Eight key strategies.* New York: John Wiley and Sons, Inc.

Birchfield, John C. 1988. *Design and layout of food service facilities.* New York: Van Nostrand Reinhold.

Chalmers, Irena, comp. 1990 *The food professional's guide: The James Beard foundation directory of people, products, and services.* New York: John Wiley and Sons, Inc.; New York: American Showcase.

———. 1994. *The great food almanac: A feast of facts from A to Z.* San Francisco: Collins Publishers.

Dittmer, Paul R., and Gerald G. Griffin. 1989. *Principles of food, beverage, and labor cost controls for hotels and restaurants.* 4th ed. New York: Van Nostrand Reinhold.

Drummond, Karen Eich. 1992. *The restaurant training program: An employee training guide for managers.* New York: John Wiley and Sons, Inc.

Egerton-Thomas, Christopher. 1994. *How to open and run a successful restaurant.* 2nd ed. New York: John Wiley and Sons, Inc.

Emerson, Robert L. 1990. *The new economics of fast food.* New York: Van Nostrand Reinhold.

Feltenstein, Tom. 1992. *Foodservice marketing for the '90s: How to become the number one restaurant in your neighborhood.* New York: John Wiley and Sons, Inc.

Fisher, M. F. K. 1990. *The art of eating.* New York: Collier Books.

Fussell, Betty. 1992. *The story of corn.* New York: Alfred A. Knopf.

Gilleran, Susan. 1993. *Kids dine out: Attracting the family foodservice market with children's menus and pint–sized promotions.* New York: John Wiley and Sons, Inc.

Gray, William S., and Salvatore C. Liguori. 1990. *Hotel and motel management and operations.* 2nd ed. Englewood Cliffs, NJ: Regents / Prentice Hall.

Greenstein, Lou. 1992. *A la carte: A tour of dining history.* Glen Cove, NY: PBC International, Inc.

Grotz, Peter. 1990. *Successful cold buffets.* New York: Van Nostrand Reinhold.

Halvorsen, Francine. 1994. *Catering like a pro: From planning to profit.* New York: John Wiley and Sons, Inc.

Herbst, Sharon Tyler. 1990. *Food lover's companion: Comprehensive definitions of over 3000 food, wine and culinary terms.* Barron's cooking guide. Hauppauge, NY: Barron's Educational Series, Inc.

Hospitality research journal. Washington, D.C.: Council on Hotel, Restaurant and Institutional education.

Hotel and motel management: A newspaper for the lodging industry. Cleveland, OH: Advanstar communications.

Hotels: The international magazine of the hotel and restaurant industry. Des Plains, IL: Cahners Publishing.

Kazarian, Edward A. 1989. *Food service facilities planning.* 3rd ed. New York: Van Nostrand Reinhold.

Ketterer, Manfred. 1991. *How to manage a successful catering business.* 2nd ed. New York: Van Nostrand Reinhold.

Khan, Mahmood A. 1991. *Concepts of food service operations and management.* 2nd ed. New York: Van Nostrand Reinhold.

King, Carol A. 1988. *Professional dining room management.* 2nd ed. New York: Van Nostrand Reinhold.

Kotschevar, Lendal H. 1988. *Standards, principles, and techniques in quantity food production.* New York: Van Nostrand Reinhold.

Kroc, Ray, and Robert Anderson. 1987. *Grinding it out: The making of McDonald's.* New York: St. Martin's Paperbacks.

Lawrence, Elizabeth. 1992. *The complete caterer.* Rev. ed. New York: Doubleday.

Lieberman, Judy Serra. 1991. *The complete off-premise caterer.* New York: Van Nostrand Reinhold.

Litrides, Carol A., and Bruce H. Axler. 1994. *Restaurant service: Beyond the basics.* New York: John Wiley and Sons, Inc.

Marvin, Bill. 1992. *Restaurant basics: Why guests don't come back . . .and what you can do about it.* New York: John Wiley and Sons, Inc.

———. *From turnover to teamwork: How to build and retain a customer-oriented foodservice staff.* New York: John Wiley and Sons, Inc.

McGee, Harold. 1984. *On food and cooking: The science and lore of the kitchen.* New York: Collier Books.

Meyer, Cynthia, Edy Schmid, and Christel Spuehler. 1991. *Professional table service.* Translated by Heinz Holtmann. New York: Van Nostrand Reinhold. Originally published as *Service-Lehrbuch* (Zurich: Verlag Schweitzer Wirteverband, 1987).

Nation's restaurant news: The newsweekly of the foodservice industry. New York: Lebhar-Friedman, Inc.

Robertson, Lynne Nannen. 1991. *Productivity in food service.* Ames, IA: Iowa State University Press.

Root, Waverley, and Richard de Rochemont. 1976. *Eating in America: A history.* New York: The Ecco Press.

Rubin, Laurie, photographer. 1992. *Food tales: A literary menu of mouthwatering masterpieces.* New York: Viking Studio Books.

Rutherford, Denny G., ed. 1990. *Hotel management and operations.* New York: Van Nostrand Reinhold.

Scanlon, Nancy Loman. 1992. *Catering menu management.* New York: John Wiley and Sons, Inc.

Shock, Patti J., and John M. Stefanelli. 1992. *Hotel catering: A handbook for sales and operations.* New York: John Wiley and Sons, Inc.

Sokolov, Raymond. 1993. *Why we eat what we eat: How Columbus changed the way the world eats.* New York: Touchstone Books.

Splaver, Bernard. 1991. *Successful catering.* 3rd ed. Edited by William N. Reynolds and Michael Roman. New York: Van Nostrand Reinhold.

Tennyson, Jeffrey. 1993. *Hamburger heaven: The illustrated history of the hamburger.* New York: Hyperion.

Toussaint-Samat, Maguelone. 1994. *A history of food.* Translated by Anthea Bell. Cambridge, MA: Blackwell Publishers. Originally published as *Histoire naturelle et morale de la nourriture* (Paris: Bordas, 1987).

Weiss, Edith, and Hal Weiss. 1991. *Catering handbook.* New York: Van Nostrand Reinhold.

Yudd, Ronald A. 1990. *Successful buffet management.* New York: Van Nostrand Reinhold.

Zaccarelli, Brother Herman. 1991. *Foodservice management by checklist: A handbook of control techniques.* New York: John Wiley and Sons, Inc.

Zee, A. 1990. *Swallowing clouds: Two millenia of Chinese tradition, folklore, and history hidden in the language of food.* New York: Simon and Schuster.

The Allied Industries

LEARNING OBJECTIVES

1. *To discuss the importance of allied industries to commercial recreation and tourism.*
2. *To explore the Standard International Classification of Tourism Activities (SICTA) as developed by the World Tourism Organization.*
3. *To exhibit positive examples of some of the allied businesses that are important to commercial recreation and tourism.*
4. *To introduce alternative career options and opportunities that are available in the allied industries.*

Introduction

The word "allied" in its simplest form means "connected." In many highly educated societies and in Western societies in particular, we tend to study and view the world in terms of categories. This may be an effective approach for dividing up issues and ideas for the purposes of studying them and making them easier to understand, but it certainly makes it difficult to see the big picture.

The foreword of this book contains the poem, "The Blind Men and the Elephant." Written in the 1800s by John Godfrey Saxe, this poem summarizes the state of commercial recreation and tourism (or whatever else we might choose to label this industry) as it is today. Each participant in this emerging and powerful area of business claims to know the dimensions and boundaries of an industry that none of us has truly seen. Each of us feels an ear, leg, tail, side, knee, or tusk, and yet does not fully comprehend the whole.

The Supply Side of Commercial Recreation and Tourism

Large amounts of time are spent talking about and analyzing the demand component of the industry, and the importance of the concept of service to our industry. Very little attention is paid to the supply side. Perhaps this is because the word supply reminds us of our old industrial nation label, and we feel that we are beyond all that at this point—we are a service economy now. But, commercial recreation and tourism is connected (allied) to many other industries. Without them and without their products, the nature and quality of what we do would be vastly different.

Have you ever been somewhere and had the power supply suddenly go off? If it was evening, do you remember what it was like without lights, without heat, fans, or air conditioners? How about without your radio, stereo, or television? The "power" that fuels our industry comes from our suppliers. What would the industry be like without them? How would we run a concert? How would we produce that concert if it was held outside?

First, remove the stage, risers, fencing, chairs, portable toilets, and food carts. Next, take down any fancy banners or signage made for this event along with the tents rented to supply shelter in case of inclement weather. Then, forget about the lasers, lights, special-effects machines, amplifiers, microphones, and other products needed for the concert. What does this leave us? Well, how about Tibetan throat singing?

Tibetan Throat Singing

Just as the Benedictine monks from the Abbey at Silos in Spain have issued a hit record of Gregorian chant, Tibetan throat singing, or *dbyangs*, a type of Tibetan Buddhist chant, has become popular as a form of New Age music. Although throat singing, called such because of the constricted vocal production used to create the fundamental sound and its multiphonic harmonics (in this type of music each singer is actually producing more than one note at a time), is performed in alternation with an orchestra of wind and percussion instruments in its use as part of a religious service, it is the unique vocal production that has captured the attention of western ears. This unique sound has become a commodity in which people are interested, thus making it marketable. All that is required for a concert of Tibetan throat singing is a Tibetan monk or group of monks who are conversant with the vocal techniques necessary to produce the appropriate sounds (Balestracci 1994).

Although Tibetan throat singing may have garnered a following, it is more of a look into our past than a statement about our future. Most of us like the glitz, glamour, whistles, and bells that are standard fare at the concerts of today. Technological evolution fueled by the belief that we just cannot live without "it" has generated new (and expanded old) industries that rely totally, or in part, on tourism and profit-oriented recreation. These are our suppliers—our allied industries.

The World Tourism Organization (WTO) has recognized the importance of this group to the total industry and has established the "Standard

International Classification of Tourism Activities" (SICTA). The SICTA is an attempt to measure the economic power of tourism and the service industry in general.

> While tourism cannot abandon the demand-side definition of its scope, it must seek to more clearly delineate a supply-based conceptual structure for its activities, because that is the source of most national economic statistics. Properly incorporated into the supply-based statistical structure, tourism's relationship to other economic sectors and its proper importance relative to other sectors can be recognized. A central element in the undertaking is the delineation of a Standard International Classification of Tourism Activities (SICTA) (United Nations 1993: 23).

The Standard International Classification of Tourism Activities is not a classification of industries, goods, or services but is a classification system based on economic **activity.**

> It is the intent of the SICTA to be responsive to both supply-side and demand-side definitions of statistical units. In defining SICTA classes and sub-classes linked to tourism, either as a primary economic activity or as a share of overall activity, linkages must be established . . . (United Nations 1993: 58).

The formulation of SICTA was based on Standard Industrial Classification (SIC). The primary purpose of SIC is to categorize all parts of economic activity in a comprehensive and consistent fashion. Although no system is perfect, SIC and International Standard Industrial Classification (ISIC) were used as the basis for SICTA. SICTA is divided into divisions, groups, and classes.

SICTA Divisions and Names

A Agriculture[+]

B Fishing[+]

C Mining and Quarrying[+]

D Manufacturing[+]

E Electricity, Gas, and Water Supply[+]

F Construction[*]
Commercial facilities—hotels, retail, etc.
Recreational facilities—ski areas, golf courses
Civil works—transportation facilities, terminals, dams
Resort residences—second homes, weekend homes

G Wholesale and Retail[*]
Sale and maintenance of motor vehicles and fuels
   Motor vehicle sales including recreational vehicles
   Sale, maintenance, and repair of motorcycles and snowmobiles

Nonspecialized retail trade
Retail food sales
Retail-specialized food sales
Retail food sales
Other retail, specialized
Retail sale of travel accessories
Textiles
Clothing
Footwear and leather goods
Luggage
In specialty stores (travel alarms, converters)
Other retail sales in specialized stores
Skin diving and scuba equipment
Ski equipment
Camping and hiking equipment
Hunting and fishing equipment
Photographic sales and services
Gift and souvenir shops
Other transport vehicles (boats, yachts, aircraft)

H   Hotels and Restaurants *
Hotels, camping sites, and other commercial accommodations
Hotels and motels with restaurants
Hotels and motels without restaurants
Hostels and refuges
Camping sites including caravan sites
Health-oriented accommodations
Other provisions of lodging (railroad sleeping cars)
Restaurants, bars, and canteens
Bars and other drinking places
Full-service restaurants
Fast-food restaurants and cafeterias
Institutional food service, caterers
Food kiosks, vendors, refreshment stands
Night clubs and dinner theaters

I   Transport, Storage, and Communication *
Land transport, transport via pipelines
Transport via railways
Interurban rail passenger services
Special rail tour services
Other land transport
Scheduled interurban buses
Long-distance tour buses
Specialized scheduled vehicles
Local tour vehicles
Charter buses, excursions (same-day visits)

Sea and coastal water transport
  Cruise ships
  Ship rental with crew
Inland water transport
  Inland water passenger transport with accommodations
  Inland water local tours
  Inland water taxis, ferries
Air transport
  Scheduled air passenger service
  Nonscheduled air passenger transport
  Aircraft rental with crew
Supporting and auxiliary transport activities
  Travel agents
  Tour operators, packagers, and wholesalers
  Ticket offices not a part of transport companies
  Guides

J Financial Intermediation*
Financial intermediation not insurance/pensions
  Exchange of currencies
Insurance and pension funding
  Travel insurance

K Real Estate, Renting, and Business Activities*
Real estate activities with own or leased property
  Buying or selling of own or leased property
Real estate activities on a fee or contract basis
  Letting of own or leased tourism property
Real estate agencies
  Real estate agencies for tourism properties
  Tourist property management
Renting of transport equipment
  Automobile rental
  Motorcycle rental
  Recreational vehicle, camper, caravan rental
  Renting of air transport equipment for personal use
Renting of personal and household goods
  Rental of watercraft and related facilities
    Saddle horses
    Bicycles
    Ski equipment
    Tourist-related goods not elsewhere classified
Research and development
  Tourism research
Other business activities
  Tourism market research
  Tourism business and management consultancy services

Architectural, engineering, and other technical activities
    Tourism architecture and engineering
Advertising
    Tourism advertising
Business activities not elsewhere classified
    Translation services

L   Public Administration*
Administration of the state
    Customs administration
    Taxation, fees, fines, tariffs
    Information bureaus
    Provision of transport-related functions
    Provision of cultural, recreational services
    Tourism administration
    Regulation of private transport activities
    Fishing/hunting regulation
    Regional and economic development administration
Provision of services to the community
    Visa issuance, consular affairs
    Special police, border guards, airport security

M Education*
    Higher education
    Hotel schools
    Tourism education programmes
    Recreation and park schools
    Ski instruction
    Swimming, scuba instruction
    Flying instruction
    Boating instruction

N   Health and Social Services[+]

O   Other Community Social and Personal Services*
Activities of business, employers, and professional organizations
    Visitor and convention bureaus
    Activities of professional organizations
    Activities of tourism-related professional organizations
    Activities of tourism industry-related trade unions
    Travel clubs
    Travelers aid societies
Recreational, cultural, and sporting activities
    Motion picture projection
    Radio and television activities
    Dramatic arts, music, and other art activities
    Operation of ticket agencies
    Amusement parks
Libraries, archives, museums, and other cultural activities
    Museum activities and preservation of historical sites and buildings

Museums of all kinds and subjects
Historical sites and buildings
Botanical and zoological gardens and nature reserve activities
Botanical and zoological gardens
Nature and wildlife preserves
Sporting and other recreational activities
Sporting activities
Physical-fitness facilities
Operations of sporting facilities
Activities related to recreational hunting
Operations of recreation parks and beaches
Activities related to recreational fishing
Gambling and betting operations, casinos
Operation of recreational fairs and shows
Operation of ski lifts

P Private Households with Employed Persons+

Q Extra-Territorial Organizations and Bodies*
Extra-territorial organizations
International tourism bodies

(Adapted from *Recommendations on Tourism Statistics, 1993*).
+Indicates no listings under division heading.
*Indicates listing of subcategories that are most relevant to commercial recreation and tourism

Many of the areas listed above are involved in the sale, marketing, or distribution of goods, but they are also responsible for product development and production. Someone develops and produces the hiking boots, motorcycles, boats, recreational vehicles, equipment, and even the airplanes that we use. Who *are* these people and what do they do? Hera are some industry examples.

Food and Beverage

Ben and Jerry's

It may seem strange to include this company as an allied industry, but this is a company that definitely has exhibited a playful attitude. This attitude has been displayed in their business practices, by their production of special events, and by the creation of innovative marketing and management policies. Besides producing a winning product, Ben and Jerry's practices caring capitalism and has demonstrated corporate responsibility—all while having fun.

Two old friends, Ben Cohen and Jerry Greenfield, founded the company in 1978. By 1985 a 43,000-square-foot plant began operation in Waterbury, Vermont (the site of their corporate headquarters). In the first six months of the operation of the plant, company officials were dumbfounded to realize that they had admitted 41,000 **tourists.** This shock was surpassed in 1991 when 220,000 tourists took the tour and made Ben & Jerry's Homemade (their official name) the number one tourist attraction in the state.

What has made this company so successful is its philosophy, which was summed up in two statements. One was made by Ben: "Business has a responsibility to give back to the community." The other comment was made by Jerry: "If it's not fun, why do it?" (Scott and Rothman 1994: 48).

> Full-color life-sized cutouts of James Dean, John Wayne, and other movie stars, each wearing the pastel hair covering that is required headgear in all food-preparation areas, adorn numerous offices throughout the organization. White trash cans, emblazoned with the black markings of dairy cows, are everywhere. Wild and crazy artwork personalizes practically every work area. And if all that weren't enough, an officially designated group called the Joy Gang regularly sponsors a variety of companywide events, including a miniature car derby and an Elvis look-alike contest (Scott and Rothman 1994: 57).

So amazed were the two partners by their success that they celebrated their first year in business by giving away ice cream cones. This tradition has continued and been joined by free summer movies and a yearly fall festival for families, called Fall Down Festivals.

Ben and Jerry not only have fun but do give back to both their local community and the community at large. The company formed a nonprofit corporation to give away 7.5 percent of their pretax profits. Ben and Jerry are excellent examples of individuals who know how to make a quality product, to be socially responsible while they make this product, and to follow through on the philosophy that business has a responsibility to give something back.

Wynkoop Brewing Company

John Hickenlooper was a geologist without a job in the mid-1980s. With the help of several partners, he refurbished the lower two levels of an old warehouse built in 1899 and opened the first brewpub in the state of Colorado. Besides creating a commercially successful restaurant and local brewery, Hickenlooper has worked to preserve and restore the historic neighborhood where Wynkoop is located. He will provide free beer to local nonprofit organizations that want to sponsor a benefit to raise money. In 1991, Wynkoop Brewing Company donated 300 kegs to help these groups. In addition, Hickenlooper developed a nonprofit organization called the Chinook fund. The fund has been able to raise approximately 80,000 dollars annually, which it distributes as small grants ($1,500 to $3,000) to community groups.

Coca-Cola

John Styth Pemberton, an Atlanta pharmacist, invented Coca-Cola in 1886 when he decided to mix up a batch of special syrup in a big pot in his backyard. Pemberton mixed water, sugar, cinnamon, nutmeg, lime juice, vanilla, guarana, and glycerin together and added a secret ingredient extracted from the leaves of coca plants. The purpose of this new syrup was to cure headaches, tiredness, indigestion, and the results of overindulgence. During the first year of sale of this new product an average of nine drinks a day were sold. Two years after inventing his syrup, which he dubbed Coca-Cola, Pemberton died. He would never know how his invention would change the beverage industry.

Pemberton's syrup was acquired by another Atlanta pharmacist, Asa Candler. Candler realized the potential of Coca-Cola as a soda fountain drink, marketed it as such, and poured large amounts of money into promoting the product. By 1895 the sale of Coca-Cola had spread to every U.S. state and territory.

> Asa Candler made the syrup but didn't bottle it. In 1899 he signed a contract giving two lawyers the rights to bottle Coca-Cola in the entire U.S. for one dollar. The lawyers were the middlemen, buying the syrup from the Coca-Cola Company and reselling it to local bottlers. This franchise system continues today . . . (Moskowitz 1990: 59).

Coke further moved into the collective American consciousness during World War II. Robert Woodruff, the head of the company, stated: "We will see that every man in uniform gets a bottle of Coca-Cola for 5-cents wherever he is and whatever it costs" (Moskowitz 1990: 60). Coca-Cola bottling plants rose near the battle fronts; sixty-four overseas plants were in place when the war was over. In addition, thousands of GI's returned home looking for places that sold Coca-Cola.

Coca-Cola is a company that has remained close to its roots by keeping its headquarters in Atlanta and is known as a benevolent company. Coke in its many forms has become the biggest beverage in the world, except for water, and is closely associated with sports and special events both locally and worldwide. The product has become so ingrained in American culture that those requesting any kind of cola drink often ask for a coke, meaning a Coca-Cola.

Athletic Footwear

Nike, Inc.

Nike dominates the global athletic footwear market with 30 percent of market share. The company, formed by Phil Knight and Bill Bowerman in 1964, was originally called Blue Ribbon Sports. In 1968, the two men formed Nike, naming the company after the Greek goddess of victory whose name was supposed to have been evoked by the legendary runner from Marathon.

Today Nike also makes fitness wear and accessories and has a line of casual and dress shoes. In 1993, the international sales from all aspects of the business was more than 1 billion dollars (Hoover et al. 1994: 814). Nike has been designated as the exclusive outfitter of the U.S. track and field team through the year 2000. Most of their shoes are produced outside of the United States, with approximately 98 percent of the shoe manufacturing occurring in Asia. The company does business in 81 countries, has 49 retail stores, and administrative offices in the United States, Hong Kong, Brazil, and the Netherlands. One of Nike's biggest competitors is Reebok.

Reebok International, Ltd.

Reebok led the pack of athletic footwear producers in the late 1980s by introducing a women's oxford-style sneaker called the Freestyle. The timing for the introduction of the Freestyle was perfect and coincided with the enormous interest in aerobics. The Freestyle became one of the largest selling shoes in history, but Reebok eventually lost market share and dropped to the number two position behind Nike.

The company, named after a speedy African antelope, has pledged to return to the number one position again and has said that it will pass NIKE by 1996. Most of Reebok's sales in 1992 (65 percent) were from sales of products in the United States. In an effort to gain name recognition and market share in Europe, Reebok has agreed to outfit and sponsor the 1994 and 1996 Russian Olympic team. Reebok has a diversified line of shoes and apparel and sells its products in 140 countries. Total sales for 1992 was 3,023 million dollars (Hoover et al. 1994: 915).

Transportation

Airbus Industrie

Airbus Industrie is a European consortium of aerospace firms. It is the second-largest manufacturer of aircraft. With 20 percent of the market worldwide, Airbus has four industrie (sic) partners and two associate members. Two of the partners are Aerospatiale of France and Deutsche Airbus of Germany; each has a 37.9 percent interest in the company. The two additional partners, British Aerospace and Construcciones Aeronauticas (CASA) of Spain, have a 20 percent and 4.2 percent interest, respectively. The two associate members, Belairbus of Belgium and Fokker of the Netherlands, participate in some but not all projects.

Headquartered in Blagnac Cedex, France, Airbus does not officially report its profits and losses, but had an estimated operating surplus of 275 million dollars in 1991 (Chai 1993: 120). One of the reasons given for the success of the company has been the subsidizing of development costs by the governments of the consortium. Government participation of up to 75 percent of the total of the costs has been reported. In 1992, a long-standing dispute was settled when the United States and the European Union (EU) set limits of 30 percent to 33 percent on future development subsidies. Airbus customers in North America include Air Canada, Continental, Federal Express, and Mexicana. The Boeing Company is the chief competitor of Airbus Industrie.

The Boeing Company

Founded in 1916, Boeing has had a long and interesting history. The company has two assembly plants, both in the state of Washington.

> Everett, 30 miles north of Seattle, is the world's largest enclosed space—taller than an 11-story building, one-half mile wide and the length of 40 football fields. To see what's going on, supervisors need binoculars. To light this 780-acre complex requires the power used to electrify 32,000 average American homes (Moskowitz et al. 1990: 535).

Boeing is so large that it has built half of the jet airplanes ever flown and buys parts and components from nearly 4,000 companies. When the company built the 757, approximately 1,300 parts and components were used to complete the project. However, four companies, Pratt & Whitney, Rolls-Royce, Honeywell, and Rockwell, were responsible for supplying 53 percent of the components and parts used for the plane. The Boeing reputation and legacy is so strong that in the first six months of 1990, they accepted new orders for 214 planes. These orders, worth 19.3 million dollars, will keep the company busy through the year 2000.

Greyhound

Greyhound is number one in the manufacturing of buses and deodorant soaps, as well as in trade show decorating. They are number two in airline catering. Founded in 1914, the company changed its name in 1990 from Greyhound to Greyhound-Dial. This change reflected the difference in company holdings and interests. The company began to expand into airline and airport catering by acquiring Dobbs and Carson International, and moved into bus manufacturing by adding the RTS modular bus formerly made by General Motors.

Recreational Vehicles

Fleetwood Enterprises

The nation's leading producer of recreational vehicles (RV's) and manufactured housing is Fleetwood Enterprises, Inc. The company has a diversified line of recreational vehicles that have wide market appeal. John Crean, the founder and current chairman of the board and chief executive officer, started by assembling and selling venetian blinds to the "trailer" manufacturing industry. Founded under meager circumstances, this venture led to the vision of manufacturing mass-produced housing. Today Fleetwood is the largest producer of housing in the United States and produces approximately 35,000 homes each year in an effort to make the American dream of home ownership a reality.

In 1964, Crean entered the recreational vehicle industry when he acquired a small plant that produced the Terry travel trailer. Today

Fleetwood operates ten travel trailer plants (including one in Ontario, Canada) and is the leading producer of travel trailers in the United States. Expanding their recreational line occurred in 1990 when the company entered the truck camper market and began to produce slide-in truck campers under the brand names of Caribou and Elkhorn.

A small motor home company acquired in 1969 moved the company into the "powered" aspect of recreational vehicles. Fleetwood is currently the largest motor home manufacturer in the United States and has six motor home plants. It has built well over 257,000 motor homes. A folding trailer division was added to the business in 1989 when Fleetwood assumed the folding trailer division of the Coleman Company (noted for lanterns, canoes, and outdoor stoves). This gave the company a 30 percent market share of this part of the industry and moved it into first place in the manufacturing of folding trailers.

Two additional aspects of the business, a supply division responsible for the comany's fiberglass and lumber operations and Fleetwood Credit Corporation (FCC), rounded out the company. Started so that retailers would have an efficient and consistent source of financing for customers at competitive rates, the FCC has become a nationwide RV finance company (table 8.1).

Ad for folding trailer.
Courtesy Fleetwood Enterprises, Inc. Riverside, California.

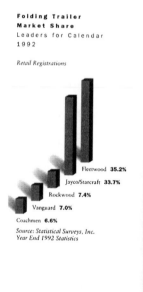

Folding Trailer Market Share
Leaders for Calendar 1992

Retail Registrations

Fleetwood **35.2%**
Jayco/Starcraft **33.7%**
Rockwood **7.4%**
Vanguard **7.0%**
Coachmen **6.6%**

Source: Statistical Surveys, Inc. Year End 1992 Statistics

Spaciousness and towing stability are key features that appeal to buyers of fifth-wheel travel trailers such as this popular Prowler model. Prowler is the No. 1 selling brand in the U.S.

Table 8.1 Fleetwood Operating Revenues and Units Shipped

Operating Revenues Years ended April	1993	1992	1991	1990	1989
	(Dollars in thousands)				
Recreational vehicles:					
North American sales—					
Motor homes	$625,145	$592,792	$502,401	$654,306	$719,264
Travel trailers*	405,505	330,409	259,405	313,087	334,502
Folding trailers	64,454	48,852	34,887	10,846	—
European sales	18,923	—	—	—	—
Total RV sales	1,114,027	972,053	796,693	978,239	1,053,766
Manufactured housing	774,784	574,149	566,564	532,917	535,339
Supply operations	19,088	11,855	11,465	15,186	17,168
Total manufacturing sales	1,907,899	1,558,057	1,374,722	1,526,342	1,606,273
Finance revenues	34,022	31,291	26,172	23,082	12,250
Total	$1,941,921	$1,589,348	$1,400,894	$1,549,424	$1,618,523

Units Shipped Years ended April	1993	1992	1991	1990	1989
Recreational vehicles:					
North American Shipments—					
Motor homes	13,941	13,739	12,247	16,459	18,731
Travel trailers	31,396	26,226	21,775	28,461	31,046
Folding trailers	16,393	13,012	9,576	2,975	—
Slide-in truck campers	1,515	1,444	815	—	—
European shipments	132	—	—	—	—
Total	63,377	54,421	44,413	47,895	49,777
Manufactured housing:					
Single-section	24,120	19,173	18,471	18,183	19,571
Multi-section	20,643	16,478	16,446	16,575	17,132
Total	44,763	35,651	34,917	34,758	36,703

Courtesy Fleetwood Enterprises, Inc. Riverside, California.
*Includes sales of slide-in truck camper units.

    Additional growth opportunities were provided for Fleetwood in 1992 when the company acquired an 80 percent share of a German partnership that owns and operates the Niesman and Bischoff motor home company. Located in Koblenz, Germany, this producer of luxury motor homes is highly regarded in the European community.

    Fleetwood has its headquarters in Riverside, California. It controls its plants by the use of divisional management teams and lets local management at each site make autonomous decisions that are in line with corporate policies and procedures. Fleetwood does not operate retail stores, and product distribution is handled by approximately 3,500 independent dealer locations in Canada and the United States. RV products are sold under the following brand names:

Motor Homes	American Eagle, Bounder, Coronado, Flair, Jamboree, Limited, Pace Arrow, Southwind, and Tioga
Travel Trailers	Avion, Prowler, Terry, Wilderness
Folding Trailers	Coleman
Truck Campers	Caribou, Elkhorn

Fleetwood products have been sold in Japan, South America, the Middle East, and Mexico, as well as in North America and Europe. It is interesting to note that although the sales of the RV's manufactured by Fleetwood would be directly counted as an economic activity in SICTA, indirect economic activity would not. The indirect economic activity from a multinational corporation of this size would be substantial.

Specialized Recreational Equipment

Yakima Products

Yakima Products was founded by Otto Bagervall, a native of Germany, and purchased by Don Banducci and Steve Cole in 1979. Under Otto's direction, Yakima made foot braces used to secure feet in kayaks and canoes. They also made music stands, snow shovels, canoe racks, and crossing flags for the local schools. Don and Steve had become friends when they met in Arcata, Oregon, and formed a company called Six River Float Trips. This company reflected the pair's love of white-water rafting and was started to help Don and Steve pay for their own activities.

In 1978, they received a letter from Otto stating that he was going out of business because the government wanted the company to pay too many taxes and enough was enough. Banducci and Cole called to ask if the company was for sale and were invited to come to Yakima, Washington for one month to be apprentices. Both men and their wives accepted Otto's invitation.

What Banducci and Cole found when they arrived in Yakima was a disorganized, dangerous operation.

> We learned right away that this man was quickly losing his memory. He had no memory and worked in a chaotic, nonsensical manner. The operation was like a Santa's workshop . . . There were no guards on the saws, and everything was made by hand (Scott and Rothman 1994: 154).

Banducci and Cole survived Otto's scrutiny and bought Yakima in 1979 for 80,000 dollars—then they moved the business from Yakima to Arcata. They quickly learned that the operation had to be streamlined. Otto had not made a profit, because he had been selling his products for less than cost. Cole, the mechanically oriented end of the partnership, redesigned and streamlined the roof rack that Otto had been selling, which was used to transport canoes.

Soon after doing this, he developed attachments so that bikes could be transported on the same rack. Though a number of companies built racks to transport bikes and canoes, there was no company that built one rack that could accommodate a variety of products. Today Yakima manufactures state-of-the-art roof racks designed to fit all vehicles. The racks hold sports equipment, including snowboards, kayaks, sailboards, canoes, skis, and bicycles.

Yakima, like Ben and Jerry's has become a good neighbor in the town of Arcata and believes in worker empowerment. The company offers full medical and dental benefits, has paid for employee drug and alcohol recovery programs, and has hired developmentally challenged workers. Otto has since died but is remembered on the company letterhead, which carries the words often spoken by him, "Let us serve with honesty, wisdom, and skill."

Multidimensional Corporations

Reed International P.L.C.

Reed International is a world leader in publishing and information systems. It is an international company with an established base in the United Kingdom, United States, and Australia, and it is expanding its operations in Asia and continental Europe. The company has six business segments that include consumer publishing, business to business publishing, exhibitions, reference publishing, books, and travel and information services.

Consumer publishing is comprised of IPC Magazines and Reed Regional Newspapers. IPC Magazines has fifty-four titles in its portfolio, including the hobby-related publications *Amateur Gardening, Golf Monthly, Amateur Photographer, Yachting World, Angler's Mail,* and *Cycling Weekly.*

Business to business publishing is handled by Reed Business Publishing (RBP) with a portfolio of eighty-eight titles, including *Flight International* and *Caterer & Hotelkeeper.* Most of these titles are published in the United Kingdom. The remainder are published in France, Holland, and Australia. The U.S. publications are handled by Cahners Publishing Company and include *Sail, Variety, Hotels,* and *Restaurants & Institutions.*

Reed Exhibition Companies (REC) is one of the leading organizers of exhibitions and handles over 287 events in 25 countries. In 1992, they organized exhibitions in North America, Europe, and Asia/Pacific that drew approximately 7.5 million customers and attracted over 60,000 companies that wished to exhibit (Reed International 1992: 22). Exhibitions included Asian Aerospace, Singapore, World Travel Market, London, International Stationery and Office Product, Tokyo, the Canadian High Technology Show, and Hotelympia. Hotelympia has been in existence and is the United Kingdom's largest single event for the hotel and catering industry. It attracted a record 57,500 buyers in 1992.

Reed Reference Publishing (RRP) published business reference materials, biographical and bibliographical books, and nonprint media including

CD-ROM. Publications of interest include the *Standard Directory of Advertising Agencies, Broadcasting & Cable Market Place,* the *Yearbook of International Organization,* and corporate information for public and private companies (*Directory of Corporate Affiliations* and *Directory of Leading Private Companies*).

The last Reed business segment, Reed Telepublishing, contains three divisions. The largest of these divisions is Reed Travel Group, the world's largest travel publishing company. The main products for this division are the *ABC World Airways Guide, Hotel & Travel Index,* and Utell (an independent hotel representation and reservation group). Reed Travel Group has 70 offices in 35 countries. Two periodicals (*Travel Weekly* and *Meetings & Conventions*) and two guides (the *Official Meeting Facilities Guide* and the *Official Hotel Guide*) make Reed International a world leader in publishing and providing industry-related information.

These are examples of small and large companies that manufacture and sell industry-related products. Some are more socially responsible than others. Some exist with small, relatively flat organizational structures, and others mirror the corporate image that most of us have of businesses in North America. They are a minuscule sample of the thousands of other companies in North America and around the world that develop and manufacture industry-related products.

Interesting, but So What?

James Burke, in his book *Connections,* details the evolution of the ideas and inventions that have resulted in today's technology. Burke's book and his award-winning television series of the same title explore the development of the computer, production line, telecommunications industry, airplane, atomic bomb, plastics industry, guided rocket, and television. The book "untangles the pattern of interconnecting events, the accidents of time, circumstance, and place that gave rise to these inventions and a host of related discoveries along the way" (Burke 1978: back cover). It is this same concept of interconnection and interrelatedness that we need to explore and apply to commercial recreation and tourism. It is the marriage of an idea with technology, and the resulting application to commercial recreation and tourism businesses by the allied industries, that determine tomorrow's recreational products and ultimately its services.

At this very moment there are people thinking about how to make a better athletic shoe, fishing pole, roller coaster, sound system, or snow ski. They want a golf ball that will fly farther, a sailboat that will go faster, a tennis racket that will annihilate their opponent, or a special effect that will wow the crowd. Perhaps they have been watching children play (or better yet) maybe they have been playing with the children and to get an idea for a new or better toy or game. They have all kinds of ideas (although one good one will do) about how to make a product better or how to create a new product that consumers will readily receive. These are the people who create and then produce industry products. They may distribute these products themselves or sell them to others for distribution. One thing is for sure, without their products the industry would be a lot less interesting and a lot less profitable.

Some of you may be excited about the opportunities available in commercial recreation and tourism but are not really sure how to integrate them into your life. What you have read in this text so far does not quite match up with your background, interests, and skills—yet, it sounds exciting. You are interested in producing, not selling or servicing, recreational products. The idea of creating a new and better product, or refining an old product, appeals to you. The allied industries may be your area—perhaps you have found your niche?

Summary

The word allied means connected. For commercial recreation and tourism, the allied industries are those that design, manufacture, and distribute the products that are needed to deliver programs and satisfy customers.

The allied industries are often overlooked as an important part of the total spectrum of commercial recreation and tourism. They are essential to the workings of the industry. Most people like and want what is new and innovative. Having, selling, or renting the fastest set of snow skis, the lightest touring bicycle, or the most spectacular pyrotechnic display is what gives one commercial recreation and tourism business the edge. The allied industries are responsible for providing the tools for the safe, innovative, and creative delivery of commercial recreation and tourism businesses.

The World Tourism Organization (WTO) has recognized the importance of the allied industries and has established the Standard International Classification of Tourism Activities (SICTA). Although the main purpose of SICTA is not to classify industries, goods, or services, but rather to track economic activity, it does identify many of the areas that contain the allied industries.

The allied industries range in size from small entrepreneurial enterprises to large multidimensional, multinational, corporations. They may have started in business with the intent of producing products for the commercial recreation and tourism market, or they may have discovered the market by chance.

The allied industries offer additional career opportunities for those who are interested in commercial recreation and tourism. They are vital to the delivery of services and allow the industry to offer the best possible experiences, programs, and services to its customers.

Discussion Questions

1. Which allied industries are most important to commercial recreation and tourism? How did you arrive at this conclusion?
2. According to SICTA, how do we know when an industry is an allied industry for commercial recreation and tourism?
3. What other opportunities and/or allied industries could be listed in this chapter?

Chapter Exercises

1. Look in your local telephone directory. What allied industries can you find that service commercial recreation and tourism businesses in your area?
2. Visit a travel agency, CVB, airport, restaurant, hotel, or other commercial recreation and tourism site. Who are the suppliers for this business?
3. Write to a supplier of products for the delivery of services for commercial recreation and tourism and ask them for information regarding their product(s).

References

Amusement business. 31 January–6 February 1994, 7–13 March 1994.

Bauer, Janet. 1992. Accommodating travelers with disabilities. *Hotels.* (November): 137.

Brandt, Richard, Neil Grass, Peter Coy, et al. 1994. Sega: It's blasting beyond games and racing to build a high-tech entertainment empire. *Business Week* (21 February): 66–74.

Burke, James. 1978. *Connections.* Boston: Little Brown and Company.

Chai, Alan, Alta Campbell, and Patrick J. Spain. 1993. *Hoover's handbook of world business 1993.* Austin, TX: Reference Press.

Hoover, Gary, Alta Campbell, and Patrick J. Spain. 1994. *Hoover's handbook of American business 1994.* Austin, TX: Reference Press.

Jones, Constance, and The Philip Lief Group. 1993. *The 220 best franchises to buy.* New York: Bantam Books.

Lager, Fred. 1994. *Ben & Jerry's: The inside scoop.* New York: Crown Publishers, Inc.

Moskowitz, Milton, Robert Levering, and Michael Katz. 1990. *Everybody's business: A field guide to the 400 leading companies in America.* New York: Doubleday.

Recreation resources. November/December 1991, July/August 1993, September 1993, November/December 1993.

Reed International P.L.C. 1992. *Annual report.*

Sadie, Stanley, ed. 1980. *The new Grove dictionary of music and musicians.* London: Macmillan Publisher Limited.

Scott, Mary, and Howard Rothman. 1994. *Companies with a conscience.* New York: Citadel Press.

Special events. March 1994.

Strasser, J. B., and Laurie Becklund. 1993. *Swoosh: The unauthorized story of Nike and the men who played there.* New York: Harper Business.

Stynes, Daniel J. 1993. Leisure—The new center of the economy? *National Recreation and Park Association SPRE Newsletter.* (August/September): 15–20.

United Nations. 1993, *Recommendations on Tourism Statistics.* World Tourism Organization.

What's new for family fun centers. January/February 1994.

Additional Resources

Following are just a few sources for recreation-related industries. There are literally thousands of resources available. Check with your local reference librarian to find names and addresses of industries that will be useful for your specific needs or look in the yellow pages of your telephone directory.

International Robotics, Inc.
611 Broadway
Suite 422
New York, NY 10012
(212) 982–8001

Soft Play, Inc. (USA)
6801-1 North Park Blvd.
Charlotte, NC 28216
1–800–782–PLAY

Lazer Fantasy
1721 132nd Ave. NE
Bellevue, WA 98005
(206) 881–5356

Chance Rides, Inc.
P.O. Box 12328
Wichita, KS 67277–2328
(316) 942–7411

IWERKS Entertainmant (specialty movie
theater technology and films)
4540 West Valerio St.
Burbank, CA 91505
(818) 841–7766

Zamperla, Inc. (amusement rides)
49 Fanny Rd.
P.O. Box 5545
Parsippany, NJ 07054
(201) 334–8133

Landmark Entertainment Group
(design/production)
5200 Lankershim Blvd.
No. Hollywood, CA 91601
(818) 753–6700

Creative Presentations, Inc.
24907 Anza Dr.
Valencia, CA 91355
(805) 295–1983

Omni Films International, Inc.
P.O. Box 5807
Sarasota, Flordia 34277–5807
(813) 924–4239

Funtime Playgrounds, Inc.
Charter St.
Albemarle, NC 28001
(704) 982–0972

Amtronics, Inc. (digital imaging systems)
P.O. Box 24190
New Orleans, LA 70184
(504) 831–0691

JOCO Enterprises (inflatibles)
5117 West Waltann Ln.
Glendale, AZ 85306
(602) 978–3100

The Robot Works, Inc.
4366 L.B. McLeod Rd.
Orlando, Flordia 32811
(407) 648–4748

Surf Coaster Corporation
212 Crest Rd.
Cape May Court House, NJ 08210
(609) 465–8000

Audio Visual Imagineering, Inc.
Laser 3-D
7953 Twist Ln.
Springfield, VA 22153
(703) 569–7646

Proslide Technology, Inc.
98 Rue de l'Eglise
ST–Sauveur des–Monts
Quebec, Canada J0R 1R4
(819) 827–4281

Zambelli Internationale (pyrotechnics)
P.O. Box 1463
New Castle, PA 16103
(412) 658–6611

MedX (fitness)
1401 NE 77th St.
Ocala, FL 34479

Intamin AG (major amusement rides and
transportation systems)
Verenastrasse 37
Wollerau, 8832
Switzerland
41–17869111

Managing Your Career

LEARNING OBJECTIVES

1. *To discuss the competitive importance of experiential learning and career services when preparing for employment.*
2. *To introduce the concept and significance of finding a mentor.*
3. *To discuss how interests, talents, and skills relate to finding a satisfying niche in the world of work.*
4. *To instill a sense of personal responsibility for one's own career management.*

Introduction

Perhaps this chapter should be called Managing Your Life rather than Managing Your Career. While some people manage to keep their personal life and their work separate, many of us find that they often intertwine. This is not necessarily good and it is not necessarily bad, it is just something to think about when making career choices.

You have probably thought about your future. Perhaps you have identified some of the characteristics that you would want in your ideal job or your perfect partner. You might have decided where you would like to live and work, how many children you would like to have, and what kind of living arrangements would best suit the lifestyle that you would like to lead. Perhaps you have even thought about retirement.

Others of you have been busy struggling to make it through the day, week, or month. Planning for the future has been something that you will get to "later," perhaps at the end of the semester, or when you have time. Things are really hectic now, and there just does not seem to be an opportunity for you to sit down and contemplate these things. Your vision has been focused on subsisting until time presents you with the opportunity to think and talk about these decisions, but this never seems to happen. Somewhere between these two scenarios lies a more realistic model of how you should be planning for the future. What you need is a plan.

A plan is a road map that will take you from where you are now to where you would like to be in two years, ten years, twenty years, or even fifty years. But (some of you may be thinking) even with a plan, few things in life rarely happen exactly as designed. If this is true, does this mean that you do not really need a plan? No, it does not. Without a plan, you do not know where you are going. This type of life management may work well for some, but most of us need direction and purpose.

People are not static—they are subject to change. Plans are also not static; they are modified and redefined as we change and grow. As we travel to where we think we want to be, we are often presented with interesting and exciting opportunities. The ability to see how these opportunities fit into our lives, and the courage to try new and challenging experiences, is part of being human. So, how do you go about formulating your plan?

Identifying Your Career Skills

Everyone possesses interests, talents, and skills. You may share some of these attributes with members of your family. You may be a born salesperson like your father or have a gift for organizing large projects like your Aunt Nancy, but the sum total of who you are is unique. You are the product of your acquired interests, talents, and skills. All of these things have been tempered by experiences that have happened only to you—making you truly one-of-a-kind. While other people may know and love you (like your parents and family), nobody other than yourself has a better chance of knowing exactly what you are capable of doing and what you are interested in. But how well do you know yourself?

It is often difficult for us to look at ourselves. It is much easier, and a lot more fun, to look at others and determine what they are like. But you aren't stuck with them, you are stuck with yourself. Now (right now!) would be a good time for you to really get to know yourself and then get busy formulating a plan for your future.

What Interests You?

Something that interests us gets our attention. It may fascinate and excite us when we see it, hear it, or are near it. Some students are interested in traveling, being in the wilderness, going to concerts, or attending festivals and special events. You may have an interest that is very specific—a love of fishing, airplanes, shopping, or dining in interesting restaurants.

Have you thought about combining what interests you with what you will do to make your living? Some people feel that when they graduate they must get an "adult" job, put aside frivolous activities and interests, and get serious. Has it occurred to you that you might be able to work in an area that excites and interests you while making your living, and that going to work could actually be fun?

What Talents Do You Possess?

Talent is a gift that we are born with, and yes, we all have talent (although it seems to be given to us in various degrees). Talent is the ability to do something well intuitively—without thinking about it very much. Talent needs to be developed; when ignored, it can disappear. There are many talented people who never recognize, use, or develop their gift.

We usually think of a talented person as being someone who is a gifted artist, musician, writer, performer, or athlete. But having talent includes other things, such as listening to and understanding people, being creative, recognizing and solving problems, having an "ear" for languages other than our native tongue, or seeing situations from unique and unusual perspectives. Although these things can be learned to some extent, there are those among us who are very good at doing them with little practice. Do you know what talents you posses?

What Skills Have You Acquired?

Skills are acquired through education, experience, or a combination of both of these factors. Examples of skills include having good speaking and writing abilities and being able to manage time effectively. People are not born knowing how to do these things. They acquire the knowledge through education and practice.

Other skills include knowing how to use tools, run machinery, or fix things that are broken. Perhaps you know how to design theatrical sets or how to make costumes. Maybe you are a whiz at cruising along on the highways of the Internet, or at using sophisticated technology such as lasers, lighting, or sound boards. Someone probably taught you how to do these things. You probably practiced, sometimes for long periods of time, to perfect the skill that you had been taught.

How Can Knowing This Help Me?

The ability to identify your interests, talents, and skills will make you more marketable in the world of work. Employers in the '90s are looking for people who not only have college degrees and book knowledge, but who have diverse backgrounds. Knowing what you have to offer to an employer will help you explain why you are the perfect candidate for the job that is being advertised. This information will also help you:

- Identify things that you don't do well and don't care to do well.
- Identify skills that you may need but do not yet possess.
- Know when you have found a match between who you are and the type of career opportunity presented to you.
- Know when it is time to move on to another position.

If you have no interests, have not discovered your talents, and have nothing to list under the skills category, then you have a lot of work to do and had better get busy.

Career Services

Most colleges and universities provide a service to help students identify their interests and skills. Staffed by skilled counselors and available to all students, it may be called Career Planning, Career Services, or any other combination of titles. The name is not important; it is what happens there that is of value.

While services differ from university to university, many campuses will offer help with career planning. Some institutions will offer testing services to help you identify your personality traits. They might even suggest careers that may interest you based on those traits. Some of you might think that this type of testing may be interesting as a parlor game, but let me assure you that it can work in your own life and be right on target.

In undergraduate school I went to the career services office at my college and took a test to learn about my personality traits and interests. The traits identified were not much of a surprise, but the career suggestions got my attention—teacher, forest ranger, and mechanic. I had always known that I wanted to be a teacher, but a forest ranger? A mechanic!?

I left the office thinking that although the experience of taking the test had been fun, the people who had made it up must have spent too much time in the sun. My friends and family knew that I wanted to be a teacher, and I had a great time teasing them by telling everyone how, someday, I would be a forest ranger or a mechanic rather than a teacher.

I did become a teacher, and in the years since taking the test I have had to eat many of the words and swallow many of the smug comments that I had made after taking that test. I did not become a forest ranger, but I did become a ranger for the National Park Service. And although I did not become a mechanic, I do have a shop in the basement of my home, which is full of wrenches, saws, routers, sanders, biscuit joiners, square-headed screws, and other assorted tools and machines. Perhaps I was the one who had been in the sun too long?

Testing is only one aspect of what career services may offer. They probably have resources and information about graduate schools, prospective employers, etc. Sometimes they will have on-campus recruitment days, where employers come to campus to interview job applicants. They may also arrange for recruiters from graduate schools to come to campus to meet potential candidates. Audio and video information about campus majors, outside employers, and the job requirements of different positions and professions might also be available. Other services provided might include the following:

Seminars on a variety of career topics
Resume-writing workshops

Information regarding career paths
Computerized job-matching service
Individualized career counseling
An alumni network
Self-study "how to" tapes
Practice interviews

If you have a career services office or department at your college or university, you may want to stop by and see what services are available. Ask them if they are a member of the College Placement Council (CPC), Inc. This is the national association for the career planning, placement, and recruitment field. Although the mission of the CPC is to serve professionals in the field, membership indicates that your career placement office has access to the information, statistical data, and training programs that are offered.

Experiential Learning

Suppose that your experience and exposure to your potential career has been minimal or nonexistent. It is not that you haven't worked, but you just haven't worked in your declared area of interest. You have done the usual things—babysitting, paper route, cashier at a local store. How do you start to accumulate the experience that employers are going to look for when you have finally completed your course of study and are looking for that real job that we discussed earlier?

Experiential learning is the phrase that is being used to unify a concept that is called by many names. The concept is that students need to have exposure to the working world in general, and to the working world in their area of interest in particular, as they are learning in their classes. Since most students work while in college anyway, why not channel these work experiences into real-life career experiences that will be beneficial now and after graduation. The names that often appear under the heading of experiential learning include: internship, practicum, field experience, and cooperative education.

Colleges and universities in both Canada and the United States recognize the importance of experiential learning to their programs. Cooperative education the precusor to experiential learning originated in the United States in 1906. Herman Schneider, a civil engineer, is recognized as the founder of the cooperative education movement. An 1894 graduate of Lehigh University, Schneider returned to become an instructor at Lehigh after working in his field. At Lehigh, he planned and researched the "cooperative" method of training engineers. Schneider knew that most students worked at least part-time while they went to college. He also knew that some things were best learned by doing them rather than by just reading about them. Schneider wanted Lehigh to offer students an opportunity to combine their classroom learning with practical experience. Unfortunately, the university did not share Schneider's vision and rejected his proposal.

These commercial recreation and tourism students are participating in the ultimate cooperative education experience. They have traveled half-way around the world to the Madarao Kogen Resort in Iiyama-shi, Nagano-ken, Japan. Located in a rural area 4 hours north of Tokyo, the students worked for this family-oriented resort and had an opportunity to tour the rest of Japan.
Photo: Ross Miller.

In 1903, Schneider left Lehigh and went to the University of Cincinnati. By 1905 the Board of Trustees at Cincinnati had approved, with some reservations, his idea for cooperative education, and by 1906 the plan was implemented. His original plan called for two groups of students to alternate, on a weekly basis, classroom learning and experience.

> It was not long before the benefits of the cooperative plan became manifest. Classroom learning was reinforced by job responsibilities. New knowledge, understandings, and skills were developed. Students were provided extraordinary opportunities for testing the appropriateness of their career choices, their interests, their abilities, and their temperaments (Hunt 1987: introduction).

It took three years before the second cooperative education program was instituted by the Polytechnic School of the YMCA Evening Institute in Boston, Massachusetts. This school later became Northeastern University, which has been long known for its cooperative education program.

Cooperative education arrived in Canada in 1958. The Canadian Association for Co-operative (sic) Education (CAFCE) has formulated the following definition for cooperative education:

> Co-operative Education Program is a program that formally integrates a student's academic studies with work experience in co-operative employer organizations. The usual plan is for the student to alternate periods of experience in appropriate fields of business, industry, government, social services and the professions according to the following *criteria:*

i) Each work situation is developed and/or approved by the Co-operative Educational Institution as a suitable learning situation.

ii) The co-operative education student is engaged in productive work rather than merely observing.

iii) The co-operative education student receives remuneration for the work performed.

iv) The co-operative education student's progress on the job is monitored by the Co-operative Education Institution.

v) The co-operative education student's performance on the job is supervised and evaluated by the student's employer.

vi) The total co-operative work experience is normally fifty percent of the time spent in academic study, and in no circumstances less than thirty percent (*Co-operative Education* 1993: 3–4).

The benefits of participating in a cooperative education program are many. Students earn money to help defray their college expenses. They also gain experience and have opportunities to network with professionals who are in the workplace. Goodwill opportunities exist for establishing links between the university and the workplace, and feedback is given to the university by the marketplace concerning suggestions for the curriculum.

Sometimes there are other opportunities for students to gain experience, in addition to cooperative education. They may be shorter, less intense opportunities for growth, or they may be built into class requirements. Whatever they are—field experiences, practicums, class requirements, or internships—it would be wise to experience as many of them as possible during your academic career. They will help you to determine what you would ultimately like to do in the industry and they may become entries on your resume. Certainly you will meet interesting people in the field, and it is possible that one of these individuals may be the one to offer you, or help you find, your first postgraduate job.

What Is a Mentor?

One of the best definitions of the word mentor is the following: A mentor is a trusted teacher or guide. We could all use a mentor to help us in life, and you need to look for one to help you with your career. Finding a mentor is not necessarily an easy task; it is not like being assigned a faculty or departmental advisor. One of your professors may become your mentor, or perhaps it will be someone that you meet while doing experiential learning.

Mentoring involves both psychological as well as career support. This is a counseling relationship, where your mentor helps you grow in both your professional and your everyday life. Your mentor helps you develop your own identity and becomes your guide as you explore questions, discover new interests, and analyze events and occurrences. Having a mentor has been referred to as having a "career partner" (Schweitzer 1993: 50).

A mentor is someone to whom you feel connected and who feels connected to you. The mentor-student relationship can occur on several levels. It can be a very powerful relationship that can change the lives of both the mentor and the student. As you both grow, the relationship often changes and the student becomes the mentor.

Work in the New Millennium

The first thing that you need to know about work in the new millennium is that the world of work is changing. Richard Bolles refers to what is happening in the workplace as a "workquake" (Bolles 1994: 10).

A workquake is a major shake-up and reorganization of the way that work is organized. According to Bolles, today's workquake has occurred as a result of several factors. The excesses of the '80s have left us with massive debt. We have all heard the predictions concerning the uncertain state of our economy as a result of our spend-now, pay later philosophy.

The workplace has not been immune to the economic realities of the 1990s as related to debt and to competition from Asia and the developing nations. In both the public and the private sectors downsizing is the theme song of the workplace as companies and corporations seek to cut costs and create leaner, meaner organizations. Even the military has been downsizing by reducing troop size through discharge and tightened admission requirements.

Leaner paychecks and a lower standard of living have been passed down to employees. Less hiring of full-time employees and increased hiring of part-time workers and temporaries has resulted as managers try to contain expenses by controlling costs for wages and benefits. Unions have struggled to maintain their status and position, while one of the most powerful of workers' rights, job security, has eroded.

All this is not meant to sound grim. It is just a statement concerning some of the changes that are occurring. Understanding what is happening now, and looking at what may happen in the future, will help you formulate your plan.

What Will the Workplace Look Like in the Near Future?

There is no doubt that the world of work has been changing and that it will continue to change in the near future. One of the predicted changes is that, by the year 2000, women and minorities will comprise more than half of the total workforce.

> More than 21 million new workers will enter the workforce by the year 2000: 29 percent will be Hispanics, 16 percent will be African-American, 11 percent will be Asian (or other), and 44 percent will be white (Strasser and Sena 1993: 11).

This diversity of people will bring strength as well as challenge to the workers and mangers of tomorrow's businesses and corporations.

The changing face of the workforce will mean that different languages (and lunches) will be coming to work each day. Some of us will find this threatening. Others will be curious. Still others will find this an exciting opportunity to learn about those who are different from us, and some of us just will not care.

People from different cultures bring with them different values, norms, and customs, and that means that we have fewer shared experiences. Here is an example of how that works: My sister-in-law was born and raised in Dublin, Ireland. We share some common holidays, Christmas, Easter, and New Year's Eve. We do not share Thanksgiving, Fourth of July, Memorial Day, and Halloween. The first holiday that our family celebrated together in America was Thanksgiving. To my sister-in-law, this was definitely not a holiday. The concept of eating turkey with all the trimmings was totally strange to her, and although she was polite, she let me know that it was also a little silly. "Why turkey?" she asked me. "I don't know, it's tradition based upon the first Thanksgiving," I replied, "Besides, I've eaten turkey every Thanksgiving of my life and I'm not going to change now." But change I did. We talked about the significance of this holiday and added items to the menu that held some importance for everyone. Ultimately we decided that the most important issue was not the food that we ate, but the shared experience of being together to give thanks for what we had.

Christmas was the second major holiday that we celebrated together. After Thanksgiving, we were all prepared to face the prospect of "fine tuning" our Christmas customs and fashioning a new ritual that integrated the best of Irish, American, and family customs and rituals. Christmas was a shared experience for us, and although we celebrated differently, at least we were all in agreement regarding the importance of this holiday as part of our lives. The only Christmas glitch occurred not with my Irish sister-in-law, but with my sister. She had just converted to Judaism. This presented a whole new set of challenges and opportunities as well as a whole new set of holidays.

The ability to broaden your experience without losing your center is an important skill. The addition of my sister-in-law and the conversion of my sister gave me an opportunity to learn about another country and another religion. The adjustments made by everyone helped us to integrate our past experiences with our present experiences and create new customs and rituals.

The new millennium will also bring new jobs—not necessarily in numbers of jobs, but in job responsibilities and descriptions. These jobs do not exist now, but will exist in the next ten, twenty, and thirty-plus years. Maybe you know someone whose job ceased to exist and who has had to retrain for a new position. If you do not know someone personally, you have probably seen the television documentaries detailing the closing of steel mills and other large and small industries. The workers at these sites have become displaced and will not be returning to their old jobs—they need new ones. Some will successfully retrain for traditional jobs. Others may experience difficulty adjusting and become lost in the transition. And a third group will train for jobs that did not exist when they started to work. They might sell or

Industries providing services will account for about four out of five jobs by the year 2005.
U.S. Department of Labor
Bureau of Labor Statistics.

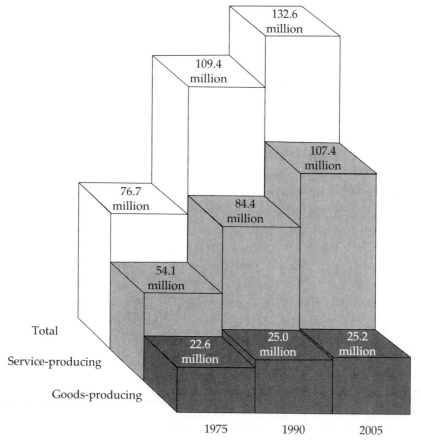

Non-farm wage and salary employment

service computers, fax machines, and other forms of new products and technologically created commodities. They may retrain for positions in the service industry and become consultants, entrepreneurs, or franchise owners.

We no longer need firemen to stoke the furnaces of coal-running trains, and business can no longer afford to protect positions that hinder productivity and make it more difficult to compete. The point is that there are no guarantees that your job, or my job, will last forever. As you prepare now for what you think you wish to do when you graduate, you must also prepare for a possible future job that does not yet exist.

Positioning Yourself for the Challenge

What Can You Do to Get Ready?

The first thing that you can do is to be selective about the courses that you take while completing your education. Every program has requirements that you must fulfill as well as electives. Pick your electives wisely by making sure that the courses that you take will help you in the future. Take the more difficult course with the more demanding professor. Remind yourself that a B in a tough challenging course is more valuable to you in the long run than an A in a course where all you are required to do is breathe.

Yes, I know that you have to work and yes, I know that your parents want you to hurry up and graduate, but stop and think about this. Graduating in four years has become the exception rather than the rule for college students. Take your time and *pay attention* to all your courses, not just the ones in your major. Consider the following:

> A student recently asked me if she was taking the "right" courses for her future in advertising. When I told her that, for the most part, the courses themselves did not matter, she said that maybe she should major in XXX so it would be easier to get a good GPA (Rotfeld 1994: 11).

Or how about the following comment:

> I once saw a letter from a top journalism graduate who lost his job after being assigned to the science beat, writing to his former teacher at Penn State: "I wish I paid better attention in Sci 4 [a general education required science course], but I never thought I'd need to know that stuff again (Rotfeld 1994: 11).

There used to be an oil filter commercial on television that used the phrase, "You can pay me now, or you can pay me later." If we all understand the benefits of changing the oil filter and oil in our automobiles now, rather than replacing our engines later, perhaps we could all understand that the same principle applies to our education. The future will be competitive, and projections indicate that while more people than ever will be entering the workforce, openings will be fewer.

Positioning yourself for the future includes joining professional organizations now. Most professionals belong to a professional association or society. We have already discussed what benefits you can derive from belonging to one and Appendix G contains a listing of professional organizations that may interest you. Your department and certainly your professors will belong to one, if not several, organizations.

Write and find out about the interests served and services provided by these organizations. Find out if there is a student rate for joining and if there is a local chapter of the parent organization near you. If there is a local chapter, attend their meetings and start to meet professionals who are in the field. Read the publications, journals, and reports that are published and distributed by them. Attend their conferences, seminars, and trade shows. "The average person has to go job-hunting eight times in his or her life" (Bolles 1994: xi), so start to network now.

Do an excellent job when participating in experiential learning programs. The world gets smaller every day and you never know when you will meet someone again. How you handle yourself says volumes about

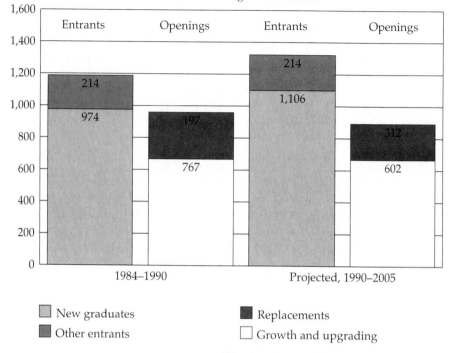

College graduates entering the labor force and job openings, 1984–1990 and projected 1990–2005.

U.S. Dept. of Labor, Bureau of Labor Statistics. The College Labor Market: Outlook, Current Situation, and Earnings—Reprinted from the Summer 1992 Issue of the Occupational Outlook Quarterly, p. 9.

Annual average in thousands

| New graduates | Replacements |
| Other entrants | Growth and upgrading |

who you are. If you find yourself working with someone who is difficult (or impossible), maintain the level of professionalism that you expect to practice for the remainder of your career. You might also want to speak with your mentor to gain some perspective on what is happening.

Meet your classmates and find out what their interests are. Look to interact with alumni from your department and/or college. Speak to students who have traveled to or lived in other countries. Travel yourself, even if you can only afford to travel locally.

Attend a festival that celebrates a culture other than your own. Read newspapers and magazines that will inform you about what is happening in the world at large. Watch television programs that are on public television or discuss current issues. Avoid programs and newspapers with headlines such as "Aliens Kidnapped Me and Stole My Blood!" Rather than watching the beautiful people on the daytime soaps, go out and get a life of your own.

Continue to work on identifying your interests and developing your talents and skills. This is a life-long process that starts, not ends, when you graduate. Someday you may decide to return to school for an advanced degree. If the thought of this does not appeal to you, then there are other options for you to take so that you can continue to learn. There are the workshops, seminars, and in-service training that may be provided through your job. There are also continuing education courses and certification programs that will help you stay current in the industry. You should never stop learning. While you are resting on your laurels, the job or the promotion will go to the person who has kept up with the changes and advances in the field.

Certification

The National Organization for Competency Assurance (NOCA) is the certifying body that sets the criteria and standards for agencies offering certification. It is the only national organization that meets the needs of certification professionals in all fields of interest. NOCA certifies the certifiers. In addition, the International Association for Continuing Education and Training (IACET) is a nonprofit organization that sets standards for the offering of continuing education units or CEU's. Taking a program that has been approved by them, or at least meets their standards, will assure that you receive a quality experience.

Learn How to Use Technology

Make friends with technology. It is here whether you like it or not. There were no personal computers, cellular phones, fax machines, and easily accessible copying machines when I started my career—and no, I am not 100 years old. There will be new technology arriving during your career, and you need to master what is currently available in order to prepare yourself for what is to come.

Technology changes exponentially. The high-tech computer of today is next year's discounted clearance model. Manufacturers race to make their products faster, more economical to own, easier to use, and indispensable to your everyday life. It is not important to know how all this happens, but it is important to know how to use all this technology to your advantage.

Using etiquette when we interact with others keeps life civilized. Communicating by computer has led to the acceptance of nettiquette for the same purpose. Common nettiquette tells us to keep messages short so that we don't tie up the system, to watch what we say and NOT TO SHOUT WHEN WE SPEAK ON THE COMPUTER. *"Nettiquette."*

The problem of not being able to hear the intonations used when communicating or to see body language, has been compensated for by the use of symbols. Here are some popularly used symbols.

:-X	I won't tell	:-@	Scream
%-)	I'm so confused	:-(	I'm upset/depressed
:-D	That's funny	;-)	I'm flirting or sarcastic
>:-<	I'm very angry	:-)	I'm joking or happy
:*	Kiss	>:->	This is a devilish comment

To see how the symbols represent emotions, turn your book sideways.

Without a doubt, the personal computer has become one of the most powerful tools of the twentieth century. It permeates not only our homes but also our workplaces. Word processing, mail merge, and spreadsheet programs have made it easier to correspond with people, to keep records of all kinds, and to crunch out presentation-ready charts and graphics. The use of electronic mail (E-mail) has eliminated much of the snail mail (paper mail) that used to be our main way of sending messages to one another both internally (in the workplace) and externally (to the world at large). Talking directly to individuals, interest groups, or local bulletin boards via computer gives us access to vast amounts of information. Individuals who are shy or who have difficulty making first contact with others find that using a computer is a great way for them to gain entrance to information and to communicate with other people. You can send and receive information, make inquiries, and meet others who may help you locate jobs or put you in contact with potential opportunities. Cruising the Internet creates even greater opportunities and challenges.

The Internet is an international communication system that allows you to cruise the computer highways around the world. It is the ultimate networking tool. The promise of the Internet is access to all kinds of information and the ability to correspond with people from all over the world. The problem with the Internet is that it becomes easy to get so busy cruising those highways and talking to those people, that we do not have time to do other things.

Know What Employers Want

Employers are looking for a set of skills rather than a particular major. Management trainee positions are vanishing, and companies and corporations are looking for individuals who possess skills that they can readily use. You are most likely to get hired if you have professional experience, and many employers use experiential learning situations to prescreen potential hirees. This means that the selection of an experience that is challenging and has the potential for growth, rather than one that is repetitive but pays well and is close to home, is more likely to pay off in the long run.

Employers are looking for employees who are well written and well spoken. Being multilingual is another desirable and marketable quality. Computer literacy, self-motivation, being a team player, and being a generalist with technical skills are all attributes that prospective employers seek in new employees.

Putting It All Together

No career or job decision is forever. Tens of thousands of workers spend their days plotting their escape from jobs that they view as oppressive and/or boring. They live for the two days of each week, and the two weeks each year, when they are liberated from their desks and their duties.

Calvin and Hobbes

by Bill Watterson

Supposedly you are in school to get an education so that you will be able to use this education to increase the quality of your life. Increasing the quality of your life happens two ways, financially and mentally in the awakening of your consciousness to the possibilities that are available to you. Strasser and Sena tell us:

> The purpose of education is to liberate you, to free you from your former limitations—allowing you to undertake any manner of career, do any type of job, even ones that do not yet exist. So don't panic, and don't sell yourself short. If you have developed the ability to think logically, to analyze coherently, and to express your thoughts cogently and persuasively, you are qualified for the vast majority of jobs out there (Strasser and Sena 1993: 25).

They further remind us that our work is what we do and it is not what or who we are (Strasser and Sena 1993: 23).

You will be faced with countless decisions during your academic journey. Should I take the easier course? Should I go to the party rather than write that paper that is due? If everyone else does it, why shouldn't I do it as well? In the end it all comes down to the fact that book knowledge without self-knowledge and self-respect is nothing. You are responsible for the managing of your own career. Be the best manager that you possibly can be :-)

Summary

The world of work has been rapidly changing and will continue to change throughout your lifetime. Although we can only speculate about what work will be like in the future, we can state with some certainty that many of the skills that you acquire now will be transferable.

No career or job description lasts forever. In addition, thousands of people spend their days silently plotting their escape from what they perceive as tedious and unrewarding job experiences. It is not inevitable that work be like this. Proper management and cultivation of your career now, can lead you to an appropriate career match when you finish your education. In the end it is important for you to remember that you are personally responsible for your own career management.

In order to prepare yourself for the future, you need to have a plan. Part of your plan should consist of identifying and understanding your interests, skills, and talents. This is important, because you will be able to work on areas that need improvement and to honestly state to potential employers what strengths you possess. In addition, understanding this information will help you match your personal requirements and abilities with an appropriate career opportunity.

In addition to exploring your personal qualities, you should take advantage of the available services offered by your college or university that can help you prepare for work. Experiential learning programs and career services are two programs that can be very helpful. Additional choices that you can make include taking courses that will help you later, rather than taking courses that fit nicely into your schedule, and meeting a variety of different individuals. Understanding others from your own country and from other parts of the world will broaden your horizons and will help you prepare for the larger world community.

Discussion Questions

1. What kinds of courses should students who are studying commercial recreation and tourism take to complement their major courses?
2. What kind of life strategy would help you to remain prepared for the changes that will be happening in the world of work during your lifetime?
3. How will the fact that more than half of the workforce will consist of women and minorities by the year 2000 change the workplace?
4. If you do not have career services or cooperative education at your school, how can you acquire the information and experiences that you will need to be successful?

Chapter Exercises

1. Divide a piece of paper into two halves. On one half list your talents and on the other half list your skills.
2. Make your own list of attributes that you would look for in a prospective employee.
3. Visit the offices and people on your campus responsible for student placement in experiential learning or who give assistance with career planning. What services are available to you from these places?
4. Think about what your ideal job would be like. Write down a description of this job. Make a list of what you can do during the next month to help you achieve this vision. Try to extend your plan for the remainder of this course. How about for the next twelve months?

References

Barrows, Clayton W., Charles G. Partlow, and Rhonda J. Montgomery. 1993. Student's perceptions of career opportunities in club management. *Educator* 5, no. 4: 17.

Barrows, Clayton W., and Marise Unkauf. 1993. Enhancing the industry/academe relationship through joint classroom projects. *Educator* 5, no. 4: 21.

Bojanic, David C., and Elizabeth A. Dale. 1993. A survey of convention sales career opportunities. *Educator* 5, no. 4: 41.

Bolles, Richard Nelson. 1994. *What color is your parachute?* Berkeley, CA: Ten Speed Press.

Brownell, Judi. 1993. Addressing career challenges faced by women in hospitality management. *Educator* 5, no. 4: 11.

Butler, Steven, and Susan V. Lawrence. 1993. The lure of the Orient." *U.S. News & World Report* (22 November): 34.

Carlson, Judith B. 1993. Working to learn—The apprenticeship experience. *JOPHERD* (October): 57.

Church, George J. 1993. Jobs in an age of insecurity. *Time* (22 November): 34.

Co-operative education. 1993. Ontario: College Co-operative Educators of Ontario.

Cornish, Jill Martineau. Association jobs offer exciting opportunities. *Job Choices: 1994.* 37th ed. Bethlehem, PA: College Placement Council, Inc.: 9–11.

Epperson, Arlin. 1993. Job competencies of corporate travel executives. *ACTE Quarterly* 5, no. 2: 10.

Heffernan, Cameron J. 1993. Networking: A key to your career. *Hosteur* 3, no. 2: 11.

Hunt, D. C. 1987. *50 views of cooperative education.* Detroit, MI: University of Detroit.

International Association for Continuing Education and Training. 1993. *The continuing education unit criteria and guidelines.* 5th ed. Dubuque, IA: Kendall/Hunt Publishing Company.

Kilborn, Peter T. 1994. College graduates find more jobs but modest pay. *The New York Times* 30 April: 1.

Lazarus, Freyda. 1993. Learning in the academic workplace: Perspectives of cooperative education directors. *Journal of Cooperative Education* 28, no. 1: 67–76.

Lowstuter, Clyde C., and David P. Robertson. 1992. *In search of the perfect job.* New York: McGraw-Hill, Inc.

McKeta, Bob. 1993. Be an intern with the army. *Parks & Recreation* (October): 30.

Montgomery, Rhonda J., and Tom Van Dyke. 1993. An experiential learning activity for a conference and meeting planning course. *Educator* 5, no. 4: 63.

Petras, Kathryn, and Ross Petras. 1993. *Jobs '94.* New York: Simon and Schuster.

Rotfeld, Herbert. 1994. What do students want? *Montclair State University Office of Institutional Assessment Outcomes Bulletin* 6, no. 1: 10–11.

Ryder, Kenneth G., and James W. Wilson. 1987. *Cooperative education in a new era.* San Francisco: Jossey-Bass Publishers.

Schweitzer, Cathie Ann. 1993. Mentoring future professionals. *JOPHERD* (September): 50.

Sciarini, M. 1993. How to develop your network. *Hosteur* 3, no. 2: 5.

Strasser, Stephen, and John Sena. 1993. *From campus to corporation.* Hawthorne, NJ: Career Press.

U.S. Department of Labor. Bureau of Labor Statistics. *Tomorrow's jobs.* Reprinted from the *Occupational outlook handbook,* 1992–93 edition. Washington, D.C.: Government Printing Office. Bulletin 2400-1.

U.S. Department of Labor. Bureau of Labor Statistics. 1992. *The college labor market: Outlook, current situation, and earnings.* Reprinted from *Occupational outlook quarterly* (Summer). Washington, D.C.: Government Printing Office.

Verner, M. Elizabeth. 1993. Developing professionalism through experiential learning. *JOPHERD* (September): 41.

Watkins, Beverly T. 1992. Getting a jump on jobs. *Chronicle of Higher Education* 24 November: A19–20.

Additional Resources

Berman, Jay M., and Theresa A. Cosca. 1992. The job outlook in brief. *Occupational Outlook Quarterly* (Spring): 7–41.

Covey, Stephen R. 1989. *The seven habits of highly effective people: Restoring the character ethic.* New York: Simon and Schuster.

Miller, Mary Fallon. 1991. *How to get a job with a cruise line.* St. Petersburg, FL: Ticket to Adventure, Inc.

Phillips, Linda, Wayne Phillips, and Lynne Rogers. 1990. *The concise guide to executive etiquette.* New York: Mean Street Books.

Soden, Garrett. 1994. *I went to college for this? True stuff about life in the business world and how to make your way through it.* Princeton, NJ: Peterson's.

Stevens, Laurence. 1988. *Your career in travel, tourism, and hospitality.* 6th ed. The Travel Management Library Series. Albany, NY: Delmar Publishers, Inc.

Tichy, Noel M., and Stratford Sherman. 1994. *Control your destiny or someone else will.* New York: Harper Business.

Vance, Sandra S., and Roy V. Scott. 1994. *Walmart: A history of Sam Walton's retail phenomenon.* New York: Twayne Publishers.

Looking Toward the Future

LEARNING OBJECTIVES

1. *To examine the process and purpose of prediction.*
2. *To examine current events in the world at large to see what impact they may have on the future of commercial recreation and tourism.*
3. *To discuss the impact of the coming of the new millennium on the future plans for commercial recreation and tourism enterprises.*
4. *To predict some future trends for commercial recreation and tourism.*

Prediction

Thinking about the future is interesting, because it involves prediction. Other words for prediction are forecast, outlook, projection, prognostication, prophecy—and guess.

How often have you heard the words "the government predicts that . . . ?" Substitute any word that you want for the word government—president, CEO, World Bank, United Nations, manager, it really doesn't matter. The end result is the same. We listen to the prediction (which almost always comes from a powerful person or group), as if it were a fait accompli.

We think of ourselves as modern and scientific people. We use large, sophisticated computer models to forecast weather. We talk about the financial outlook for the coming quarter or fiscal year, and crunch out population projections for the next century, but what we really are doing is guessing. Guessing is acceptable. In fact, at the moment, guessing is the only option.

Responsible people and groups use models rather than crystal balls to make their predictions. They study probability and statistics. They review past performance and trends, and create complicated computer programs to explore all the "what ifs." What if the winter is unusually cold? How will this affect our energy consumption and therefore our pricing? What if the dollar falls and loses purchasing power against the yen, pound, or Deutsch mark? What effect, if any, will this have on travel trends? The "what ifs" are endless.

Prediction is important, but it is not an exact science. One of the variables that keeps muddling up the predictions is the unpredictable nature of human beings. The fall of the Berlin Wall, the radical change in both form and philosophy of the former Soviet Union, and the oil embargoes of the '70s were the results of bold human actions. These kinds of actions are very difficult to predict.

Still, we need to predict possible outcomes. Responsible predictions are informed and educated guesses made by knowledgeable people about what probably will happen. In spite of the fact that it is still a guess, exploring what may happen and being prepared to meet the possibilities is far better than remaining ignorant. After all, some predictions come true, and looking at the future gives hope as well as warning.

The year A.D. 2000 marks the passage from one millennium to another. The world has experienced this event only once before, in the year A.D. 999. Life was radically different then. The period known as the Dark Ages was finally ending in Western Europe, disease and famine were common, and anyone who lived to be fifty was considered to be very old. The world was plagued by tyranny. It was also ethnically divided, economically precarious, and according to the thinkers of the day, flat. The passage of the world into the first millennium in A.D. 999 was measured by a concept of time based on an approximation of how long it would take to walk to the next village, rather than by how many hours and minutes it will take to fly half way around the world.

For the people celebrating New Year's Eve in the year A.D. 1999, the event heralds a double celebration. It signals not only the arrival of a new century but a new millennium as well. Unlike New Year's Eve of A.D. 999, New Year's Eve, A.D. 1999, promises to be outrageous (at least for some of us).

Special event companies, travel and tour agencies, destination resorts, and other commercial recreation and tourism companies and individuals are already planning the events to celebrate this phenomena. Future plans for New Year's Eve, A.D. 1999, include the chartering of the *Queen Elizabeth II* by the Millennium Society.

The Millennium Society was founded by American college students. In 1979, they started dreaming about and preparing for the arrival of the millennium. With a worldwide membership of approximately 6,000, the Millennium Society is planning to welcome the new millennium by transporting 1,750 people from New York City to Alexandria, Egypt. Once there, they will continue to the Great Pyramid of Giza to welcome and toast the new millennium. The price tag for this gala is an estimated 10,000 dollars per person. If this is too rich for your budget, you can attend one of the satellite-linked parties that they will be sponsoring. These parties will be happening at major sites around the world. Potential sites include the Taj Mahal, Eiffel Tower, and Stonehenge. Satellites will link all sites to one another via audio and video connections, and the party will continue until all revelers around the world have welcomed the new millennium. Besides having fun, there is another agenda for this group; they hope to raise 75 million dollars to fund international student exchanges (Smolowe 1992: 10).

Other people are also making plans. Japan is thinking about sailing six cruise ships toward the international dateline. The passengers aboard the ships would be among the first people to cross into the new millennium. While that is happening, others will attend a party at 60,000 feet, aboard the Concorde. Those who wish to remain earthbound will celebrate at the world's most glamourous hotels where their reservations were made years ago. Festivities will happen all over the world as, for the first time, satellites and television allow us to welcome the arrival of a century and a millennium together.

Besides being a wonderful opportunity for fun and celebration, perhaps the most important aspect of this event is its significance as a marker. Just as each New Year's Eve prompts us to reflect on where we have been and where we are going, the arrival of a new century and a new millennium is so unique that it merits special attention and reflection. Will the advances made during the next 1,000 years be as dramatic as the events of the last 1,000 years? What will the celebrants of the year A.D. 2999 see when they look back at us?

We know that the future will be different. Change is happening constantly, and those who are tuned in to what is happening are better predictors, particularly in the short run. The farther we look ahead, the more difficult it is to make an accurate prediction. For most of us our window of concern extends from today until the end of this year, the next five years, the decade, or until retirement. It may be fun to speculate about the year A.D. 2999 but, unless you plan to be there, this becomes nothing more than an interesting exercise.

A more practical activity would be to explore the following question: What are the events that are happening around us now that can help us predict the future form of the commercial recreation and tourism industry?

The Americans with Disabilities Act

The Americans with Disabilities Act (ADA) was signed into law on July 26, 1990, by President George Bush. The ADA did not just suddenly appear but was the result of previous legislation concerning accessibility and the rights of individuals with disabilities. One of the earlier acts was the Architectural Barriers Act of 1968. Under this legislation, all buildings that were constructed, altered, or financed with federal monies after 1969 were to be accessible to individuals with physical disabilities. This act was followed by the formation in 1973 of the Architectural and Transportation Barriers

Compliance Board. The purpose of the board was to develop and enforce standards that would make public places accessible to disabled persons. The standards were to go into effect in 1982. The work of this board, as well as the Architectural Barriers Act of 1968, had little impact on the private sector.

The ADA combined two pieces of legislation, the Civil Rights Act of 1964 and the Rehabilitation Act of 1973, to provide a civil rights act for people with disabilities. Five areas, employment, public accommodations, public services, telecommunications services, and transportation, are covered under the ADA.

Source: Newhouse News Service.

Armed with a copy of the law, disabled traveler gets his chair

By PAUL NOVOSELICK
Newhouse News Service

I made a point of carrying a copy of the law with me.

And it was a good thing I did.

I was going to fly with my family to Florida for a vacation at Walt Disney World. I wanted my wheelchair stored on board the aircraft with us, because airlines have a notorious reputation for losing or damaging wheelchairs stored in cargo bays.

And according to the federal Air Carrier Access Act, my request was not unreasonable.

"In aircraft in which a closet or other approved storage area is provided in the cabin for passengers' carry-on items, of a size that will accommodate a folding wheelchair, the carrier shall designate priority stowage space ... for at least one folding wheelchair," the federal law says.

A folding wheelchair may be stowed in the closet "with priority over carry-on items," the law says.

If more than one person requests the on-board stowage, the law says they will be served on a "first-come, first-served" basis.

Here's how our experiment with the law on Northwest Airlines went in early January:

At Kent County (Mich.) International Airport, a Northwest employee first told me "that wheelchair will never fit" on a DC-9, even after I had dismantled it to show how it would. Fortunately, another Northwest ground staffer came by, grabbed the wheelchair, and said "Come with me." He put the wheelchair in the plane's closet.

"I've had relatives who used wheelchairs," he said as I walked behind him with my cane. "I know what it's like."

At Detroit Metro Airport, the Northwest personnel denied my request for on-board wheelchair storage. I asked for the airline's "Complaint Resolution Officer" — a designated employee the law says must be available in person or by phone at each airport at all times to handle these kinds of disputes — and all I got were blank stares.

Then a supervisor arrived and told me that wheelchairs go in the cargo bay. She said she had never heard of a provision in the law for on-board storage.

I hauled out my copy of the law. She read a section I had highlighted as yet another supervisor peeked over her shoulder.

They agreed the wheelchair should go on board.

For the return trip, I called the airport in Tampa 24 hours in advance to confirm reservations and request on-board stowage for my wheelchair.

We checked in an hour early to "pre-board," as the law dictates. But when we got to the gate, things turned bizarre.

A ground crew employee and the flight crew supervisor created an embarrassing scene as my wheelchair was pushed and shoved into the closet. I was humiliated by their rude behavior.

"In 14 years of flying, I've never had a wheelchair brought on board," the supervisor said to me loudly after we had been seated. After I tried to tell her it was within my rights to have the wheelchair on board, she curtly snapped:

"Sir, you have been served."

At Detroit Metro, I decided to forgo the on-board stowage hassles. I agreed to check the wheelchair in with my luggage when a Northwest employee told me there wasn't room for it on board. I had grown weary of the fight.

But then, to my pleasant surprise, a flight attendant volunteered to help stow the wheelchair in the closet, on board.

It figures. The one time I did not press for on-board storage, I got it without a hitch.

Four flights, four surprises. You'd think what I was doing was something new. But the Air Carrier Access Act regulations went into effect on March 6, 1990.

It would seem that after almost three years, airline personnel should be aware of the law.

Sources

Two free brochures are available on the Air Carrier Access Act: "New Horizons for the Air Traveler With a Disability," published by the Department of Transportation, Office of Consumer Affairs, 400 Seventh St. S.W., Washington, D.C. 20590, and "The Air Carrier Access Act: Making It Work for You," by the Paralyzed Veterans of America, 801 Eighth St. N.W., Washington, D.C. 20006 (1-800-424-8200).

People protected under the ADA include individuals with a physical or mental impairment. This impairment may be either visible or hidden and is defined as a condition that limits one or more of a person's major life activities. Visible impairments include conditions that limit a person's ability to carry out manual tasks such as using equipment or opening doors. Hidden impairments may include conditions that limit a person's ability to see or to be mobile. They may also limit a person's ability to carry out manual tasks. Hidden impairments may also include a speech or hearing impairment, or a medically controlled condition such as diabetes, epilepsy, or HIV/AIDS. Also protected under the ADA are individuals who are regarded as having impairments such as severe visible facial scars, involuntary head and body movements, or disfigurements.

The ADA protects individuals against employment discrimination. Qualified people who have a disability and who can perform the functions of a job with no ancillary provisions, or with reasonable accommodation, should not be disqualified because of their condition. In addition, public accommodations including hotels, restaurants, theaters, retail stores, museums, libraries, parks, and other public areas should be made accessible to them. Private clubs and religious organizations do not need to comply with the ADA.

Public transportation including airplanes, ships, buses, and trains, are covered under the ADA. Most CVBs will provide copies of accessible hotels, restaurants, and transportation options to individuals interested in visiting the area that they serve. Industries, as well as CVBs, may gather information regarding accessibility and publish pamphlets and booklets that are available on request. One such organization is the Airports Council International-North America (ACI-NA), which publishes a booklet detailing the accessibility of airport terminals. The booklet lists all accessible features, services, and facilities at over 553 airport terminals worldwide.

The ADA is important for able-bodied individuals for several reasons. First, statistics tell us that at one time or another, there is a good possibility that each of us will experience at least a temporary disability. Second, if you are planning on becoming older, say twenty, thirty, or forty years older, you will experience to some degree the conditions previously mentioned. The print on the menu mysteriously gets smaller, the stairs become longer and steeper, and it is harder to mobilize your body in general. The sensitivities shown to those who need them now, will serve all of us later. Finally, the bottom line is that we need to include everyone and allow them to reach their maximum potential so that collectively we are all stronger. It is a matter of courtesy and common sense.

Work and Leisure

World economies are changing, and as they change, so does the world of work and leisure. The rise of the Pacific Rim, the formation of the European Union (EU) and the newly found independence of many Eastern European

U.S. Department of Justice
Civil Rights Division
Coordination and Review Section

Americans with Disabilities Act Requirements
Fact Sheet

Employment

✓ Employers may not discriminate against an individual with a disability in hiring or promotion if the person is otherwise qualified for the job.
✓ Employers can ask about one's ability to perform a job, but cannot inquire if someone has a disability or subject a person to tests that tend to screen out people with disabilities.
✓ Employers will need to provide "reasonable accommodation" to individuals with disabilities. This includes steps such as job restructuring and modification of equipment.
✓ Employers do not need to provide accommodations that impose an "undue hardship" on business operations.
Who needs to comply:
✓ All employers with 25 or more employees must comply, effective July 26, 1992.
✓ All employers with 15-24 employees must comply, effective July 26, 1994.

Transportation

✓ New public transit buses ordered after August 26, 1990, must be accessible to individuals with disabilities.
✓ Transit authorities must provide comparable paratransit or other special transportation services to individuals with disabilities who cannot use fixed route bus services, unless an undue burden would result.
✓ Existing rail systems must have one accessible car per train by July 26, 1995.
✓ New rail cars ordered after August 26, 1990, must be accessible.
✓ New bus and train stations must be accessible.
✓ Key stations in rapid, light, and commuter rail systems must be made accessible by July 26, 1993, with extensions up to 20 years for commuter rail (30 years for rapid and light rail).
✓ All existing Amtrak stations must be accessible by July 26, 2010.

Public Accommodations

✓ Private entities such as restaurants, hotels, and retail stores may not discriminate against individuals with disabilities, effective January 26, 1992.
✓ Auxiliary aids and services must be provided to individuals with vision or hearing impairments or other individuals with disabilities, unless an undue burden would result.
✓ Physical barriers in existing facilities must be removed, if removal is readily achievable. If not, alternative methods of providing the services must be offered, if they are readily achievable.
✓ All new construction and alterations of facilities must be accessible.

State and Local Government

✓ State and local governments may not discriminate against qualified individuals with disabilities.
✓ All government facilities, services, and communications must be accessible consistent with the requirements of section 504 of the Rehabilitation Act of 1973.

Telecommunications

✓ Companies offering telephone service to the general public must offer telephone relay services to individuals who use telecommunications devices for the deaf (TDD's) or similar devices.

This document is available in the following accessible formats:
- Braille
- Large print
- Audio tape
- Electronic file on computer disk and electronic bulletin board. (202) 514-6193

For more information about the ADA contact:
U.S. Department of Justice
Civil Rights Division
Coordination and Review Section
P.O. Box 66118
Washington, D.C. 20035-6118
(202) 514-0301 (Voice)
(202) 514-0381 (TDD)
(202) 514-0383 (TDD)

This symbol tells a person with a disability, particularly one using a wheelchair, a facility is physically accessible and can be entered and used without fear of being blocked by architectural barriers.

Standard ADA Symbols.

Reproduced from *A Guide to Accessibility of Terminals— Access Travel: Airports.* Airports Council International—North America.

This symbol is used for people with hearing losses to indicate there are devices and services available in the facility that will assist them in performing communication activities.

This symbol is used to identify volume controlled telephones that amplify sound for voice communications.

This symbol indicates a facility has Telecommunications Devices for the Deaf (TDDs) available for communicating on the telephone with people who are deaf or hard of hearing.

This symbol shows there are services in a facility for people who are visually impaired.

countries will have an impact on the globe for years. The movement of workers across borders and the cooperation, even on a minimal level, of independent nations into a united body, will affect North America and other parts of the world well into the next century. Use of a common form of money, the formation of a unified governing body, easier visa and entry requirements for EU members into EU countries, and easier trading policies and restrictions will help make the EU a dominant power. The exchange of ideas and belief systems from the different cultures involved in this transition will shape a different world of work and leisure.

Eastern Europeans who emigrated from their native lands in the not-too-distant past are returning to see the relatives who were left behind and to visit the towns and villages where they were born. Some of these pilgrims are taking their children and grandchildren back with them. They need places to stay and to eat. They need rental cars, ground transportation, guides, and structured tours. They are looking to return with souvenirs as well as memories. Entrepreneurs in the host countries will soon discover the power of tourism revenue to help build the infrastructure that will be needed for these tourists. The same infrastructure will benefit the citizens as well as the visitors. Jobs will be created and people will discover that peace is more advantageous than war.

Hard-working peoples and nations will discover that there is another dimension to living besides work. That dimension includes travel and recreation. In Japan, a work-oriented society, the Japanese consciousness regarding the benefits of leisure time is waking. In 1992, the Five Year Economic Plan, which is concerned with increasing the quality of life for Japanese citizens around the globe, was published. One of the targets for the plan is the reduction of the number of average hours worked. This reduction will allow for the inclusion of vacation and weekend time so that families and individuals can relax. Amusement parks, virtual reality centers, pay and play golf centers, and other commercial recreation ventures are experiencing rapid growth in Japan (Allanson 1993: 24).

Although there has been slow growth in the building of amusement parks in North America, there is high growth in Japan, the Asian continent, parts of South America and Mexico, and the Middle East. The Saudi Amusement Centers Company was established in 1983 by a group of Saudi businessmen who recognized the value of recreation to a society. Today they own two major amusement parks, Prince Mohamed Bin Fahd Amusement Park and Gulf Amusement Park. Attendance at the parks was highest in 1988 (600,000 people) but fell drastically during the Gulf War of 1991. Visitation returned after the end of the war, with 400,000 guests expected in 1993. Admission is restricted to families, and Islamic traditions are observed in the park (Saudi Amusement Centers Company 1993: 16).

The concept of year-round school will continue to be debated and may become a national reality. The cycle of the original school calendar was determined when we were an agrarian society. The planting, harvesting, and cultivation of crops was vital to our existence, but we no longer need time off to care for crops. As large conglomerates take over the business of feeding people and the farms of today become more highly automated, the small independent farmer has become an endangered species.

As of December, 1992, there were 28 states that held school year-round. These states contained 2,024 schools with 1,570,154 pupils (Hartman, 1993: 50). The establishment of the year-round school will make it difficult for seasonal businesses such as resorts, theme parks, ski areas, and swim clubs to hire part-time summer staff. Seasonal passes and family attendance may be in jeopardy. The debate on the pros and cons of year-round school is just

States with year-round schools.
Source: Funworld, 1993.

Numbers inside each state indicate number of year-round schools and (number of pupils enrolled in year-round schools)

Totals as of December 1992: 28 states with year-round schools, 2,024 year-round schools, 1,570,164 pupils on the year-round calendar

getting under way, and the impact on the industry will be dramatic, especially in those areas with short seasonal windows.

Where we work as well as when we work will change. The electronic cottage described by John Naisbitt in *Megatrends* has failed to materialize.

> Because we want to be with each other, I don't think many of us will choose to work at home in our electronic cottages. . . . Very few people will be willing to stay home all of the time and tap out messages to the office. People want to go to the office. People want to be with people; and the more technology we pump into society, the more people want to be with people (Naisbitt 1982: 43).

Home has not become the center of our workplace. What we have done instead is to drag our toys, the fax machine, cellular phone, and microcomputer, into our homes from the office. Home has not replaced the office, it has become part of it.

Women will continue to enter the workforce. In 1955 27 percent of the women with children under the age of 18 worked. By 1991 that figure had risen to 66.6 percent (*The 1993 Information Please Almanac* 1992: 56). The continued presence of women in the workforce will help to give rise to, and acceptance of, gender-neutral occupations. When this occurs, the difference between the wages paid to males and the wages paid to females will close.

In *The Popcorn Report*, Faith Popcorn talks about "cocooning." This concept, named and predicted by Popcorn, describes the trend to stay at home and not go out.

> Everyone was looking for haven at home—drawing their shades, plumping their pillows, clutching their remotes. Hiding. It was a full-scale retreat into

the last controllable (or sort of controllable) environment—your own digs. And everybody was digging in. The word Cocooning struck such a collective chord in the American psyche that it entered the national—and the international—vocabulary (Popcorn 1991: 27).

The cocooning phenomena was fueled by the availability of VCR's, cable television, video stores, and the feeling that being inside was safer than being outside.

The car-jackings, mall violence, and kidnappings of the '90s did nothing to dispel the feeling that inside *was* safer. The problem became one of figuring out how to get people out of their cocoons. Industry response was to make the environment safer by stationing police and security guards at the mall, and by luring people out of their homes with multiple attractions facilities.

Naisbitt was right. While it might be all right to be in our electronic cottage for part of the time, in the long run, people want to be around other people. Electronic cottages and cocoons may be comforting for a while, but eventually we all need to come out. It is the interactive experience with others at the movies, the mall, the restaurant, and on the tour in another country that makes for a total experience. The question of safety and of world response to terrorism is one that needs to be continually addressed.

Changing Roles

There is no doubt that the roles and rules for families and individuals are changing. We can easily observe these changes by looking at recent demographics. It appears that the concept of what constitutes the nuclear family is undergoing restructuring. The "Leave it to Beaver" vision of the fifties is fading, and Leslie Wolfe of the Center for Women Policy Studies suggests that the nuclear family of the fifties might have been the exception rather than the rule. Today's families include stepchildren, half brothers and sisters, and married same-sex partners who are looking for the same benefits held by opposite-sex married couples. There are surrogate mothers, lesbian mothers, single mothers, and postmenopausal mothers. There are interracial, interfaith, and intercultural marriages. The possibilities for family composition and structure appear to be endless.

Unlike marriage in the past, divorce and splitting up will be more prevalent. Ken Dychwald, a San Francisco consultant who specializes in the impact of longevity, feels that it may become normal to have several marriages that suit our various stages of life. He points to Margaret Mead, the late anthropologist, as an example of someone who married based on the stages of her life.

Mead liked to say that she was married three times, all successfully. Mead's husbands suited her needs at different points in her long and varied life. Her first partner, whom she called her 'student husband,' provided a conventional and comfortable marriage. As her career progressed, however, she sought a traveling partner who was interested in her field work. Finally, she found a romantic and intellectual soul mate (Wallis 1992: 43).

The very fact that people live longer will change the way that they live and the way that we provide services and programs for our customers. Will the amusement parks of today that specialize in "throw-up" rides be attractive to the deluge of baby boomers about to hit the market?

People are living longer as the result of more stable living conditions and medical advances. We have had to redefine our concept of what constitutes old. In 1901, the average life expectancy was 49.24 years (Carruth 1991: 669). Today men can expect to live approximately 71.5 years and women 78 years (*The Economist* 1990: 134). Although disease is still with us, it does not hold the power over us that it did at the turn of the century. Some of you reading this book would have been dead if you had lived 100 years ago. Have you had pneumonia? Measles? Chicken pox? A bad infection requiring antibiotics? Do you have diabetes? Respiratory problems? Have you had an operation or been in a bad accident? If your answer is yes to any of these questions, there is a good possibility that you would not have survived.

Medical research will continue to develop ways to save, prolong, and enhance the quality of life. The difficult questions to be answered are not the ones that consist of how we will do this, but the ones that involve the price to be paid, the moral and ethical "rightness" of the procedures, and the difficulty of deciding who will benefit. This debate is already under way.

The genetic engineering of people, animals, and plants is a difficult topic that challenges our religious values and our belief systems. We now have the ability to clone like animals and to genetically engineer disease-resistant foods.

> In 15 or 20 years, predicts biologist Leroy Hood of the California Institute of Technology, doctors will be able to take a blood sample from a newborn infant, extract DNA from the blood and insert it into a machine that will analyze 100 or so genes. 'That will give us DNA fingerprints of genes that predispose us to common kinds of disease' (Jaroff 1992: 58).

The ability to do these types of things could change the composition of our society and the world at large. The state of our planet may be dictated by the size of our population. By 2020, it is projected that 8.5 billion people will inhabit our earth (*The Economist* 1990: 12). The implications for outdoor recreation, natural resources, and quality of life are obvious.

Consumer Awareness

It is difficult for small businesses to compete with larger ones. Large businesses can advertise to a broader audience. They can deliver a standardized level of service and use economies of scale to their advantage. They are also more resilient to economic variations and other adversities.

Today, large corporations are gobbling up smaller companies in the travel, amusement, entertainment, and lodging, food, and beverage industries. They are doing this because there is money to be made and because they want to diversify. In the United States, five major corporations dominate the amusement industry in the late 1990s—Anheuser-Busch, Disney, Time-Warner, Paramount Communications, and Universal.

Accompanying this phenomenon is distrust regarding the protection of consumers and consumer rights. This is not a new issue. What is new is that these issues have become fueled by the litigious nature of a society that seems to have forgotten the principles of consumer protection *and* personal responsibility. The courts have become clogged with lawsuits brought on behalf of litigants. Some of them have merit and some do not. The aggressive marketing of individual lawyers and law firms is accompanied by the promise that "there is no commission unless you win." The inclination to sue and to get what we deserve is compelling. The choice of settling out of court has become the route that many take. Often it is cheaper than defending oneself. We are all losers in frivolous litigation. Things cannot continue like this.

Sophisticated marketing techniques are not as effective as they once were. We know about subliminal marketing. We understand that sex sells alcohol, cigarettes, underwear, cars, jeans, and toothpaste. Commercials have become more entertaining than the television shows they sponsor. Meanwhile, we have learned to read labels and to insist that those labels be written truthfully and in a comprehensible manner. We no longer buy Fords because we have always had Fords, or use Tide because we have always used Tide. Brand-name loyalty is dead. Perhaps this is because we have learned the concept of shopping for price *and* quality. We have been "fouled" one too many times. Consumer awareness and power is here to stay—we will not be going back.

Population Mobility

In the United States, the "center of population" has been moving steadily west. The center of population is "that point at which an imaginary flat, weightless, and rigid map of the United States would balance if weights of identical value were placed on it so that each weight represented the location of one person on the date of the census" (U.S. Bureau of the Census 1992: 9). On August 2, 1790, the center of population was 23 miles east of Baltimore, Maryland. By April 1, 1990, it had shifted to 9.7 miles southeast of Steelville, Missouri. There is no doubt that our population is going westward. It is also going south.

Those states experiencing the most drastic increase in population between 1980 to 1990, were in the west and the southwest. Four states on the East Coast—New Hampshire, Virginia, Georgia, and Florida also experienced rapid growth. It should not be surprising that this occurred. The decline in the infrastructures of eastern cities, high land prices, restrictive

No. 3. Center of Population: 1790 to 1990

["Center of population" is that point at which an imaginary flat, weightless, and rigid map of the United States would balance if weights of identical value were placed on it so that each weight represented the location of one person on the date of the census]

YEAR	North latitude			West longitude			Approximate location
	°	'	"	°	'	"	
1790 (August 2)	39	16	30	76	11	12	23 miles east of Baltimore, MD
1850 (June 1)	38	59	0	81	19	0	23 miles southeast of Parkersburg, WV
1900 (June 1)	39	9	36	85	48	54	6 miles southeast of Columbus, IN
1950 (April 1)	38	50	21	88	9	33	8 miles north–northwest of Olney, Richland County, IL
1960 (April 1)	38	35	58	89	12	35	In Clinton Co. about 6 1/2 miles northwest of Centralia, IL
1970 (April 1)	38	27	47	89	42	22	5.3 miles east–southeast of the Mascoutah City Hall in St. Clair County, IL
1980 (April 1)	38	8	13	90	34	26	1/4 mile west of De Soto in Jefferson County, MO
1990 (April 1)	37	52	20	91	12	55	9.7 miles southeast of Steelville, MO

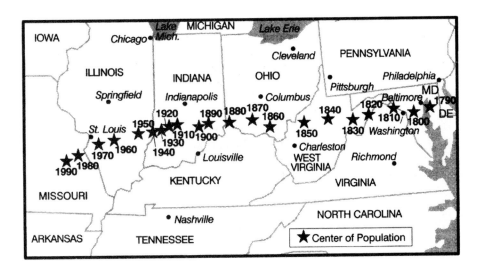

No. 4. U.S. Population Abroad, by Selected Area: 1992

[In thousands. As of June 3. Data compiled as part of noncombatant personnel evacuation requirements report]

business practices, and congestion sent many businesses west and south. Where they went, workers and their families followed.

The future mobility of populations worldwide will be determined by the same considerations. The availability of adequate living space and the ability to acquire an education, to be safe, and to make a reasonable living concern all peoples. This is called quality of life. Regardless of nationality, everyone wants the same chance to pursue a reasonable quality of life. The United States has seen this happen as auto companies, both American and from abroad, look to the south and the southwest to establish their assembly plants. Detroit, New York, and other larger, older cities have neither the

Percent change in state population: 1980 to 1990.
Statistical Abstract of the United States, 1992.

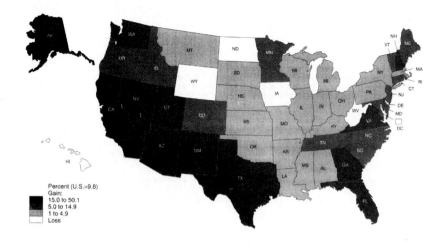

Percent (U.S.=9.8)
Gain:
15.0 to 50.1
5.0 to 14.9
1 to 4.9
Loss

land nor the infrastructure to compete. The population of the member countries of the EU will also be shuffling around, as the individual members of less affluent countries take advantage of their right to travel and work in their new community.

The Global Village

We have become voyeurs. We like looking at one another (if only to confirm the superiority of our system). There is something that is fascinating and at the same time disturbing. Perhaps the problem is that by viewing one another by instantaneously conveyed satellite transmissions, we get to remain in the shadows. It is like watching a murder on TV—we all know that it is not real.

But what is happening around us *is* real and the future of the global village lies in all of us coming out of the shadows to meet one another. Although it may sound trite, we *are* one people, one planet. There is very little choice.

Nature does not obey any law passed by *Homo sapiens*. Perhaps in the distant future, we will figure out a way to control, or at least bend, natural forces in our favor. But in the immediate future, the one that we will all inhabit, this is doubtful. The issues of war and of the stewardship of our planet need to be addressed by all members of the global village.

Some people feel that future wars will be economic, not military. Let us hope that they are correct. Future military wars, if allowed to occur, will be high-tech and long distance. We will sit in our bunkers and aim the newest and most efficient of weapons at one another. There are an infinite number of ways that we can kill each other; poison gases, biological warfare, lasers, nuclear bombs, and killer spores are only a few of the choices. We can also make the choice not to do this. In order to make this choice we are going to have to get to know one another "up front and personal." At first this will be a little bit like the seventh grade dance, but, with practice, we can do it.

We need to become better stewards of our planet. The future holds new promises for energy that include solar, hydro, geothermal, tidal, and wind power. We can also look forward to fusion instead of fission as a more benign source of nuclear energy. But what do we do in the interim while we are waiting for all of this to happen? How can we, as the largest consumers of energy on the face of the planet, convince some slash and burn farmer in South America that he should not cut down the rain forest? He would like a TV, video recorder, washer, dryer, refrigerator, and microwave oven. Are we willing to modify the way that we live? Do we really need to do this and give up some of our creature comforts?

The key to unifying and making peace in the global village is education and exposure. We need to meet the other members of our planet and remember that this is their planet too. It is easy to hate a faceless, nameless person whom we will never see. It is harder to hate once we meet face to face. While we may never completely understand or agree with one another, we can achieve a level of mutual respect and tolerance. Maybe that will be what the celebrants of the next millennium in A.D. 2999 will see as the legacy of the previous 1,000 years—peace and cooperation.

Technology

Technology is wonderful, and the future promises to deliver even better technological advances in all parts of our lives. The commercial recreation and tourism industry knows of our love affair with technology and pays close attention to how it can be incorporated into the industry.

The amusement industry has eagerly embraced new technology. They know that consumers seek out those experiences that are new, exciting, and lifelike. Virtual reality will continue to get "virtually" better as computer technology improves and allows for the use of more sophisticated programs. The virtual reality systems of today will someday look as antiquated and obsolete as the original video game—Pong. We will wonder how we ever put up with them.

Special effects will become even more special. It will no longer be sufficient to see and hear what is happening. We will want to smell, taste, and touch, as well. When we watch the skier race down the slope, we will want the snow in our face, the wind pressing against our bodies, and the coldness of the mountain air all around us. As the monster sneaks up behind the beautiful heroine, we will want to smell him and to feel his hot breath on our neck (at least some of us will).

Holography, including holographic television, will allow us to enter into three-dimensional worlds. Holographic suites where we can relax and explore places and experiences that are unavailable to us by conventional methods will be possible. We will be able to visit historical sites and speak with past presidents. The Hall of Presidents at EPCOT will join Pong as a relic of our past. We expect this to happen. After all, it happens on the starship *Enterprise*.

The way we travel will change. We have the technology available today to pinpoint our exact position on our globe. Soon it will be commonplace for us to do this from our cars. Those of us who do not like to ask for directions will not have to do this anymore; those of us who get lost will no longer have an excuse. Smart roads with sensors will communicate to us the best routes from point A to point B, regulate traffic—and even drive the car.

Supersonic, suborbital planes will make it possible to get anywhere in the world in two hours (although getting out of the airport is another issue). Perhaps those of us who are really adventurous will someday allow our atoms to be disassembled, transported, and reassembled rather than taking the plane. Just as we now take vacations underwater, space vacations will be possible in the future. People are already signing up for them.

Today we have simulators for golf, skiing, and tennis. We also have artificial beaches and ski slopes. In July, 1993, the southern Japanese island of Kyushu became home to the Seagaia Ocean Dome. The dome is less than 300 yards from the ocean and 15 kilometers from a real bathing beach. It can be open 365 days a year, 24 hours a day regardless of weather. There are no bugs, insects, or wind, and no threat from sunburn (False Beaches and Skiing 1993: 26).

Wild Blue Yokohama, also in Japan, is another artificial facility that boasts rubber sand and plastic palm trees. It can accommodate 5,000 people at a time, has a flowing river, waterslides, outdoor pool, and a fake rain forest. The same company that runs Wild Blue Yokohama also runs an indoor ski center in Funabashi, Japan. That facility has two chair lifts and two slopes, intermediate and advanced. Each slope is 535 meters long, 160 meters wide, and drops 80 meters from top to bottom (False Beaches and Skiing 1993: 26).

Today we have new wonder fibers and fabrics that protect us in the outdoors. There is a two-wheel-drive bicycle that parallels the concept of the four-wheel-drive car, and although there are no Dick Tracy wrist phones, there are picture phones available for our homes. Things are constantly changing.

As in the past, technology will be the driver of the future. The question is how will it be used? Will we lose sight of the real world in the virtual world and forget that the world is not a theme park? Let us hope that our emotional and social development keeps pace with our intellectual ability to conceptualize and create new technologies. Many of these predictions will not happen in our lifetime. When, how, and if they happen will depend on the priorities that we set.

A Final Note

On December 8 through 10, 1993, *U.S. News & World Report* polled 1,000 registered voters. Fifty-nine percent of those surveyed thought that we should be extremely worried about the future of the country. Thirty-seven percent felt that their children would be worse off than they were, while only 29 percent thought that they would be better off (State of the Union 1993: 40).

A Time/CNN poll of 800 adult Americans taken on July 22 through 23, 1992, found that 41 percent thought that the world would be in better shape at end of the twenty-first century, 32 percent thought that it would be worse, and 15 percent felt that it would be about the same. While the majority polled felt that there would be more environmental disasters (59 percent), poverty (61 percent), and disease (53 percent), 62 percent still had hope for the future (The Future Poll 1992: 13).

What do these polls tell us? Surely, they are not scientific. At most they reflect the feelings of a small group of people at a specific moment in time. The future is not determined by what they say, but it may be determined by how they feel and what they do. To a large extent your future is determined by how you feel. It is also determined by what you know and the actions that you take based on this information.

You have chosen to become part of an industry called commercial recreation and tourism. Part of your job as a member of the industry, and as a citizen of this world, is to stay current and to be informed about the world and the events happening around you. It is easy for us to bury our heads in our desks, to be overcome with self-importance, and to lose sight of the whole. Faith Popcorn refers to this as cultural autism.

> This kind of cultural autism is numbing corporate America. Brain Reserves's antidote: to scan today's culture for signs of the future. I think of this as 'brailling' the culture, reaching out to touch as many parts of it as possible— to make sense of the whole. Compensating for tunnel vision by developing a different sensitivity, a 'feel' for what's going on (Popcorn 1991: 21–22).

It really does not matter whether the glass before you is half empty or half full. What matters is that you see the glass. The seeds of the future are all around you. Open your eyes and look.

Summary

Thinking about the future involves the process of prediction. Another word for prediction is "guess." Although predictions are necessary to help us analyze possibilities and formulate contingency plans, prediction is, by no means, an exact science. The unpredictability of people is only one of the factors that makes accurate prediction difficult. Still, we need to engage in prediction—it is our only option for viewing the future.

Prediction and knowing what will or is likely to happen in the future allows us to prepare for changes in the variables that affect the delivery of our services. It also allows us to plan future programs. The passage from one millennium to another in the year 2000 has already started individuals and companies thinking and planning about ways to mark this historic event.

We know that nothing stays the same and that businesses that refuse to acknowledge and adapt to the changes that may occur may find that they have difficulty competing in the future. Already we know that the Americans with Disabilities Act, the rise of the Pacific Rim, and the formation of the European Union are affecting the way that business is conducted. The variables discussed in chapter 2 will continue to force changes in the way that we think about our world and in the manner that the industry conducts business. As always, technology will be the catalyst, or driver, for much of the change.

The future is not preordained and is full of promise as well as dread. We have the ability to use the events and changes that are happening today and that will happen tomorrow to make a better industry and a better world for all of us.

Discussion Questions

1. What impact might the assimilation of small independent amusement parks and enterprises by established corporations have on the amusement industry?
2. How might the threat of litigation and the awarding of large settlements to plaintiffs affect the types of programs and services offered by commercial recreation and tourism operators.
3. What is brand loyalty and does it exist for recreational products and services?
4. What predictions discussed in this chapter do you feel might come true?
5. How far do you think that hotels, restaurants, and other commercial recreation and tourism businesses should go to accommodate people with disabilities?

Chapter Exercises

1. Read one of the books mentioned in this chapter that deals with prediction. Do you believe that the author has painted a reasonable and realistic view of the future?
2. Make a list of types of information that you consider to be vital for making an accurate prediction. Where could you find these sources?
3. Make three predictions for the future of commercial recreation and tourism. Support your predictions by citing the current trends and conditions that led you to arrive at your conclusions.
4. Go to the library, or other source, and find a prediction that was made more than twenty years ago. Did the prediction come true? Why or why not?
5. Find out if your campus has a department or program concerned with providing services for a population that is covered under the ADA. List the number and types of programs available. How accessible is your campus for these, and other people with disabilities?

References

Aburdene, Patricia, and John Naisbitt. 1992. *Megatrends for women.* New York: Fawcett Columbine.

Airports Council International. 1993. *A guide to accessibility of terminals—access travel: Airports.* 6th ed. Washington, D.C.: Airports Council International—North America.

Allanson, Norman. 1993. Land of the rising sun. *Leisure Management* (July): 24–25.

Brammall, Sherrie. 1993. Seeing the light. *Funworld* (July): 8–10.

Brill, Louis.1993. Get real. *Funworld* (July): p. 22+.

———. 1993. HDTV highly developing theater value. *Funworld* (July): 86–88.

Brooks, Patrick. 1993. The world of amusement and the European Community. *Park World* (September): 64–67.

Butler, Steven. Will Japan Inc. boom again in '94? *U.S. News & World Report* (27 December 1993/3 January 1994): 71.

Carruth, Gorton. 1991. *What happened when—A chronology of life and events in America.* New York: Signet.

Collins, Terry. 1993. The practical side of animation. *Funworld* (July): 42–43.

Drucker, Peter F. 1992. *Managing for the future.* New York: Penguin Books.

Elmer-Dewitt, Philip. 1992. Dream Machines. *Time Beyond the Year 2000* (Fall): 39–41.

Elson, John. 1992. The millennium of discovery. *Time Beyond the Year 2000* (Fall): 16–21.

False beaches and skiing. 1993. *Park World* (September): 26.

Hartman, Margaret. 1993. What if school never ends? *Funworld* (July): 50+.

Huck, Cathleen Baird. 1992. Conrad Hilton and the Americans with Disabilities Act: "Human dignity is paramount." *Hospitality and Tourism Educator* (May): 45–46.

Januarius, Mary. 1993. The third age. *Leisure Management* (June): 30–32.

Jaroff, Leon. 1992. Seeking a godlike power. *Time Beyond the Year 2000* (Fall): 58

Lacayo, Richard. 1992. Future schlock. *Time Beyond the Year 2000* (Fall): 90.

Lasch, Christine. 1992. Is progress obsolete? *Time Beyond the Year 2000* (Fall): 71.

Lemonick, Michael D. 1992. Tomorrow's lesson: Learn or perish." *Time Beyond the Year 2000* (Fall): 59–60.

Linden, Eugene. 1992. Too many people. *Time Beyond the Year 2000* (Fall): 64–65.

Morrow, Lance. 1992. A cosmic moment. *Time Beyond the Year 2000* (Fall): 6–9.

Naisbitt, John. 1982. *Megatrends.* New York: Warner Books.

Naisbitt, John, and Patricia Aburdene. 1990. *Megatrends 2000.* New York: Avon Books.

Nash, J. Madeleine. 1992. The frontier within. *Time Beyond the Year 2000* (Fall): 81–82.

Nelan, Bruce. 1992. How the world will look in 50 years." *Time Beyond the Year 2000* (Fall): 36–38.

Novoselick, Paul. 1993. Armed with a copy of the law, disabled traveler gets his chair. *Sunday Star-Ledger* 21 February.

Overbye, Dennis. 1992. Is anybody out there? *Time Beyond the Year 2000* (Fall): 78–80.

Peters, Thomas J., and Robert H. Waterman, Jr. 1982. *In search of excellence.* New York: Warner Books Inc.

Platts, Martyn. 1993. Evocative, exotic and ripe for development. *Park World* (September): 46–48.

Platts, Martyn. 1993. Finale Martyn Platts presents the "alternative" industry view. *Park World* (September): 86.

Popcorn, Faith. 1991. *The popcorn report.* New York: Doubleday.

Roberts, Steven. State of the union. *U.S. News & World Report* (27 December 1993/3 January 1994): 38–41.

Saudi Amusement Centers Company. 1993. *Family Entertainment Center* 1: 16–17.

Smolowe, Jill. 1992. Tonight we're gonna party like it's 1999. *Time Beyond the Year 2000* (Fall): 10–11.

Snook, David. 1993. Theme parks in the 21st century. *Park World* (September): 50–53.

State of the union. *U.S. News & World Report* (27 December 1993/3 January 1994): 38–41.

The 1993 information please almanac. 1992. Boston: Houghton Mifflin Company.

The Economist. 1990. *Book of vital world statistics.* New York: Times Books.

The future poll. 1992. *Time Beyond the Year 2000* (Fall): 12–13.

Toffler, A. 1990. *Powershift.* New York: Bantam Books.

————. 1970. *Future shock.* New York: Bantam Books.

U.S. Bureau of the Census. 1992. *Statistical abstract of the United States: 1992.* Washington, D.C.: U.S. Government Printing Office.

U.S. Equal Employment Opportunity Commission and the U.S. Department of Justice, Civil Rights Division. 1991. *The Americans with Disabilities Act questions and answers.* Washington, D.C.: U.S. Government Printing Office.

U.S. Department of Justice, Civil Rights Division, Coordination and Review Section. 1991. *The Americans with Disabilities Act.* Washington, D.C.: U.S. Government Printing Office.

U.S. Department of Transportation. 1991. *New horizons for the air traveler with a disability.* Washington, D.C.: U.S. Government Printing Office.

Wade, Betsy. 1993. Practical travelers: New proposals for the disabled. *The New York Times.* 19 December.

Wallis, C. 1992. The nuclear family goes boom! *Time Beyond the Year 2000* (Fall): 42–44.

Zoglin, R. 1992. Beyond your wildest dreams. *Time Beyond the Year 2000* (Fall): 70.

Additional Resources

Boyett, Joseph H., and Henry B. Conn. 1992. *Workplace 2000: The revolution reshaping American business.* New York: Penguin Books.

Burrus, Daniel, and Roger Gittines. 1993. *Technotrends: How to use technology to go beyond your competition.* New York: Harper Business.

Deal, Terrence, and Allan A. Kennedy. 1982. *Corporate culture: The rights and rituals of corporate life.* Reading, MA: Addison Wesley Publishing Company.

Miller, Eric. 1991. *Future vision: The 189 most important trends of the 1990s.* Naperville, IL: Sourcebooks Trade.

Morrison, Ian, and Greg Schmid. 1994. *Future tense: The business realities of the next ten years.* New York: William Morrow and Company.

Peter, Laurence J., and Raymond Hull. 1972. *The Peter Principle: Why things always go wrong.* New York: Bantam Books.

Poon, Auliana. 1993. *Tourism, technology and competitive strategies.* Wallingford, U.K.: C.A.B. International.

U.S. Architectural and Transportation Barriers Compliance Board. 1994. *Recommendations for accessibility guidelines: Recreational facilities and outdoor developed areas.* Washington, D.C.: U.S. Government Printing Office.

U.S. Architectural and Transportation Barriers Compliance Board. 1994. Americans with Disabilities Act accessibility guidelines for buildings and facilities; recreation facilities and outdoor developed areas; proposed rule. *Federal Register* (21 September): 48542–48546.

APPENDIX A Meeting Planning Functions and Independent Conditions

Meeting Planning Functions

1. Establishing meeting design and objectives (7–11 questions)
2. Selecting site and facilities (7–11)
3. Negotiating with facilities (7–11)
4. Budgeting (7–11)
5. Handling reservations and housing (4–6)
6. Choosing from transportation options—air and ground (1–2)
7. Planning program (7–11)
8. Planning guidebook/staging guide/documentation of specifications (4–6)
9. Establishing registration procedures (7–11)
10. Arranging for and using support services: convention bureau, outside services, hospitality committee (4–6)
11. Coordinating with convention center or hall (4–6)
12. Planning with convention services manager (7–11)
13. Briefing facilities staff—pre-meeting (4–6)
14. Shipping (4–6)
15. Planning function room setups (7–11)
16. Managing exhibits (4–6)
17. Managing food and beverage (7–11)
18. Determining audiovisual requirements (7–11)
19. Selecting speakers (4–6)
20. Booking entertainment (102)
21. Scheduling promotion and publicity (4–6)
22. Developing guest and family programs (1–2)
23. Producing and printing meeting materials (4–6)
24. Distributing gratuities (1–2)
25. Evaluating—post-meeting (4–6)

Independent Conditions Which Affect
Meeting Planning Functions

1. Time of year/dates (seasonal, holiday, negotiation, climate)
2. Labor conditions (union status of contract, nonunion, availability)
3. Length of meeting
4. Size of attendance (single event, multiple events)
5. Site/facility location and type (convention centers, hotel, downtown, resort)
6. Objective (education, incentive, exhibit, business sales, information)
7. Type of organization (association or society, corporation, religious, government)
8. Location/geography (city, resort, international, off-shore)
9. Budget (subsidized, breakeven, profit, sponsorship)
10. Participant funding (self, organization, meeting support, restrictive per diem)
11. Management responsibility (staff, volunteer, contract service)
12. Space requirements (sleeping rooms, meeting rooms, banquet space, exhibit space)
13. Transportation variables (ground operator, airlines, accessibility)
14. Participant demographics (gender, age)
15. Social events (type, timing, availability)
16. Special requirements (tradition, handicapped, politics)
17. Weather
18. Legal (contracts/liability law/Americans with Disabilities Act)
19. Ethics
20. Technology
21. Current events
22. Risk management

Information Provided by the Public Relation's Division of Meeting Professionals International's Marketing Department.

APPENDIX B
Code of Conduct for Commercial Tour Operations in Gwaii Haanas/South Moresby British Columbia

Preamble

This Code of Conduct has been developed by the commercial operators and resource guides listed as participants in the Appendix. It has been developed, primarily, to regulate our own activities in Gwaii Haanas/South Moresby, and those of our guests.

The guiding spirit of this Code of Conduct is to ensure that we cause minimal impacts to the wildlife, wilderness, natural habitats, and the archaeological, cultural, and historical sites of Gwaii Haanas/South Moresby. We seek to preserve and protect this special place as it now is for the appreciation, enjoyment, and enrichment of future generations.

The intent of this Code is to guide and regulate our own commercial operations. We also wish to inform, educate, and voluntarily involve all other commercial operators and private visitors who wish to protect in perpetuity, the opportunity for, and the quality of the exceptional experiences found in Gwaii Haanas/South Moresby. We will provide this Code to others when appropriate.

Etiquette

Most of GH/SM is a wilderness area where people expect to have little or no evidence or signs of human activity. Most visitors want to experience the peace, quiet, and solitude of nature. We recognize the necessity to ensure that everyone can have this kind of experience. Specifically, we will:

1. Keep noise levels at a minimum in anchorages, campsites, on trails, etc. We will discourage loud music, limit excessive engine noises, and keep noise confined to our own group as is possible.

2. Whenever possible, communicate anchorage or campsites to other parties in advance and find another site if one is already occupied.
3. Not take pets (onshore).
4. Store personal gear together in an unobtrusive place when ashore.
5. Co-operate and communicate in a friendly and professional manner with other operators or parties.
6. Limit the size of our groups to 20 people and ensure that we have a knowledgeable guide for every 10 people.
7. Bathe in streams at the mouth, not upstream nor near frequented drinking water sources.
8. Be accurate and responsible with our advertising.
9. Discourage the collection of natural matter (such as shells, rocks), and forbid the collection of fossils.
10. Record and communicate to proper authorities (CHN, CPS, DFO, CCG), any questionable, problematic, or unsafe activities.

Wildlife

Part of the experience for visitors is to observe close-hand birdlife, and marine and land mammals. In order to cause the least intrusion and disturbance to the natural patterns and behavior of wildlife, we will at all times approach with care and sensitivity all sighted wildlife. We will:

Whales/Dolphins

1. From a distance, determine the travel direction and diving sequence of the whales.
2. Approach them slowly from the side and slightly to the rear, but not directly from the front or rear and position the boat parallel to the whales at a distance no closer than about 100 meters, at a speed that matches theirs, and avoid rapid changes in vessel course or speed—let the whales make the decisions.
3. Be careful not to separate nor come between a calf and cow.
4. Not interfere with the natural behavior of whales, i.e., when orcas hunt and kill other mammals, or when they are resting.
5. Move away slowly when finished whale watching.
6. Be aware of what other operators are doing, communicate our intentions to each other and not box the whales in.
7. Record sightings and observations in log.

Seabird Colonies, Bird Nesting Sites, Raptor Eyries

We recognize that the Queen Charlotte Islands are one of the major nesting areas for seabirds, shorebirds, raptors, etc., many of which nest in ground burrows. Birds are extremely vulnerable during nesting season and can be damaged or disturbed by human visitation at this time. All operators are encouraged to become knowledgeable about seabird colonies. Therefore, we specifically will:

1. Have a knowledgeable guide accompany visitors onto seabird nesting areas.
2. Obtain a map (such as Queen Charlotte Island Seabird Colonies map from Environment Canada) which shows types of birds, colony location, and nesting dates.
3. Limit time spent ashore near open nesting sites. Particularly, avoid causing birds to fly off their eggs or leave their chicks, for example at any of the gull, cormorant, or murre colonies, or when near oyster catchers, etc.
4. Refrain from visiting sensitive sites such as: Anthony Islets, Rankine, Kerouard, E. Copper, Jeffrey, and Slug Islands.
5. Not camp nor have fires or bright stationary lights near known nesting sites.
6. Not climb trees that contain eagle nests. Eagles are known to abandon nests when disturbed.
7. Not climb cliffs near Peregrine falcon eyries.
8. Not discharge firearms near nesting sites.
9. Have no low fly-overs by aircraft of falcon eyries and eagle nests.
10. Limit number of visitors in colony to ten at any one time.

Seals and Sea Lions

1. Not have low fly-overs (under 500 ft.) by aircraft, or close approaches by vessels that disturb animals at rookeries and haulouts.
2. Be alert to animal movements and leave immediately if more than two to three animals dive into the water.
3. Take extreme care to not surprise animals—proceed slowly from a direction where animals can see the boat. Approach from downwind.

Bears

1. Not feed or allow close approach to bears.
2. Store food caches at least seventy-five meters from tent sites.
3. Keep food cache covered and hung in a tree when not attended.
4. Never store food in kayaks or boats that are on the beach.
5. Ensure tents are not set on bear trails.
6. Be careful to not disturb nor come near bears during salmon spawning season.
7. Remain alert to bear sign and activity at all times, and be sensitive to the bear routes and patterns.
8. Report sites where bears have had problems with people.

Deer

1. Not touch or pick up any fawn even if it appears abandoned.

Visitor Safety

All commercial operations are conducted surrounded by the marine environment of the North Pacific. Unpredictable local weather conditions, frequent high winds, strong currents, and extreme tides combine to create dangerous hazards for the unprepared visitor. We encourage the adaptation by all operators of the highest degree of responsible operations, vessel standards, and crew/guide training. Some suggestions:

1. All vessel operators have experience with the waters of GH/SM before commencing a commercial venture.
2. All commercial vessels to be seaworthy, well maintained, well equipped, and meet all coast guard standards.
3. All crew to be trained in first aid (preferably advanced), hold radio operator's license and to be trained in marine emergency duties and have C.G. certification where required.
4. Vessels and aircraft to be available in an emergency situation, i.e., marine search and rescue or vessel in distress. Know how to prepare for a medical air evacuation.
5. Crew to monitor C.G. VHF Ch. 16.
6. We encourage all vessels (or groups of vessels) to have EPIRBs, or VHFs and extra safety equipment for emergencies (extra pumps, towing lines, smoke flares, etc.).

Guides

The need for guide standards has been discussed. Demonstrated skill, experience, training, local knowledge of GH/SM, including knowledge of its natural and cultural history, ability to lead a group, first aid, etc., are essential.

Archaeological, Cultural, and Historical Sites

We acknowledge and respect the Haida Nation's concerns regarding visitors to Haida archaeological and cultural sites. Therefore, we will:

1. Attempt to make radio contact with Haida Watchperson before arrival or go ashore and make contact, in order that Watchperson can coordinate with other visitors to limit the number of visitors in a site at any one time.
2. Have one guide per ten guests when onshore. Limit group size to approximately twenty.
3. Not camp on archaeological or sacred sites, i.e., Sgun Gwaii, Hotspring, House Island; not camp within 1 km of any Haida village site.

4. Not dig into middens or in any archaeological site; not touch nor remove any artifact, cultural or historical; not enter burial grounds.
5. Leave no garbage nor human waste in these sites.
6. When on Hotspring Island, no more than fourteen people in three pools at one time, no more than twenty people onshore at one time. If another group is waiting, limit stay to three hours or less. Emphasize spiritual and botanical values of the island as opposed to a party and bathing attitude.
7. Remind any commercial photographers who are our guests that they should receive permission from the band council for taking pictures to be sold.

Burnaby Narrows

Burnaby Narrows exhibits one of the special biological phenomenon in the Charlottes and is a popular site. As we are concerned about the possible deterioration of the site because of visitation and to lessen the impacts on marine life by heavy foot traffic, we will:

1. Advise all our guests of the possible impacts of foot traffic on marine life.
2. Attempt to use glass bottom viewers for nonwalking, float-through tours of the Narrows.
3. Not gather, collect, nor harvest marine life in the Narrows.
4. Minimize camping activities and anchoring of vessels in the immediate vicinity.

Food Gathering

As part of our guests' experience we do catch and gather some fish and seafood. We will educate and encourage our guests to limit their catch in order to ensure preservation of the resource, to reduce impacts on traditional fisheries, and to maintain the quality of the experience for the future. We support the conservation of marine resources as there is already a depletion of certain species, i.e., abalone, coho, rock scallops, and bottom fish in GH/SM. We will:

1. Limit our catch to what we can eat on the trip.
2. Discourage harvesting of purple hinged rock scallops.
3. As a result of coastwide closure, there is no harvest of abalone (until 1995).
4. Refrain from "catch and release" of salmon.
5. Be certain every person who fishes possesses a valid DFO license.
6. Maintain in our logs a record of fish and shellfish caught.
7. Limit the catch of salmon to one per license per day.
8. Discourage the harvest of shellfish in fragile areas.
9. Be aware of health risks associated with eating shellfish such as P.S.P. and allergies.
10. Discourage collecting of seafoods while diving.

Garbage

With increased visitation in GH/SM by boats, aircraft, and people, there will be more garbage and human waste. We will operate utilizing `no trace' practices. Specifically, we will:

1. Burn paper and organics below the high tide mark.
2. Dispose of our organics overboard when away from anchorages and moorings, preferably well off-shore.
3. Pack out all cans, plastics, bottles, and nonbiodegradables.
4. Not discharge holding tanks while in anchorages or moorings.
5. When onshore or in campsites near the ocean, encourage the use of lower intertidal areas for a disposal of human waste. When latrines need to be established away from the shore, they will be at least 200 meters from any freshwater sources.
6. Use biodegradable soaps for dishes, bathing, laundry.

Camping

Most suitable camping site (protected beach, good anchorage, water source, etc.) are also Haida archaeological sites which visitors should be aware of. We will:

1. Make sure all campsites are left in `no trace' condition.
2. Build fires in foreshore, below high tide mark, away from driftwood. Make sure fires are extinguished when unattended. Use only driftwood for fires.
3. On popular, heavily used campsites, we support the construction and use of latrines (outhouses).
4. Limit durations of stay to one week.

Local Involvement

Recognizing our involvement with the economy and people of the Queen Charlotte Islands, we will attempt to:
1. Hire local people in our operations.
2. Buy supplies and materials locally.
3. Participate in local events and promote them to our guests.
4. Encourage the on-island provision of pertinent crew and guide training courses and programs.
5. Improve communication between local people and ourselves.

Credit: The Travel and Tourism Research Association-Canada Conference Proceedings, 1991. Accompanying summary of address by Brian Palconer "Tourism and Sustainability: The Dream Realized."

APPENDIX C   Official Hotel Guide Classification System

- **Superior Deluxe:** An exclusive and expensive luxury hotel, often palatial, offering the highest standards of service, accommodations, and facilities—Elegant and luxurious public rooms—A prestige address—Establishments in this category are among the world's top hotels.

- **Deluxe:** An outstanding property offering many of the same features as Superior Deluxe—May be less grand and offer more reasonable rates than the Superior Deluxe properties, yet in many instances may be just as satisfactory—Safe to recommend to most discriminating clients.

- **Moderate Deluxe:** Basically a Deluxe hotel, but with qualifications—In some cases, some accommodations or public areas may offer a less pronounced degree of luxury than that found in fully Deluxe properties—In other cases, the hotel may be a well-established famous name, depending heavily on past reputation—The more contemporary hotels may be heavily marketed to business clients, with fine accommodations and public rooms offering Deluxe standards in comfort, but with less emphasis on atmosphere and/or personal service.

- **Superior First Class:** An above average hotel—May be an exceptionally well-maintained older hotel, more often a superior modern hotel specifically designed for the first-class market, with some outstanding features—Accommodations and public areas are expected to be tastefully furnished and very comfortable—May be a good value, especially if it is a commercial hotel—May be recommended to average clients and in most cases will satisfy the discriminating ones.

- **First Class:** A dependable, comfortable hotel with standardized rooms, amenities, and public areas—May have superior executive level or wing—May be safely recommended to average clients not expecting Deluxe facilities or special services—Should also be satisfactory for better groups.

- **Limited-Service First Class:** A property offering full first-class quality accommodations, but limited public areas, food service, and facilities—Usually moderate in size, the hotel often utilizes a residential scale and architecture and many offer complimentary breakfast and evening cocktails in the lobby or in a small, informal restaurant—Geared to the individual business/pleasure traveler.

- **Moderate First Class:** Essentially a First Class establishment with comfortable but somewhat simpler accommodations and public areas—May be lacking in some features (e.g., restaurant)—Some of the rooms or public areas, while adequate, may tend to be basic and functional—Usually suitable for cost-conscious clients.

- **Superior Tourist Class:** Primarily a budget property with mostly well-kept, functional accommodations, some up to First Class standards—Public rooms may be limited or nonexistent—Often just a place to sleep, but may have some charming or intimate features—May be a good value—Should satisfy individuals (sometimes even discriminating ones) or groups on a budget.

- **Tourist Class:** Strictly a budget operation with some facilities or features of Superior Tourist Class, but usually no (or very few) First Class accommodations—Should under no circumstances be recommended to fussy or discriminating clients—Should generally be used with caution.

- **Moderate Tourist Class:** Low-budget operations, often quite old and may not be well-kept—Should only be used in a pinch if no others are available—Clients should always be cautioned what to expect.

A Note On Unclassified Hotels.   It is the policy of the Official Hotel Guide to classify hotels based on a comprehensive body of information encompassing a selection of reliable sources and contacts. If, however, that information is insufficient, incomplete, or in any way ambiguous, a hotel may be listed without a classification, but this in no way reflects negatively on the property.

APPENDIX D   The Organizing Committee for the XVIII Olympic Winter Games, Nagano 1998

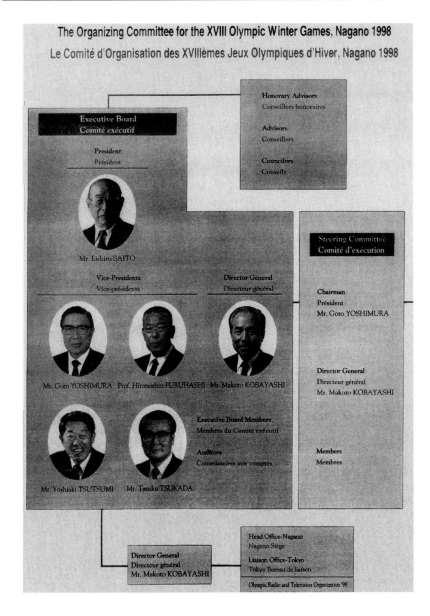

Courtesy NAOC.

Commissions
Commissions

Names of the Commission and Chairman / Noms de la Commission et du Président	Responsibility / Responsabilité

Finance & Planning
Finance et Planning — Mr. Osamu KEGAI

1. General plan for the management of the Games
   Plan général de l'administration des Jeux
2. Operational plan for the management of the Games
   Plan opérationnel de l'administration des Jeux
3. Financial plan for the Games
   Plan financier des Jeux
4. Coordination of the Commissions
   Coordination des Commissions
5. Matters not pertaining to any other Commission
   Affaires non ressortissantes à aucune autre Commission

Sports
Sports — Mr. Yushiro YAGI

1. Plan for the competitions and training schedule
   Plan des compétitions et de l'entraînement
2. Plan for regulations of the management of each competition
   Plan des règles administratives de chaque compétition
3. Organization plan for the officials of the competitions
   Plan de l'organisation des responsables des compétitions

Facilities
Installations — Mr. Yushuro YAGI

1. Plan for the sports facilities
   Plan des installations sportives
2. Supervision of the sports facilities
   Supervision des installations sportives
3. Plan for the temporary facilities
   Plan des installations temporaires

Mark Protection
Protection des marques — Mr. Muneyoshi UEDA

1. Protection of the marks and related items
   Protection des marques et articles concernés
2. Production of the emblem of the Games
   Production de l'emblème des Jeux
3. Production of the mascot of the Games
   Production de la mascotte des Jeux

Marketing
Marketing — Mr. Muneyoshi UEDA

1. Marketing plan
   Plan de marketing
2. Operational plan for overseas marketing
   Plan opérationnel du marketing à l'étranger
3. Operational plan for domestic marketing
   Plan opérationnel du marketing intérieur

International Relations
Relations Internationales — Mr. Ichiro OGIMURA

1. Matters concerning relations with the IOC, IFs, NOCs, and
   other organizations concerned
   (including reports to the IOC)
   Affaires concernant les relations avec le C.I.O., les F.I., les
   C.N.O. et les autres organisations concernées
   (rapports au C.I.O. inclus)

Cultural Programme
Programme Culturel — Mr. Masao YAMAMOTO

1. Plan for the cultural programme
   Plan du programme culturel
2. Plan for the Youth Camp
   Plan du Camp de la jeunesse
3. Promotion of exchange among athletes and officials
   Promotion d'échanges parmi les athlètes et les officiels

Olympic Village
Village Olympique — Mr. Ken-ichi CHIZUKA

1. Plan for the composition of the Olympic Village
   Plan de la composition du village olympique
2. Plan for the management of the Olympic Village
   Plan de l'administration du village olympique

Transportation & Security
Transport et Sécurité — Mr. Tadao NAKAMURA

1. Transportation plan
   Plan de transport
2. Security plan
   Plan de sécurité

Accommodation
Hébergement — Mr. Heishiro NISHIYAMA

1. Accommodation plan
   Plan d'hébergement
2. Plan for the management and supervision of accommodation
   Plan de l'administration et la supervision de l'hébergement

Medical Services
Services Médicaux — Prof. Yoshio KURODA

1. General plan for medical services
   Plan général de services médicaux
2. Plan for health control
   Plan de contrôle sanitaire
3. Plan for doping control
   Plan de contrôle anti-dopage
4. Plan for gender verification
   Plan de vérification de sexe
5. Operational plan for medical services
   Plan opérationnel de services médicaux
6. Plan for the maintenance of hygienic conditions
   Plan de l'entretien de conditions hygiéniques

Public Relations
Relations Publiques — Mr. Tsunekazu TAKEDA

1. Plan for public relations
   Plan de relations publiques
2. Operational plan for overseas public relations
   Plan opérationnel de relations publiques à l'étranger
3. Operational plan for domestic public relations
   Plan opérationnel de relations publiques intérieures

Media
Medias — Mr. Yasuaki SUDA

1. Plan for media services
   Plan de services pour les medias
2. Plan for setting up the Main Media Center
   Plan de l'établissement du Centre Principal de Medias
3. Plan for the management of the Main Media Center
   Plan de l'administration du Centre Principal de Medias

Ceremonies
Cérémonies — Mr. Hideo KAGAMI

1. Plan for the Opening and Closing Ceremonies
   Plan des cérémonies d'ouverture et de clôture
2. Plan for the victory ceremonies
   Plan des cérémonies des vainqueurs
3. Plan for the torch relay
   Plan du relais de la torche

APPENDIX E State and Territorial Travel Offices

States

Alabama Bureau of Tourism and Travel
P.O. Box 4309, Dept. TIA, Montgomery, AL 36103–4309
Tel: (205) 242–4169
Toll Free: 1–800–ALABAMA

Alaska Division of Tourism
P.O. Box 110801, TIA, Juneau, AK 99811–0801
Tel: (907) 465–2010

Arizona Office of Tourism
1100 West Washington, Phoenix, AZ 85007
Tel: (602) 542–8687

Arkansas Tourism Office
One Capitol Mall, Dept. 7701, Little Rock, AR 72201
Tel: (501) 682–7777
Toll Free: 1–800–NATURAL

California Office of Tourism
P.O. Box 9278, Dept. TIA, Van Nuys, CA 91409
Tel: (916) 322–2881
Toll Free: 1–800–TO–CALIF

Colorado Tourism Board
P.O. Box 38700, Denver, CO 80238
Tel: (303) 592–5410
Toll Free: 1–800–COLORADO (1–800–265–6723)

Connecticut Department of Economic Development, Tourism Division
865 Brook Street, Rocky Hill, CT 06067
Tel: (203) 258–4355
Toll Free: 1–800–CT–BOUND

Delaware Tourism Office
99 Kings Highway, Box 1401, Dept. TIA, Dover, DE 19903
Tel: (302) 739–4271
Toll Free: 1–800–441–8846

Florida Division of Tourism
126 West Van Buren Street, FLDA, Tallahassee, FL 32301
Tel: (904) 487–1462

Georgia Department of Industry, Trade & Tourism
P.O. Box 1776, Dept. TIA, Atlanta, GA 30301
Tel: (404) 656–3590
Toll Free: 1–800–VISIT–GA

State of Hawaii Department of Business, Economic Development & Tourism
P.O. Box 2359, Honolulu, HI 96804
Tel: (808) 586–2423

Idaho Division of Tourism Development
700 W. State Street, Dept. C, Boise, ID 83720
Tel: (208) 334–2470
Toll Free: 1–800–635–7820

Illinois Bureau of Tourism
100 W. Randolph, Suite 3-400, Chicago, IL 60601
Tel: (312) 814–4732
Toll Free: 1–800–223–0121

Indiana Department of Commerce/Tourism and Film Development Division
One North Capitol, Suite 700, Indianapolis, IN 46204–2288
Tel: (317) 232–8860
Toll Free: 1–800–289–6646

Iowa Division of Tourism
200 East Grand, TIA, Des Moines, IA 50309
Tel: (515) 242–4705
Toll Free: 1–800–345–IOWA

Kansas Travel and Tourism Division
400 West 8th Street, 5th Floor, Dept. DIS, Topeka, KS 66603–3957
Tel: (913) 296–3009
Toll Free: 1–800–252–6727

Kentucky Department of Travel Development
2200 Capitol Plaza Tower, Dept. DA, Frankfort, KY 40601
Tel: (502) 564–4930
Toll Free: 1–800–225–TRIP

Louisiana Office of Tourism
Attn: Inquiry Department, P.O. Box 94291, LOT, Baton Rouge, LA 70804–9291
Tel: (504) 342–8119
Toll Free: 1–800–33–GUMBO

Maine Office of Tourism
189 State Street, Augusta, ME 04333
Tel: (207) 289–5711
Toll Free: 1–800–533–9595

Maryland Office of Tourism Development
217 East Redwood Street, 9th Floor, Baltimore, MD 21202
Tel: (410) 333–6611
Toll Free: 1–800–543–1036

Massachusetts Office of Travel and Tourism
100 Cambridge Street, 13th Floor, Boston, MA 02202
Tel: (617) 727–3201
Toll Free: 1–800–447–MASS (For ordering vacation kit only) (*U.S. only*)

Michigan Travel Bureau
P.O. Box 30226, Lansing, MI 48909
Tel: (517) 373–0670
Toll Free: 1–800–5432–YES

Minnesota Office of Tourism
375 Jackson Street, 250 Skyway Level, St. Paul, MN 55101
Tel: (612) 296–5029
Toll Free: 1–800–657–3700

Mississippi Division of Tourism
P.O. Box 22825, Jackson, MS 39205
Tel: (601) 359–3297
Toll Free: 1–800–647–2290

Missouri Division of Tourism
P.O. Box 1055, Dept. TIA, Jefferson City, MO 65102
Tel: (314) 751–4133
Toll Free: 1–800–877–1234

Travel Montana
Room 259, Deer Lodge, MT 59722
Tel: (406) 444–2654
Toll Free: 1–800–541–1447

Nebraska Division of Travel and Tourism
301 Centennial Mall South, Room 88937, Lincoln, NE 68509
Tel: (402) 471–3796
Toll Free: 1–800–228–4307

Nevada Commission of Tourism
Capitol complex, Dept. TIA, Carson City, NV 89710
Tel: (702) 687–4322
Toll Free: 1–800–NEVADA–8

New Hampshire Office of Travel and Tourism Development
P.O. Box 856, Dept. TIA, Concord, NH 03302
Tel: (603) 271–2343

New Jersey Division of Travel and Tourism
20 West State Street, CN 826, Dept. TIA, Trenton, NJ 08625
Tel: (609) 292–2470
Toll Free: 1–800–JERSEY–7

New Mexico Department of Tourism
1100 St. Francis Drive, Joseph Montoya Building, Santa Fe, NM 87503
Tel: (505) 827–0291
Toll Free: 1–800–545–2040

New York State Department of Economic Development
One Commerce Plaza, Albany, NY 12245
Tel: (518) 474–4116
Toll Free: 1–800–CALL–NYS

North Carolina Division of Travel and Tourism
430 N. Salisbury Street, Raleigh, NC 27603
Tel: (919) 733–4171
Toll Free: 1–800–VISIT–NC

North Dakota Tourism Promotion
Liberty Memorial Bldg., Capitol Grounds, Bismarck, ND 58505
Tel: (701) 224–2525
Toll Free: 1–800–HELLO–ND (435–5663) (U.S. and Canada)

Ohio Division of Travel and Tourism
P.O. Box 1001, Dept. TIA, Columbus, OH 43211–0101
Tel: (614) 466–8844
Toll Free: 1–800–BUCKEYE (Continental U.S., Ontario, and Quebec)

Oklahoma Tourism & Recreation Department Travel and Tourism Division
500 Will Rogers Bldg., DA92, Oklahoma City, OK 73105–4492
Tel: (405) 521–3981
Toll Free: 1–800–652–6552 (Info. Requests Only)

Oregon Economic Development Department, Tourism Division
775 Summer Street, NE, Salem, OR 97310
Tel: (503) 373–1270
Toll Free: 1–800–547–7842

Pennsylvania Bureau of Travel Marketing
130 Commonwealth Drive, Warrendale, PA 15086
Tel: (717) 787–5453
Toll Free: 1–800–VISIT–PA

Rhode Island Tourism Division
7 Jackson Walkway, Dept. TIA, Providence, RI 02903
Tel: (401) 277–2601
Toll Free: 1–800–556–2484

South Carolina Division of Tourism
Box 71, Room 902, Columbia, SC 29202
Tel: (803) 734–0235

South Dakota Department of Tourism
711 E. Wells Avenue, Pierre, SD 57501–3369
Tel: (605) 773–3301
Toll Free: 1–800–843–1930

Tennessee Department of Tourism Development
P.O. Box 23170, TNDA, Nashville, TN 37202
Tel: (615) 741–2158

Texas Department of Commerce, Tourism Division
P.O. Box 12728, Austin, TX 78711–2728
Tel: (512) 462–9191
Toll Free: 1–800–888–0511

Utah Travel Council
Council Hall/Capitol Hill, Dept. TIA, Salt Lake City, UT 84114
Tel: (801) 538–1030

Vermont Travel Division
134 State Street, Dept. TIA, Montpelier, VT 05602
Tel: (802) 828–3236
Toll Free: 1–800–338–0189 (Trade Only)

Virginia Tourism
1021 East Cary Street, Dept. VT, Richmond, VA 23219
Tel: (804) 786–4484
Toll Free: 1–800–VISIT–VA

Washington State Tourism Development Division
P.O. Box 42513, Olympia, WA 98504–2513
Tel: (206) 586–2088 or (206) 586–2012
Toll Free: 1–800–544–1800

West Virginia Division of Tourism & Parks
2101 Washington Street, East, Charleston, WV 25305
Tel: (304) 348–2286
Toll Free: 1–800–225–5982

Wisconsin Division of Tourism
P.O. Box 7606, Madison, WI 53707
Tel: (608) 266–2161
Toll Free: In-state: 1–800–372–2737
Out-of-State: 1–800–432–TRIP

Wyoming Division of Tourism
I-25 at College Drive, Dept. WY, Cheyenne, WY 82002
Tel: (307) 777–7777
Toll Free: 1–800–225–5996

District of Columbia

Washington, D.C. Convention and Visitors Association
1212 New York Avenue, NW, Washington, D.C. 20005

Tel: (202) 789–7000

U.S. Territories

American Samoa Government Office of Tourism
c/o McClellan Corporation International, 21318 Dumetz Road, P.O. Box 4070, Woodland Hills,
    CA 91365
Tel: (818) 884–0480

Guam Visitors Bureau, United States
c/o Mr. Richard Keating, Marketing Representative
425 Madison Avenue, New York, NY 10017
Tel: (212) 888–4110
Toll Free: 1–800–228–GUAM

Marianas Visitors Bureau
P.O. Box 861, Saipan, MP 96950
Tel: (670) 234–8325/6/7

Puerto Rico Tourism Company
P.O. Box 5268, Dept. TH, Miami, FL 33102
Tel: (212) 223–6530
Toll Free: 1–800–866–STAR, Ext. 17

U.S. Virgin Islands Division of Tourism
P.O. Box 6400, VITIA, Charlotte Amalie, St. Thomas, USVI 00801
Tel: (809) 774–8784
Toll Free: 1–800–372–8784

APPENDIX F Information about Americans with Disabilities Act Requirements

This document is available in the following alternate formats:

- Braille
- Large Print
- Audiotape
- Electronic file on computer disk and electronic bulletin board (202) 514–6193

For more specific information about ADA requirements affecting Public Services and Public Accommodations contact:

Office on the Americans with Disabilities Act
Civil Rights Division
U.S. Department of Justice
P.O. Box 66118
Washington, D.C. 20035–6118
(202) 514–0301 (Voice)
(202) 514–0381 (TDD)
(202) 514–0383 (TDD)

For more specific information about ADA requirements affecting employment contact:

Equal Employment Opportunity Commission
1801 L Street NW
Washington, D.C. 20507
(202) 663–4900 (Voice)
800–800–3302 (TDD)
(202) 663–4494 (TDD—for 202 Area Code)

For more specific information about ADA requirements affecting transportation contact:

Department of Transportation
400 Seventh Street SW
Washington, D.C. 20590
(202) 366–9305 (Voice)
(202) 755–7687 (TDD)

For more specific information about requirements for accessible design in new construction and alterations contact:

Architectural and Transportation Barriers Compliance Board
1111 18th Street NW
Suite 501
Washington, D.C. 20036
800–USA–ABLE (Voice)
800–USA–ABLE (TDD)

For more specific information about ADA requirements affecting telecommunications contact:

Federal Communications Commission
1919 M Street NW
Washington, D.C. 20554
(202) 632–7260 (Voice)
(202) 632–6999 (TDD)

Source: Americans with Disabilities Act Office
The Americans with Disabilities Act
Questions and Answers
U.S. Government Printing Office: 1991-299–558

APPENDIX G Directory of Professional Associations and Organizations

Air Transport Association of America (ATTA), 1301 Pennsylvania Ave., Suite 1100, Washington, D.C. (202) 626–4000

American Alliance for Health, Physical Education, Recreation, and Dance (AAHPERD), 1900 Association Drive, Reston, VA. (703) 476–3400

American Coaster Enthusiasts (ACE), P.O. Box 8226, Chicago, IL 60680.

American Hotel and Motel Association (AH&MA), 1201 New York Ave. Suite 600 N.W., Washington, D.C. 10005. (202) 289–3100 FAX (202) 289–3199

American Ski Federation, Constitution Ave, Washington, D.C. 20002. (202) 543–1595

American Society of Association Executives (ASAE), 1575 Eye St. N.W., Washington, D.C. 20005. (202) 626–2803 FAX (202) 371–8825

American Society of Travel Agents (ASTA), 1101 King St. Alexandria, VA 22314. (703) 739–2782 FAX (703) 684–8319

Association of Conference and Events Directors—International (ACED), Colorado State University, Rockwell Hall, Fort Collins, CO 80523. (303) 491–5151 FAX (303) 491–0667

Association for Convention Operations Management (ACOM), 1819 Peachtree St. N.E., Suite 560, Atlanta, GA 30309. (404) 351–3220

Convention Liaison Council (CLC), 1575 Eye St. N.W., Washington, D.C. 20005. (202) 626–2764

Exposition Service Contractors Association (ESCA), 400 South Houston St., Suite 210, Dallas, TX 75202. (214) 742–9217

Health Care and Exhibitors Association (HCEA), 5775 Peachtree-Dunwoody Rd., Suite 500D, Atlanta, GA 30342. (404) 252–3663 FAX (404) 252–0774

Hospitality Sales and Marketing Association International (HSMAI) 1300 L St. NW, Suite 800, Washington, D.C., 20005. (202) 789–0089 FAX (202) 789–1725

Institute of Association Management Companies (IAMC), 5820 Wilshire Blvd., Suite 500, Los Angeles, CA 90036.

International Association of Amusement Parks and Attractions (IAAPA), 1448 Duke St., Alexandria, VA 22314. (703) 836–4800 FAX (703) 836–4801

International Association of Auditorium Managers (IAAM) 4425 W. Airport Freeway, Suite 590, Irving, TX 75062.

International Association of Conference Centers (IACC) (243) North Lindbergh Boulevard, Suite 315, St. Louis, Mo., 63141. (314) 993–8575 FAX (314) 993–8919

International Association of Convention and Visitors Bureaus (IACVB) P.O. Box 6690, Champaign, IL 61820. (217) 359–8881 FAX (217) 359–0965

International Association of Fairs and Expositions (IAFE) P.O. Box 985, Springfield, MO 65801. (417) 862–5771 FAX (417) 862–0156

International Congress and Conference Association (ICCA), J.W. Brouswerplein 27, P.O. Box 5343, Amsterdam, The Netherlands.

International Festivals Association (IFA), P.O. Box 2950, Port Angeles, WA 98362. (206) 457–3141 FAX (206) 452–4695

International Food Service Executives Association (IFSEA) 1100 S. State Rd. 7, Suite 103, Margate, FL 33068. (305) 977–0767 FAX (305) 977–0876

International Special Events Society (ISES), 9202 North Meridian St., Suite 200, Indianapolis, IN 46260.

Meeting Professionals International (MPI), 1950 Stemmons Freeway, Suite 5018, Dallas, TX 75207. (214) 712–7700 FAX (214) 712–7770

National Association of Catering Executives (NACE), 304 W. Liberty St., Suite 201, Louisville, KY 40202. (502) 583–3783 FAX (502) 589–3602

National Association of Black Hospitality Professionals (NABHP), P.O. Box 5463 Plainfield, NJ 07060. (908) 354–5117 FAX (908) 354–8804

National Recreation and Park Association (NRPA), 2775 S. Quincy St., Suite 300, Arlington, VA 22206. (703) 825–4940

National Restaurant Association (NRA) 1200 17th St. NW, Washington, D.C., 20036. (202) 331–5900 FAX (202) 331–2429

Professional Convention Management Association (PCMA), 100 Vestavia Office Park, Suite 220, Birmingham, AL 35216. (205) 823–7262 FAX (205) 822–3891

Religious Conference Management Association (RCMA), One Hoosier Dome, Suite 120, Indianapolis, IN 46225. (317) 632–1888

Resort and Commercial Recreation Association (RCRA), P.O. Box 1208, New Port Richey, FL 34656. (813) 845–7373

Society of Corporate Meeting Planners (SCMP), 2600 Garden Rd., Suite 208, Monterey, CA 93940. (408) 649–6544 FAX (408) 649–4124

Society of Government Meeting Planners (SGMP), 219 E. Main St., Mechanicsburg, PA 17055. (717) 795–7467

Society of Incentive Travel Executives (SITE), 21 West 38th St., New York, NY 10016. (212) 575–1838 FAX (212) 575–1838

Society for Food Service Management (SFM) 304 W. Liberty St., Suite 201, Louisville, KY 40202. (502) 583–3783 FAX (502) 589–3602

Travel Industry Association of America (TIAA), 2 Lafayette Center, 133 21st St. NW, Suite 800, Washington, DC 20036.

World Waterpark Association (WWA), P.O. Box 14826, Lenexa, KS 66214. (913) 599–0300 FAX (913) 599–0520

APPENDIX H   Recreation: A Select Chronology

3200 B.C.E.	• Egyptians invent the sail.
776 B.C.E.	• First recorded Olympic games. Sports included horse racing, wrestling, boxing, pentathlon, and running. Women not admitted as spectators.
c. 300 B.C.E.	• Ball games, dice playing, and board games well known to the Greeks and Romans.
264 B.C.E.	• First Roman gladiatorial games.
71–80 C.E.	• Colosseum built in Rome.
c. 380	• Theodosius forbids the Olympic Games.
527	• First animal-driven paddle-wheel boats.
550	• Beginnings of chess game in India.
1000	• Chinese perfect their invention, gunpowder.
1094	• First record of gondolas in Venice.
1100s	• Arabian *carosello*, or war games including jousting practice. This developed into the medieval tournament and into the amusement ride, the carousel.
1151	• First game of chess arrives in England.
1174	• Earliest horse races in England.
c. 1200	• First jesters appear in European courts.
1269	• First toll roads in England.
1271	• Marco Polo, a Venetian, travels to China, in the court of Kublai Khan (1275–1292), returns to Genoa (1295), and writes his *Travels*.
c. 1300	• Development of *Noh* drama in Japan. • Skittle becoming popular in Europe.
1377	• Playing cards overtake dice in popularity in Germany.
1400–1500	• Card games gain popularity throughout Europe.
1418	• Portugal's Prince Henry the Navigator sponsors exploration of coastal Africa, beginning the Age of Exploration.
1450s	• Florence becomes the center of Renaissance arts and learning under the Medicis. • Mocha in southwestern Arabia becomes main port for coffee export.

1465	• Edward I passes an edict banning "hustling of stones" and other bowling-type sports.
1490	• Beginnings of ballet at the Italian courts.
1492	• Columbus sails to the New World.
	• The profession of book publisher emerges.
1495	• Hieronymus Bosch paints altarpiece "Garden of Earthly Delights," showing perverse versions of various forms of popular recreation as a scene of Hell.
1502	• "Nuremberg Egg," the first watch, is constructed by clock maker Peter Henlein.
1517	• Coffee introduced in Europe.
1520	• Chocolate brought from Mexico to Spain.
	• Henry VIII orders bowling lanes to be built in Whitehall.
1532	• Sugar cane first cultivated in Brazil.
1535	• First diving bells.
1536	• Indian rubber mentioned for the first time.
1539	• First Christmas tree, at Strasbourg Cathedral.
	• A public lottery held in France.
1542	• Heavy taxes on drinks in Bavaria.
1545	• First European botanical gardens at Padua, Italy.
1550	• Billiards played for the first time in Italy.
1551	• First licensing of alehouses and taverns in England and Wales.
1552	• St. Andrew's Golf Club founded. Mary, Queen of Scots, was probably the first woman golfer.
1555	• Tobacco brought from America to Spain.
1565	• Tobacco and sweet potatoes introduced into England.
1566	• *Notizie Scritte*, one of the first newspapers, appears in Venice.
1568	• Bottled beer invented.
1580	• Francis Drake returns to England after circumnavigating the globe.
1589	• Forks used for the first time at the French court.
1596	• Tomatoes introduced in England.
1606	• Extensive program of road building begins in France.
1607	• Jamestown, Virginia, established—first permanent English colony on the American mainland.
1608	• First checks, "cash letters," in use in the Netherlands.
1609	• Dutch East India Company ships tea to Europe for the first time.
1618	• James I: "Book of Sports," the Puritans object to the playing of popular sports.
1620	• Oliver Cromwell denounced because he participated in "the disreputable game of cricket."
1622	• Papal chancellery adopts January 1 as beginning of the new year. Up to this time it had been March twenty-fifth.
1625	• Hackney coaches appear in the streets of London
	• Tobacco tax and tobacco monopoly in England.
1630	• Invention of the card game cribbage.

1631	• The first public thanksgiving, a fast day, was celebrated in Massachusetts Bay Colony.
1635	• Speed limits on hackney coaches in London established, 3 mph.
	• Sale of tobacco in France limited to apothecaries—only on doctor's prescriptions.
1637	• The first public opera house, Teatro San Cassiano, opens in Venice.
1647	• First newspaper advertisement (for the book *The Divine Right of Church Government*, appearing in the newspaper *Perfect Occurences of every Daie Journall* [sic] *in Parliament*).
1654	• First American toll bridge—over the Newbury River at Rowley, Massachusetts.
1657	• First stockings and fountain pens manufactured in Paris.
1661	• Vauxhall Gardens opens.
1663	• Turnpike tolls introduced in England.
1664	• British take New Amsterdam from the Dutch.
	• First organized sport in America: horseracing at Newmarket course at Hempstead Plains, Long Island, New York.
1666	• Cricket Club founded at St. Albans, Hertfordshire, England.
1677	• Ice cream becomes popular as a dessert in Paris.
1690	• The first newspaper in America—*Publick Occurences,*—lasted for four days. Benjamin Harris did not have permission to publish.
1702	• Queen Anne of England gives royal approval to horseracing and originates the idea of the sweepstakes—racing for a cash award.
1704	• The first ongoing newspaper in America—*Boston News Letter.*
1710	• Post road system developed in the United States to aid mail delivery.
1711	• Ascot races established.
1715	• Vaudevilles, popular entertainments, appear in Paris.
1720	• First yacht club established at Cork Harbor, Ireland.
1722	• *Grand Tour*, a travel handbook, published by French painter Hyacinthe Rigaud.
1724	• Daniel Defoe: *A Tour through the Whole Island of Great Britain* published.
1725	• First public concerts held in Paris.
1727	• *Racing Calendar* first published (records of previous year's horse races).
1732	• Ninepins first played in New York.
1733	• The Serpentine in Hyde Park (London) designed.
1744	• First recorded cricket match: Kent vs. All England.
1760	• Edmund Hoyle establishes rules of whist.
1765	• James Watt invents the steam engine.
1770	• Visiting cards introduced in England.
1776	• Military ski competitions in Norway.
1778	• James Cook discovers Hawaii.
	• La Scala Opera House in Milan, Italy, opens.
1779	• First velocipedes appear in Paris.
1783	• Montgolfier brothers make first hot-air balloon ascent.
1786	• Earliest attempts at internal gas lighting in England and Germany.

1791	• L'Enfant designs Washington, D.C., but plans not fully implemented until 1900.
1794	• First American hotel—City Hotel in New York.
1795	• Hydraulic press invented by Joseph Bramah.
	• First horse-drawn railroad in England.
1796	• First U.S. passports issued.
1801	• Robert Fulton, a civil engineer, produces the first submarine, the *Nautilus.*
1804	• Lewis and Clark begin exploration of what is now northwestern United States.
1807	• R. Fulton makes first successful steamboat trip between New York and Albany.
	• Street lighting by gas in London.
1810	• Phineas Taylor Barnum born.
1814	• First practical steam locomotive built by George Stephenson.
1818	• First regularly scheduled trans-Atlantic passenger service.
1819	• First steamship crosses the Atlantic.
1822	• Boston's streets lit by gas.
1823	• Rugby football originates at the Rugby School in England.
1825	• First passenger-carrying railroad in England.
1826	• The Union Oyster House, a restaurant, opens in Boston (still open today!).
1827	• *Baedecker Guides* appear, published by Karl Baedecker.
1829	• Omnibuses, designed by George Shillibaer, are put into service in London's transport system.
1831	• Horse-drawn buses appear in New York.
1834	• Charles Babbage invents "analytical engine," precursor to the computer.
1837	• First Canadian railroad.
1838	• Daguerre-Niepce method of photography presented to the Académie des Sciences and the Académie des Beaux Arts in Paris.
1839	• Charles Goodyear makes rubber a commercially viable product by discovering the process of vulcanization.
	• Cunard Line founded as the British and North American Royal Mail Steam Packet Company.
	• Abner Doubleday designs first baseball field and conducts first baseball game.
1841	• First "Cook's Tour" led by Thomas Cook to a temperance meeting in Loughborough, Leistershire, England.
	• P. T. Barnum opens his curious collection of freaks and curios called the "American Museum" in New York.
1843	• D. D. Emmett produces the first minstrel show.
	• Skiing becomes popular as a sport in Tromso, Norway.
1844	• Samuel F. B. Morse patents the telegraph.
1845	• Knickerbocker Baseball Club codifies the rules of baseball.
1849	• California Gold Rush begins.

c. 1850	• McCormack Harvesting Machine Company franchises its product.
1850	• Vauxhall Gardens closes.
1851	• The London Great Exhibition is the first world's fair, meant to demonstrate British industrial achievement and prosperity. Six million visitors in 141 days.
	• YMCA (Young Men's Christian Association) introduced in the United States. It did not become a national organization until late in the century.
1853	• Elevator invented.
	• New York City acquires land that is to become Central Park. Frederick Law Olmsted and Calvert Vaux submit winning design for the development of the park.
1855	• Paris Exposition.
1856	• YWCA (Young Women's Christian Association) started in New York as the Ladies Christian Union.
c. 1860	• Boys Club founded in Hartford, Connecticut.
1863	• Roller skating introduced in America.
1865	• George Pullman's sleeping cars first appear on American Railroads.
1868	• Badminton, the game, was developed at Badminton Hall in Gloucestershire, England.
	• First recorded bicycle race at Parc de St. Cloud, Paris.
1869	• First U.S. transcontinental rail route completed at Promontory Point, Utah.
	• Suez Canal opened.
	• First postcards introduced in Austria.
1871	• White Star Line launched the SS *Oceanic*, first of the large modern luxury ocean liners.
1872	• First international soccer game: England vs. Scotland.
	• Yellowstone inaugurated as the first U.S. National Park.
1873	• The Prater (Vienna) becomes Europe's most popular pleasure garden. Vienna World's Fair.
1875	• First Kentucky Derby.
1876	• Alexander Graham Bell invents the telephone.
	• Bayreuth Festspielhaus opens with first complete performance of Richard Wagner's *Ring des Niebelungen.*
	• World Exhibition at Philadelphia.
1877	• Thomas Alva Edison patents phonograph.
	• First All-England Lawn Tennis championship at Wimbledon, London (Spencer Grove, champion).
1878	• First commercial telephone exchange opens in New Haven, Connecticut.
1880	• First viable electric light bulb independently developed by Edison and J. W. Swan.
	• Bingo is developed from the Italian lotto game of Tombola.
	• World Exhibition in Melbourne.

1883	• Brooklyn Bridge and Metropolitan Opera House completed.
	• *Orient Express* makes its first Paris to Istanbul run.
	• World Exhibition in Amsterdam.
1884	• The London Underground (subway system) opens.
1885	• A sand garden, a precursor to the modern playground, is located in the yard of the Children's Mission on Parmenter Street in Boston.
	• The Coney Island Coaster opens.
	• Golf introduced to America.
	• George Eastman manufactures coated photographic paper.
1886	• John Styth Pemberton, an Atlanta pharmacist, mixes a batch of syrup called Coca-Cola in a pot in his back yard.
1888	• J. P. Dunlop invents the pneumatic tire.
	• First loop-the-loop coaster.
	• Eastman perfects the "Kodak" box camera.
	• Tesla builds an electric motor (manufactured by George Westinghouse).
1890	• First water slide patented.
1891	• Beginnings of wireless telegraphy.
	• Zipper invented (not in practical use until 1913).
1892	• Diesel engine patented.
	• First model playground at Jane Addams's Hull House in Chicago.
1893	• Chicago World's Fair.
	• Henry Ford constructs his first car.
1894	• First showing of Edison's kinetoscope in New York City.
	• The disc is used instead of the cylinder for the first time for sound reproduction.
1895	• First professional football game played in United States at Latrobe, Pennsylvania.
	• American Bowling Congress formed to govern the same.
	• First U.S. Open Golf Championship held.
	• Auguste and Louis Lumière invent a motion-picture camera.
1896	• Berlin World's Fair.
	• Marconi receives first wireless patent in England.
	• First modern Olympic Games held in Athens, Greece.
	• First Alpine ski school founded at Lilienfeld, Austria.
	• Helium discovered.
1897	• World Exhibition at Brussels.
	• Steeplechase, the first Coney Island amusement park, built.
1898	• First photographs taken using artificial light.
1899	• First magnetic sound recording.
1900	• The Cakewalk becomes the most fashionable dance.
	• Speech transmitted via radio waves.
	• First presentation of tennis's Davis Cup.
	• First trial flight of the Zeppelin.
1901	• First motor-driven bicycles.
1903	• Wright Brothers fly first powered, controlled, heavier-than-air flight at Kitty Hawk, North Carolina.
	• Henry Ford organizes Ford Motor Company.

1903 cont.	• First American coast-to-coast crossing by car. It takes 65 days.
	• First Tour de France bicycle race.
	• Richard Steiff designs first teddy bears.
	• Luna Park at Coney Island built.
1904	• New York City subway opened.
	• St. Louis Exposition and Olympics.
	• Dreamland (amusement park) built at Coney Island, burned down in 1911.
1906	• French Grand Prix auto race first run.
1907	• Baden-Powell founds the Boy Scout movement.
	• First daily comic strip, "Mr. Mutt" (later Mutt & Jeff) begins in the *San Francisco Chronicle.*
1908	• First "Model T" Ford produced. Fifteen million were eventually sold, revolutionizing transportation in the United States.
1910	• Boy Scouts of America incorporated.
	• The "week end" becomes popular in the United States.
	• Camp Fire Girls founded.
1912	• Girl Scouts of America founded.
	• *Titanic* sinks on maiden voyage; over 1,500 drown.
	• First successful parachute jump.
1913	• Garment workers strike in New York and Boston, winning shorter work week and increase in wages.
	• Grand Central Terminal in New York City is completed.
	• Charlie Chaplin makes his first films.
1914	• First scheduled airline flights.
1915	• The U.S. Agricultural Appropriations Act is the first legislation that specifically mentions recreation as a legitimate use in National Parks.
1916	• Daylight savings time introduced in Britain.
	• National Park Service established under U.S. Department of the Interior.
1918	• Daylight savings time introduced in the U.S.
	• Eight-hour work day established by law in Germany.
1919	• J. W. Alcock and A. Whitten Brown make first trans-Atlantic nonstop flight.
	• Sir Barton is the first horse to win all three races of the Triple Crown (Kentucky Derby, Preakness, and the Belmont Stakes). J. Loftus was the jockey in all three races.
	• Ray Allen and Frank Wright open a root beer stand that eventually grows to become 2,500 A&W stands.
1920	• First American broadcasting station opened by the Westinghouse Company in Pittsburgh, Pennsylvania.
	• Waterskiing introduced. Lake Annency, Haute Savoie, France.
	• Eighteenth Amendment to the U.S. Constitution: Prohibition goes into effect.
1923	• The Disney Company is formed when Walt Disney signs a contract with M. J. Winkler to produce a series of "Alice Comedies."
1924	• National Capital Parks Commission created around Washington, D.C.
	• There is a world craze for Mah-Jongg.
	• First Winter Olympics held.

1925	• First television transmission of recognizable human features.
	• Crossword puzzles become popular.
	• The Charleston is the most popular dance.
1927	• Charles Lindbergh flies solo from New York to Paris.
	• *The Jazz Singer*: first talking motion picture.
1928	• First scheduled television broadcast—at WGY, Schenectady, New York.
	• First color motion pictures exhibited by George Eastman.
	• "Steamboat Willie" is released at the Colony Theater in New York—the first Mickey Mouse cartoon released, and the first appearance of Minnie Mouse.
1929	• U.S. Stock Exchange collapses, causing the beginning of a worldwide economic crisis.
	• Bell Laboratories experiment with color television.
	• American manufacturers begin to make aluminum furniture.
	• Graf Zeppelin airship flies around the world.
1930	• Ellen Church hired as the first airline "stewardess."
	• Photo flashbulb comes into use.
1932	• Disney's first color film, *Flowers and Trees,* also wins the first Academy Award. Disney Studio opens an art school to train animators.
1933	• DC-1 airplane introduced.
	• First All-Star baseball game.
1934	• DC-2 airplane introduced.
1935	• The Federal Music Project, part of Franklin Roosevelt's New Deal sponsored thousands of free concerts, employing some 18,000 otherwise unemployed musicians.
1936	• DC-3 airplane introduced.
	• The ocean liner *Queen Mary* wins a trans-Atlantic speed contest.
	• The Federal Art Project, part of the New Deal, employed over 5,000 artists in 44 states.
1937	• Amelia Earhart is lost in mid-Pacific on a round-the-world flight.
	• First jet engine built.
	• Disaster of dirigible *Hindenburg* at Lakehurst, New Jersey, is described in the first transcontinental radio broadcast.
	• Billy Butlin opens first commercial holiday camp in Britain.
	• Golden Gate Bridge opens in San Francisco.
	• Disney's *Snow White and the Seven Dwarfs* is the first feature-length animated film to be released.
1938	• Douglas "Wrong Way" Corrigan flies from New York to Dublin.
	• Forty-hour work week established in the United States.
	• Toothbrushes with nylon bristles introduced as the first commercial use of nylon, the first fully synthetic fiber.
1939	• Baseball is first televised in the United States.
	• Pan-Am offers the first regularly scheduled flights between the United States and Europe.
	• Nylon stockings are introduced.

1940	• First successful helicopter flight in United States.
	• Olympic Games suspended until 1948, after World War II. Wimbledon and Davis Cup competition also suspended because of the war.
1942	• Coconut Grove nightclub fire in Boston kills 491.
	• First magnetic recording tape invented.
	• War economy measures cause college and university enrollments to plummet, but the new adult education classes become extremely popular.
1944	• End-of-war paper shortages forced publishers to experiment with soft-cover books.
1946	• ENIAC, the first electronic digital computer, is dedicated at the Moore School of Electrical Engineering in Philadelphia, Pennsylvania. It filled a 30-by-60-foot room.
	• Postwar building boom heralds the march to the suburbs in the United States.
1949	• Luna Park at Coney Island finally succumbed to fire. It also had major fires in 1944 and 1947.
	• Convention Liaison Committee (later became Convention Liaison Council) founded.
1950	• Sen. Joseph McCarthy of Wisconsin chairs a Senate special investigating committee to probe the charges of communist activity in the State Department. The committee's work resulted in the "blacklisting" of many people in the entertainment industry and the scientific and academic communities. Its results could be felt for several decades.
	• Malls start to become popular in America's suburbia.
1951	• Columbia Broadcasting System introduces the first color broadcast to the world. Unfortunately there are no color televisions owned by the public.
	• Direct-dial telephone service is introduced.
	• The first atomic-powered generator begins producing electricity at the U.S. Reactor Testing Station in Idaho.
1953	• Edmund Hillary of New Zealand and Tenzing Norkay of Nepal reach the top of Mt. Everest.
1955	• Disneyland theme park opens in Anaheim, California.
	• First broadcast of *The Mickey Mouse Club* television series.
	• Rock 'n' roll music introduced.
1956	• Creation of the U.S. Interstate Highway System.
	• IFA (International Festivals Association) founded.
	• The first trans-Atlantic telephone cable was laid.
1957	• Ringling Brothers and Barnum and Bailey Circus performs its last tented circus. Production costs force a move to performances inside permanent structures.
	• The Presidential Inauguration ceremonies are the first nationally televised videotaped broadcast.
	• *Mayflower II* lands at Plymouth, Massachusetts, after duplicating the 1617 voyage of the Pilgrims.

1958	• Cha-cha is the latest dance craze.
	• Beatnik movement spreads from California to the rest of the United States and Europe.
1959	• Pan-American World Airways initiates passenger service circling the globe.
1960	• The first commercial use of aluminum cans, which, unlike the tin-plated steel cans, are not biodegradable. At this time 95 percent of soft drinks and 50 percent of beer in the U.S. is sold in returnable bottles that are reused 50–60 times.
	• Development of the laser.
1961	• Angus G. Wynne, Jr. opens the first of the seven Six-Flags Theme Parks located near Dallas/Fort Worth, Texas. It is called Six Flags over Texas.
	• McDonald's begins its major expansion. Ray Kroc buys the hamburger chain, which has been around since 1954, from the McDonald brothers and immediately establishes over 200 stands. It will expand into a world wide chain.
	• Berlin Wall erected.
	• Last journey of the *Orient Express* (Paris to Bucharest).
	• First passenger airline hijacking.
1962	• The *Orient Express* goes out of business after nearly 79 years of service between Paris and Istanbul. It is a victim of the airplane.
	• The Lear jet is introduced. Within five years it will be the leading private jet airplane.
	• The first Wal-Mart store opens.
	• Tab openers for aluminum cans are introduced.
1964	• The Astrodome, the world's first domed stadium, is built in Houston, Texas.
1964	• The Beatles arrive in New York to begin their U.S. tour.
	• The U.S. Surgeon General's report on cigarette smoking is released.
	• The Frug, Monkey, Funky Chicken, and Watusi are popular dances. Discothèques have become popular as dance emporiums.
1965	• Steeplechase, the first Coney Island amusement park, is demolished, making it also the last of the big Coney Island amusement parks.
	• National Endowment for the Arts and National Endowment for the Humanities established by the Federal Aid to the Arts Act.
	• U.S. Banks prepare to issue their own credit cards, having seen the success of American Express and Diners Club.
	• The Blackout of 1965 darkens seven states and Ontario, Canada, affecting 30 million people in an 80,000-square-mile area. In most areas the power was out for twelve hours or more.
	• The world's first communication satellite, *Early Bird,* is put into orbit, relaying telephone calls and television programs between Europe and the United States.
	• The Grateful Dead have their beginnings in San Francisco as an acid-rock group.

1966	• Disposable diapers introduced.
	• First rare and endangered species list issued by the U.S. Department of the Interior.
	• Walt Disney dies.
1967	• McDonnell Aircraft Corp. completes successful takeover of Douglas Aircraft and creates the McDonnell-Douglas Corp.
1968	• Hershey Foods discontinues the nickel candy bar.
1969	• The *Concorde* makes its first supersonic flight.
	• Man walks on the moon for the first time.
	• Sesame Street debuts on public television.
	• Woodstock Music and Art Festival, the festival that defines a generation, takes place in the Catskills.
1970	• Boeing 747 jumbo jet goes into trans-Atlantic service.
	• Ivy League schools begin to go co-ed.
	• Theodore Roszak's *The Making of a Counter Culture* and Alvin Toffler's *Future Shock* are both written.
	• First wave pool in North America opens at Point Mallard in Decatur, Alabama.
1971	• Amtrak takes over virtually all American passenger railroad traffic in a government effort to end the decline in passenger rail service. The Amtrak takeover effectively ends service to many cities.
	• Walt Disney World in Orlando, Florida, opens.
1972	• The European Economic Community, created by treaty in 1957, accepts Britain, Ireland, Denmark, and Norway as members.
	• The San Francisco Bay Area Rapid Transit System (BART) commences service. It is the first new regional transit system in the United States in over fifty years.
	• Federal Express is founded.
	• The Munich Olympic Games are marred by the murder of eleven Israeli athletes by terrorists from the Palestine Liberation Organization.
	• Nike, Inc., is founded. By 1990 Nike will be the largest manufacturer of athletic footwear.
	• MPI (Meeting Planners International) founded.
1973	• Congress overrides the National Environmental Policy Act to allow the Alaskan oil pipeline to be built. This action is a response to oil embargoes.
	• The energy crisis is exacerbated by an oil embargo by the Arab nations.
	• Tennis "battle of the sexes" played by Bobby Riggs and Billie Jean King.
	• Arizona law bans smoking in public places.
1974	• Fifty-five mile-per-hour national speed limit signed into law. Federal highway funding is conditional on enforcement of this new speed limit. The speed limit conserves 3.4 million gallons of gasoline per year and highway fatalities fall.
	• The Heimlich Maneuver is first described in the journal *Emergency Medicine*.

1974 cont.	• London's Covent Garden fruit, vegetable, and flower market moves to South London after more than 300 years in the center of town. The Covent Garden location is converted to an upscale shopping district. • Airbus A300B is assembled in Toulouse, France, beginning the challenge to Boeing for the world aircraft market.
1975	• Lyme disease is identified in Lyme, Connecticut. The disease, spread by the deer tick, has changed how people approach hiking, camping, and other outdoor activities. • U.S. soft drinks edge past coffee in popularity and will pass milk within the next year. • The first Indoor Clean Air Act is passed in Minnesota, requiring all public places to have smoke-free areas, but enforcement is difficult.
1976	• U.S. Nuclear power reactors begin commercial production of electricity. • Energy Policy and Conservation Act sets U.S. gas mileage standards for cars. • Apple Computer is founded by Steve Wozniak and Steve Jobs in a San Jose garage. • Legionnaire's Disease, a rare form of pneumonia, kills twenty-nine members of the American Legion who are attending their annual convention in Philadelphia. • Fax machines gain ground as transmission time plummets from six minutes to three minutes per page. Machine prices fall, but quality is still poor. • Rupert Murdoch buys the *New York Post* to add to his worldwide collection of eighty-three newspapers and eleven magazines with emphasis on scandals, sex, crime, and sports. • Punk rock gains favor among England's working-class youth, then travels across the Atlantic. • As with Covent Garden in London, Boston's Quincy Market reopens as a shopping area, thereby revitalizing a run-down part of the center city. • Perrier water is introduced to the United States. • First Night is held in Boston, Massachusetts. It has since spread all over the U.S., changing the New Year's Eve partying habits of many. • United States celebrates its bicentennial. • The *Concorde* begins supersonic passenger service.
1977	• South Africa receives its first television broadcasts. The Pretoria government has finally yielded to public pressure after banning television on the grounds that it was morally corrupting. • Elvis Presley dies. • Blue jeans sales are over 500 million pairs, up from 150 million in 1957 and just over 200 million in 1967. • California experiences its worst drought. • The U.S. Supreme Court rules that the Environmental Protection Agency has authority to establish industry-wide standards for discharging pollutants into waterways. • The U.S. government recognizes the People's Republic of China.

1977 cont.	• The U.S. raises the mandatory retirement age from 65 to 70.
	• The last German Volkswagen Beetle rolls off the assembly line. The Beetle is the only car whose production surpasses the Model T Ford.
	• U.S. space shuttle *Enterprise* makes its first manned flight.
1978	• Atlantic City, New Jersey, has the first legal U.S. gambling casino outside of Nevada.
	• Aviation Act phases out Civil Aeronautics Board and begins deregulation process of airline industry.
1979	• Accident at Three Mile Island nuclear power plant in Pennsylvania. American public and government have second thoughts about nuclear power.
1980	• Cable News Network (CNN) goes on the air.
	• French Post Office develops *telématique*—a new system linking telephones with central computers to eliminate paper telephone directories.
	• Rollerblade, Inc. is founded in Minnesota by Canadian hockey player Scott Olsen after he buys a Chicago patent for in-line roller skates.
	• Fire at 7-year-old MGM Grand Hotel in Las Vegas traps 3,500 guests, kills 84. The hotel has no smoke alarms. Hotel industry rethinks safety procedures.
	• Tokyo Disneyland groundbreaking and site dedication.
1981	• France's Trés Grande Vitesse (TGV) train makes its first run from Paris to Lyons. It is Europe's first high-speed passenger train.
	• Ghermezian Brothers open the West Edmonton Mall in Canada—the largest mall in the world.
	• People Express, the discount airline that buys used airplanes from airlines with excess capacity, begins operation out of the North Terminal, an unused terminal at Newark airport in New Jersey. Six years later it will be out of business.
	• AIDS (Acquired Immune Deficiency Syndrome) begins taking a worldwide toll that will later be compared to the Black Death of the 14th century.
	• IBM introduces its first personal computer.
	• MTV (Music Television) is first broadcast to cable subscribers.
1982	• Honda begins American production of its cars in Marysville, Ohio.
	• Fax transmissions are down to twenty seconds per page (from three minutes in 1976), reducing telephone charges to under one dollar per page. There are over 350,000 fax installations in the United States.
	• EPCOT Center opens in Orlando, Florida.
1983	• Chicago motorists begin a test of cellular phone technology.
	• Tokyo Disneyland opens.
1984	• The Macintosh computer is introduced by Apple Computers.
	• Margaret Thatcher's government in England begins privatizing. Jaguar Motors is sold to private investors; British Telcom shares go on sale.
	• U.S. Supreme Court rules that home videotaping does not infringe copyrights.
	• Trivial Pursuit, developed by a Canadian entrepreneur, revives the board-game industry with U.S. sales of 777 million dollars.

1985	• Terrorism becomes rampant with attacks by Arab, French guerrilla, Islamic, and Palestinian groups.
	• Hijackers seize the cruise ship *Achille Lauro* in the Mediterranean, killing an American passenger.
	• A TWA jet flying from Athens to Rome is hijacked to Beirut, where passengers are held for seventeen days.
	• Bombs explode in Madrid, Paris, Athens, and Frankfurt, and grenades are thrown in Rome. Gunmen attack Rome and Vienna airports.
	• Coca-Cola announces a plan to change its 99-year-old formula with a sweeter version designed for younger tastes. Customer complaints force the company to reintroduce the original formula under the name Coke Classic.
1986	• Terrorism continues: A bomb aboard a TWA plane over Athens kills four Americans; an explosion in a West Berlin discothèque kills two and injures 230; guards at London's Heathrow Airport avert a tragedy when they find a bag of explosives that had been planted on a Tel-Aviv-bound flight.
	• U.S. space shuttle *Challenger* explodes, killing all seven astronauts aboard, including civilian astronaut Christa McAuliffe, a school teacher from New England, chosen in a contest to fly aboard the shuttle. The defect, discovered by Nobel laureate Richard Feynmawn, was an O-ring that did not remain elastic in the cold.
	• Jeana Yeager and Dick Rùtan take nine days to circle the globe, nonstop. They refuel in midair.
	• Grossinger's Resort in New York's Catskill Mountains is demolished after seventy-two years of serving a New York area social group that had become more and more assimilated into the American mainstream.
	• New York's Jacob K. Javits Convention Center opens, replacing the aging Coliseum.
1987	• Garbage and dead fish wash up on East Coast beaches.
	• U.S. microwave oven sales reach 12.6 million. Food companies rush to develop microwaveable food products.
	• ISES (International Special Events Society) founded.
1988	• Syringes, rubber gloves, and other medical waste arrive on mid-Atlantic beaches.
1989	• Demolition of the Berlin Wall.
	• An earthquake of 7.1 on the Richter Scale strikes San Francisco, causing over 6 billion dollars in property damage.
	• Disney-MGM Studios opens in Orlando, Florida.
	• The SkyDome in Toronto, Canada, is the first stadium with a fully retractable roof.
1990	• Germany reunites and the USSR crumbles.
	• Americans with Disabilities Act signed by President George Bush banning discrimination in employment, public accommodations, transportation, and telecommunications against the 43 million disabled people in the U.S. The law also provides protection for workers with AIDS.

1990 cont.	• Smoking is banned on all U.S. domestic flights. • The U.S. Clean Air Act becomes law, mandating reduced auto emissions. • Canadian Pacific Hotels and Resorts (CPH&R) undertakes the development of an environmental program for all of its hotels in Canada.
1991	• New York's Grand Central Station becomes strictly a commuter station as Amtrak reroutes all long-distance service to Penn Station. • Tourism Standards Consortium (TSC) formed by the Pacific Rim Institute of Tourism and the Tourism Councils of Saskatchewan, Manitoba, and Alberta, Canada.
1992	• Mall of America, the largest shopping mall in the United States, opens in Bloomington, Minnesota. This mall includes Camp Snoopy, a theme park, and over 400 stores. It has become a major tourist destination. • Windsor Castle in England damaged by fire, which will cost 90 million dollars to repair. To cover the costs of repairs, Queen Elizabeth II agrees to open parts of Buckingham Palace to tours for the first time, and to start paying taxes on her personal income. • Hurricane Andrew strikes southern Florida killing 15, leaving 250,000 homeless, and causing over 20 billion dollars in damage. • Euro Disney opens outside of Paris.
1993	• A bomb explosion at New York's World Trade Center forces 100,000 to evacuate. Arrests of Islamic fundamentalists are made, and a plot to bomb the United Nations headquarters and the Holland and Lincoln Tunnels is uncovered. • Pocket-sized telephones become common in the United States. • Major companies in the U.S. work toward creating a huge information superhighway offering on-demand video, telephone calls on cable, and TV programming on telephone lines. • First "green" Olympics, held at Lillehammer, Norway. • Seagaia Ocean Dome opens on the Southern Japanese island of Kyushu.
1994	• Chunnel (English Channel Tunnel) has various technical difficulties but opens to limited train travel. • Five major companies—Anheuser-Busch, Disney, Time-Warner, Paramount Communications, and Universal—dominate the amusement park industry. • The new Denver, Colorado, airport has postponed its opening several times, because the computerized luggage handling system does not yet function.

INDEX

Hard Rock Cafe, 160
Haunted Mansion, 30
Haunted Swing, 29
Hickenlooper, J., 176
Hilton, J., 87
Hinkel, Phillip, 27
Holiday corporation, 152
Holography
Hotel Sales and Marketing Association
        International (HSMAI), 155
Hygienic Horses, 29

Industrial Revolution, 18
Inglis artificial water slide for pleasure
        resorts, 28
Inkamp, K., 89
Inns, early, 38
Integrated facilities, 60–62
Interests, 190–191
International Association for
        Continuing Education and
        Training (IACET), 201
International Association of Auditorium
        Managers (IAAM), 117–118
International Business Machines
        (IBM), 74
International Conference on AIDS, 117
International Festivals Association
        (IFA), 117–118
International Hotel/Motel and
        Restaurant Show
        (IH/M&RS), 156
International Olympic Committee
        (IOC), 110
International Special Events Education
        Foundation (ISEF), 91–93
    certification program, 93
    first certification examination, 93
    history of, 92–93
    mission, 93
International Special Events Society
        (ISES), 82
    membership by discipline, 91
    membership categories, 92
    mission, 90
    origins of, 89–90
    principles of professional conduct
        and ethics, 90
International Standard Industrial
        Classification (ISIC), 131
International Travel Act, 126
Internet, 202
Interstate Commerce Commission, 127
Interstate highway system, 47

Jackson, R., 83
Jamieson, L., 1, 5, 10
Jannus, T., 36
Japan Olympic Committee (JOC), 113
Jet aircraft, introduction of, 33–34
Johnson & Johnson (J&J), 74

Kelly Air Mail Act, 36
Kelly, J., 1, 5, 8
Kentucky Fried Chicken, 157
Kitty Hawk, NC, 35
Knight, P., 177
Kodak, 109

Largest moving staircase in the
        world, 53
Las Vegas, 61
Legionnaires disease, 163
Leisure, changing concept of, 17, 214
Letter of eviction, 38
Licensed Beverage Education
        Consortium (LBEC), 161
Lilenthal, O., 35
Lockheed Constellation, 37
Lodging
    amenities, 148, 154
    back of the house, 154
    distribution channels, 149–151,
        153–154
    front of the house, 154
    professional associations, 155
    rating systems, 148, 154
Loop-the-loop, 28
Lusitania, 33

Madison Square Garden, 105
Mall of America, 62
Management corporations, 117
Managers
    definitions, 98–99, 104
    internal and external forces,
        101–102
    levels, 100–101
    perquisites, 98–99
    skills, 100
    types, 98
    types of activities, 99–100
Manufactured attractions, 134
Marketing, sophistication of, 19
Marriott Marquis Hotel, 154
Marxim's, 160
Mauritania, 33
McDonald's, 60, 109, 152

Meeting Professionals International
        (MPI), 76
    mission statement and supporting
        goals, 77
Meeting professionals
    gender, 81
    salaries, 81
Meetings and conventions, 72
    attributes of professional planners,
        79–80
    history of, 72–74
    skills, 77
    types of planners, 74–76
Men, redefinition of role, 18, 216–217
Mentor, 195
Mescon, M., 99
Metropolitan Atlanta Olympic Games
        Authority (MAOGA), 110
Microbreweries, 161, 162
Millennium Society, 208
Ministry of Small Business, Tourism,
        and Culture, 124
Mobil Travel Guides, 154
Models of tourism evolution, 135
Montgolfier, brothers, 35
Morrison, A., 6
Multi-dimensional corporations, 183
Multi-purpose facilities, 105–107

Nader, R., 19
Nagano Olympic Games Organizing
        Committee (NAOC), 113
Nagano Winter Games—1998, 113–114
Naisbitt, J., 215, 216
National Environmental Policy Act, 136
National Organization for Competency
        Assurance (NOCA), 201
National Park Service, 126, 127–128
National Restaurant Association
        (NRA), 152, 161
National Tourism Policy Act, 127
Natural attractions, 134
New toboggan slide for bathers, 28
Nike, Inc., 177–178
94th Squadron, 160
Norsk McLaks Meny, 109
North American waterparks, 54
Norton, R., 1, 4, 5, 9, 10

Ocean Park Hong Kong, 53–54
Ocean liners, 33
Old boys network, 81
Olympic Games 108
    Atlanta—1996, 110